TRAIL NORTH

A JOURNEY IN WORDS AND PICTURES

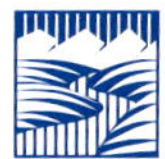

TRAIL NORTH

A JOURNEY IN WORDS AND PICTURES

BY ROBERT GUEST

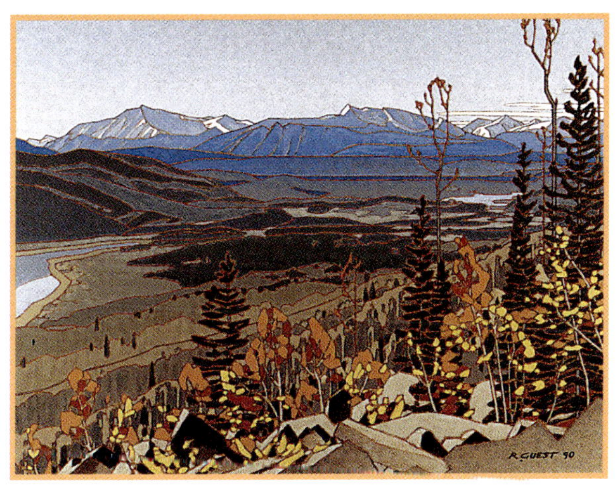

LONE PINE PUBLISHING

First printed in 1995 5 4 3 2 1
Printed in Canada

The Publisher
Lone Pine Publishing
206, 10426-81 Ave.
Edmonton, Alberta
Canada T6E 1X5

202A-1110 Seymour Street
Vancouver, British Columbia
Canada V6B 3N3

16149 Redmond Way, #180
Redmond, Washington
USA 98052

Canadian Cataloguing in Publication Data

Guest, Robert, 1938-
Trail north

ISBN 1-55105-052-8 (bound).— ISBN 1-55105-027-7 (pbk.)

1. Guest Robert, 1938- 2. Hinton Trail (Alta.) — Pictoral works. 3. Hinton Trail (Alta.) — History. 4. Alberta — History, Local. I. Title.
FC3695.H56G83 1994 971.23'3'0022 C95-910067-9
F1079.H56G83 1994

Editor-in-Chief: Glenn Rollans
Editor: Graham Sheard
Design, Layout and Production: Kim Johansen, Pièce de Résistance Ltée.
Copyediting: Jennifer Keane
Printing: Quality Colour Press Inc.

Reprinted materials and photographs in this book are used with the generous permission of their copyright holders. Pages 151 and 152 of this book, which list reprinted material sources, photo credits and permissions, constitute an extension of this copyright page.

The publisher gratefully acknowledges the assistance of Alberta Community Development and the Department of Canadian Heritage, the support of the Canada/Alberta Agreement on the cultural industries, and the financial support provided by the Alberta Foundation of the Arts.

Foreword

Throughout the years, there have been many trails leading into the Peace River country.

In 1790, Malcolm McLeod was the first Euro-Canadian to enter the region, travelling by canoe from Fort Chipewyan to a spot 12 miles north of present-day Peace River. Three years later, the exploration party of Alexander Mackenzie followed the Peace and Pine rivers on their way through the Rocky Mountains. The all-water excursion from Fort Chipewyan soon became a standard route for the eastern fur traders.

While wintering near the forks of the Peace and Smoky rivers, Mackenzie was told of an ancient Cree war road which extended there from Lesser Slave Lake. At the same time, another Cree trail extended from Lesser Slave Lake to the developing community at Sturgeon Lake. From the 1820s, a trail was used by employees of the Hudson's Bay Company to travel from their post at Fort Assiniboine to the western end of Lesser Slave Lake. During the 1860s and 1870s, gold seekers from the Caribou entered the Peace River country from the west along the Peace and Pine passes, while explorers and missionaries penetrated from the east.

Of all the ancient trails into the Peace River country, the most scenic and best preserved is the Hinton Trail. Extending north from the present site of Hinton past Nose Mountain into the district of Beaverlodge, this trail provides valuable and pleasant insight into what the environment and travelling conditions must have been like for natives, trappers, explorers and missionaries over a century ago. The Hinton Trail was never able to accomodate the four-wheeled wagons that were a necessity for settlement prior to the coming of the railroad–the terrain was simply too rugged. Yet the Trail never died, as this book points out. How much richer and fuller is our understanding of Peace River heritage because of the history of this trail.

The following pages of paintings, drawings and text provide as full and accurate an impression of the Hinton Trail–as it was then and how it is now–as it is possible to achieve without actually travelling it. Robert Guest, who has an intimate knowledge of the region south from Beaverlodge, has drawn from countless sources, both archival and personal, in depicting this trail and those who experienced it. He has married his text to a vivid visual portrayal of scenes along the way, and to other insightful illustrations.

This book should be a standard for all lovers of Western Canadiana.

Dr. David Leonard
Provincial Archivist
Provincial Archives of Alberta
December 1994

Introduction

I was raised on a farm on the banks of the Wapiti River in the community of Hinton Trail. The community was named in 1923 after the historic packtrail that went through the area. As a young person I remember that the old Trail had a certain romantic appeal, and I hoped that some day I would have the chance to follow it. In later years the chance finally came but was not what I had anticipated. I discovered it was not possible to follow the old Trail anymore, and there were only a handful of oldtimers left who knew anything about it. I was fortunate to meet some of these people, and will always appreciate their patience, stories and good advice.

My effort to produce a collection of paintings on the Hinton Trail began in 1984 with a few field sketches. It was not until 1988 that I was able to give the project my full attention. Having spent a number of seasons with the Forestry Service and having flown over the area in small planes many times, I knew the area well and decided it would make an excellent subject for an art collection and a book. The more I thought about it, the more anxious I became to complete the project before too many oldtimers had either left the area or passed on. In many cases I was already too late. While many had travelled the Trail through the years, very few people kept any kind of record. In fact, it is surprising to see how many knowledgeable people today know nothing of the Trail despite their interest in western history. Likely this was the last chance to record something of the old Hinton Trail connecting the Peace River country with the Yellowhead Pass.

Before 1900 the Hinton Trail was the best-known trail from west-central Alberta to the Peace River country. It was an important route long before there were any roads. A common mistake now is to confuse it with the Edson Trail, but the Hinton Trail was established for many years before the competing Edson Trail came into the Peace River country from farther east. The Edson Trail lasted only about six years.

The Hinton Trail passes through some of the most varied and interesting landscape in western Alberta. The country was, and still is, breathtaking, and the Trail provides an extended tour through approximately 200 miles of prime watershed. In some places it passes close to the source of significant rivers such as the Berland, the Muskeg, the Wildhay, and the Cutbank. Between the Smoky and Kakwa rivers the Trail reaches its highest point at about 1,500 metres (5,000 feet).

Much of the packtrail passes through remote and unsettled country, and it was not easy for me to reach some of the historic sites along the way. There were rivers to wade across and cliffs to climb, cold weather to contend with and a certain amount of travelling in the moonlight.

Before wandering off in the wilderness to begin my project I had to find out where to go. Since no map had been made of the Hinton Trail, I had to stop and put one together. This required meeting people who knew the country and had gone over the Trail themselves, such as native trappers, outfitters, retired forestry personnel, geologists, and early settlers. Not many of the original travellers were left, but those who were helped fill in the gaps. After about 150 interviews, and visits to the Provincial Archives of Alberta, as well as consulting with the Whyte Museum of the Canadian Rockies in Banff, I had enough material for a first version of a map. It shows the Hinton Trail at its most active period, about the mid-1930s. Putting together the map took approximately eighteen months.

Talking to people about the map often became a chance to gather other information on the Trail: travelling conditions, detours along the Trail, how to find specific river crossings and which were the most dangerous, accidents, remains of native settlements, Indian burial grounds, and much more. I was the first to record much of this information. This all helped me focus on which places to include on my long list of sites to draw and paint.

The descendants of the Trail people are as varied as the country itself, and they all have a story to tell, some based on real adventures and others on tall tales that have been passed on. I have tried to weave their lives and experiences together–they are all part of the same story. And everyone I met was willing to share.

With the map finished, I began to decide what I wanted in the paintings. My main objectives were: to try to represent the significant points of the Hinton Trail starting at the south end and working north, to try to capture as much of the variety of the changing landscape as possible from the farmland to the edge of the mountains, to try to record the seasonal changes and conditions of weather typical to the country, and to represent different times of the day and night. I also planned to record relics such as wagons, the ruins of old trading posts, trappers' cabins, campsites, a Metis log church, corrals, Indian graves, and Sundance tipis.

The success of the series would depend on two things mainly: the strength of the setting's historical context, and a durable artistic technique. I was determined to strike a balance between the factual and the expressive. For the sake of history I wanted to convey a strong sense of authenticity. And, from the artistic point of view, my intention was to emphasize the spirit of the place, or subject, by means of design, choice of colours, and symbolism.

One of my first tasks was to check each important spot in person. This required a lot of bushwhacking, and going out on many a winter's night when it was too cold to make sketches. I tried to make some anyway. In the daylight I carried a camera as well, hoping to get backup photographs which might be used for discussions or slide presentations. In nearly every case, I was aware that my first visit to an area was in all likelihood my last. For instance, the hike to the Muddywater River required about forty-five miles of walking, and the round trip took five days.

I gathered the first impressions with a pencil. I dashed off these sketches in a 9-inch-by-12-inch pad under pressure. Most of them resemble gesture drawings—just ideas. I wanted to impart a feeling of the subject, which sometimes required two or three sketches showing different angles. In addition to the main subject, the sketches I collected of plants, bear tracks, beaver stumps, blazes on trees, cloud formations, and so on would help later when trying to do an interesting painting. On long hikes, I wrapped a smaller drawing pad in plastic and carried it in a backpack. The best sketches were dated with a note on the back of each, recording the location and conditions. On most of the outings, daylight was very short, and I had to keep an eye on the weather, always thinking about the long walk back to the road. Then again, often there wasn't a road.

The next step was a small version, or mock-up, which I painted in oil or acrylic. These resembled coloured diagrams and were mostly done on 5-inch-by-7-inch panels. I also used a few 8-inch-by-10-inch panels, which I completed on location as both a sketch and a colour key—an exploration of values for the final 12-inch-by-16-inch painting. I saved many of the pre-study drawings for presentation as finished works.

For an historic project of this type I had to create a number of reconstructions in my paintings. Reconstructions, in this instance, included such things as Indian cabins, early fire lookout towers, trading posts and stores, Indian encampments, and events of historical note. I had little to go on except archival photographs and some resourceful people who provided me with photographs from their personal albums. To retain a true spirit of the subject I made trips to the actual locations for sketches.

On practical grounds, I decided to make the collection of paintings portable and durable. All paintings are the same size, 12 inches by 16 inches, and were painted with acrylics. In terms of its permanency, acrylic seems to be one of the most stable media available today, provided it is not watered down too much. Using acrylic also meant that I didn't have to worry about drying problems, unhealthy fumes, cracking of surfaces, changing colours, or awkward storage and handling.

Rather than applying paint in the usual way, using long brush strokes, I wanted something that was more complex and subtle. So, like the Impressionists, I employed pointillism. Colours are blended not by the brush, but by the eye. I used this technique throughout the entire composition, and it is meant to harmonize with the golden brown line-work. I preferred to work with thick paint, hoping for a gentle impasto surface that would have a rustic quality.

I had to test colours in advance, especially in preparation for the fast-drying acrylic medium. The range of pre-mixed colours did not apply to every painting, but they certainly helped me tackle subjects that required unusual combinations. A wide range of colour schemes for the wide range of subjects along the Trail guaranteed a variety of moods and atmospheres.

Usually the subject itself suggested a colour scheme. Some were obvious, such as a typical fall day with its reds and golds seen against blues and blue-greens. For the best colour results I preferred to complete my paintings in daylight. I found that artificial light was suitable for drawing, but not necessarily good for painting. Understandably my pace slowed down during the winter. For all the challenges the night presents, I find it incredibly sensitive, and night moods are one of the things not easily reproduced through photography. I have had a fascination for the night since childhood and it seems natural to me that a number of dark subjects are included in this collection.

I based one of the first paintings of the project, Mad Wolf's Hill, on an oil study done in 1965 when I was stationed at Copton Lookout. I was employed by the Alberta Forest Service at the time. Copton Ridge was roughly halfway along the Trail route, between the Wapiti River and the Indian village of Grande Cache. The painting portrayed a high, wind-swept hill, an important landmark that overlooked the old Trail.

On average, each of the 74 paintings required about ten days to complete, not counting the time spent visiting the sites and preparing drawings and mock-ups. I also prepared a series of iconographic illustrations, now distributed throughout the book. Most of them represent objects of the trail era, from the world of nature (such as fossils), to human artifacts. I gathered information for these drawings from my own sketches and photographs as well as from books and other historical sources. I wanted these illustrations to be able to stand alone as well as to complement the paintings.

My project took about seven years to complete–from 1987 to 1993–which was longer than I had anticipated. I had thought there would be nothing to getting a few sketches, talking to some oldtimers, and simply painting some pictures to go with their stories. The initial concept of a book didn't impose an exact number of pieces, and I found it hard to set a limit and stick with it. In order to represent a good cross-section of the Trail it was necessary to select from the full length of the map. Quite often a trip to visit someone for an interview would result in a new painting. My original goal was for about forty finished paintings. I ended up with seventy-three and a work in progress, all included in this book.

Now, in spite of the years of cold nights, bushwacking, and stretching the patience of my wife to the limit, the project seems to have been worthwhile. In addition to the satisfaction of getting the work done, there are other rewards. I enjoyed the unique experience of travelling the foothills in ways I never thought possible and to places new to me. From my isolated cabin on the banks of the Wapiti I travelled to centres as far away as Kelly Lake, McClennan, Calgary and Victoria to gather information. I met people from all walks of life, from trappers to geologists, making many new friends along the Trail. These friendships will remain long after the project is finished. Finally, I was able to introduce a larger audience to my work. A representative set of twenty-five of these paintings was shown in the Jasper Art Museum in the fall of 1992, and a larger exhibit was mounted at the Provincial Museum of Alberta in the spring of 1993, where fourteen framed study drawings were displayed with the paintings to show the evolution of the pieces.

As the title suggests, this book takes the form of a journey. The paintings are in geographic order, with the first painting of the Athabasca valley and the final one at the Trail's end at Lake Saskatoon. This approach shows the changing character of the Trail's landscape, just as those who rode the Trail northwards saw it. I have written the history of the Trail mostly as the anecdotes and tales of my fellow travellers on it.

All in all, *Trail North* has been quite an adventure. I sincerely hope it adds a vivid record to the history of the West. It's my tribute to the optimistic people who had faith in the project, and who gave their time, and friendly advice, and wonderful hot cups of tea!

Today, with this project reaching completion, I live and continue to work in semi-isolation, and being a bit of an outdoor "nut," I prefer it this way.

Robert Guest

Beaverlodge, December 1994

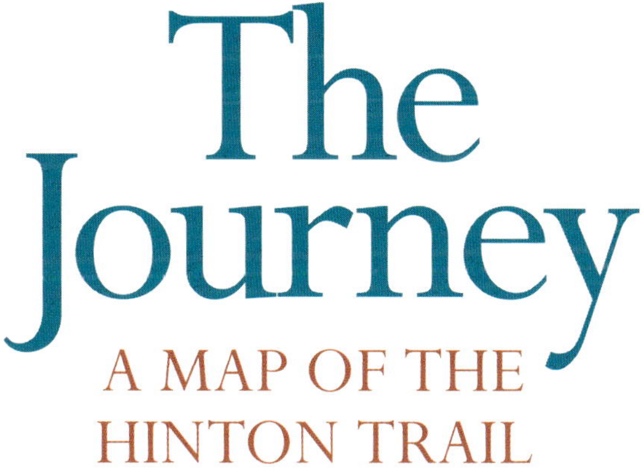

THE HINTON TRAIL
AND ITS MAIN BRANCHES TO ABOUT 1940

FROM THE YELLOWHEAD PASS TO THE PEACE RIVER COUNTRY SHOWING POINTS OF INTEREST.

0 2.5 5 7.5 10 Mi
0 4 8 12 16 Km

NORTH

120
119
118
55
54
ALBERTA-BRITISH COLUMBIA BOUNDARY

KELLY LAKE
HYTHE
BEAVERLODGE
CUTBANK LAKE
BEAR LAKE
LAKE SASKATOON
MT. VALLEY
HALCOURT
INDIAN QUARTER
SENTINEL TREE
GRANDE PRAIRIE
RIO GRANDE
KENNEY'S CROSSING
WEMBLEY
FLYINGSHOT LAKE
REDWILLOW RIVER
PIPESTONE CREEK
RIVER
ELMWORTH
HINTON TRAIL
OSBORNE'S CROSSING
HAZELMERE
SYLVESTRE
GROVEDALE
LINGRELL FLATS
JASPER CROSSING
SOUTH WAPITI
WAPITI
RIVER
SHUTTLER FLATS
PINTO CREEK
NOSE CREEK
PIERRE LAKE
LATORNELL RIVER
NOSE MTN. TOWER
NOSE CREEK SETTLEMENT
NOSE LAKE
CUTBANK RIVER
SIMONETTE RIVER
MUSREAU LAKE
NARRAWAY RIVER
REDROCK CREEK
BUFFALO HEAD CAMP
TWO LAKES
ROUND PRAIRIE
PORCUPINE CABINS
FORT PORCUPINE POST
SMOKY
KAKWA RIVER
COPTON CREEK
WINDFALL HILL
SHEEP CREEK POST
DANIEL'S FLATS
LITTLE SMOKY RIVER
SHEEP CREEK
GUSTAVE FLATS
GRANDE CACHE
McDONALD'S FLATS
MUSKEG STOPPING PLACE
SUSA CREEK
PIERRE GREY'S POST
VICTOR LAKE POST
SULPHUR RIVER GATES
BERLAND RIVER
ASA HUNTING CAMPSITE
A LA PECHE LAKE
MUSKEG RIVER
MAIN BAPTISTE CABIN
WILDHAY RIVER
SULPHUR RIVER
MOBERLY CREEK CABIN
GREGG LAKE
ATHABASCA RIVER
JARVIS LAKE
PEPPERS LAKE
ROCK LAKE
FISH LAKE FLATS
STARVATION FLATS
ATHABASCA LOOKOUT ENTRANCE
HINTON
TWINTREE LAKE
BRULE LAKE
PRAIRIE CREEK
© R. GUEST 92

43

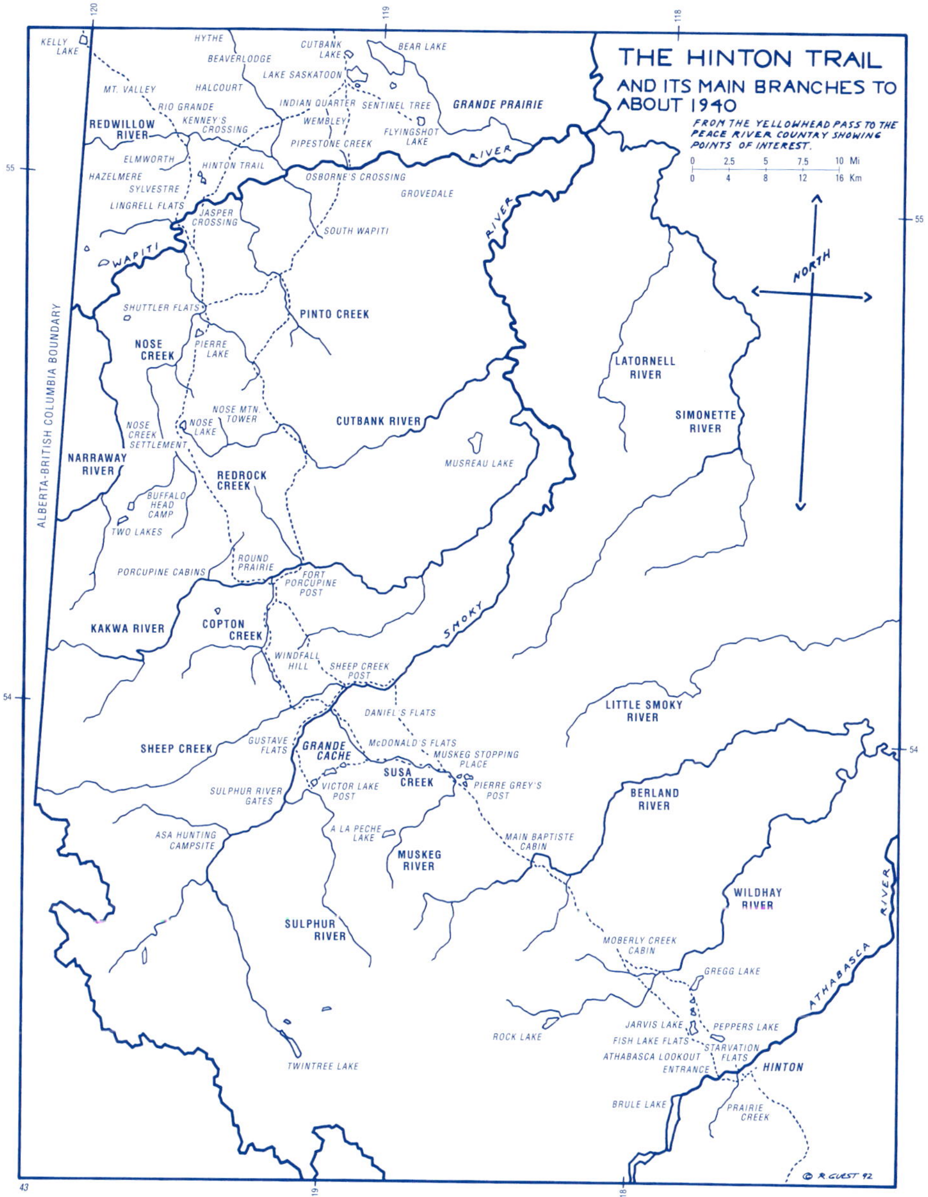

Athabasca Valley, Northwest of Hinton

The Hinton Trail we know today probably developed in the last century beneath the feet of Indians who needed pitching trails to take them to their traplines and hunting territory. It was well-travelled before the railroad came through and before the hamlet of Hinton had a name. The main trail led to the Peace River country. There were several branches, but the most important one seems to have crossed the ford on the Athabasca River at the mouth of old Prairie Creek. The setting for this painting is an evening during a cold snap in late November. The view combines a sense of history with some of the finest foothills country along the Yellowhead Pass.

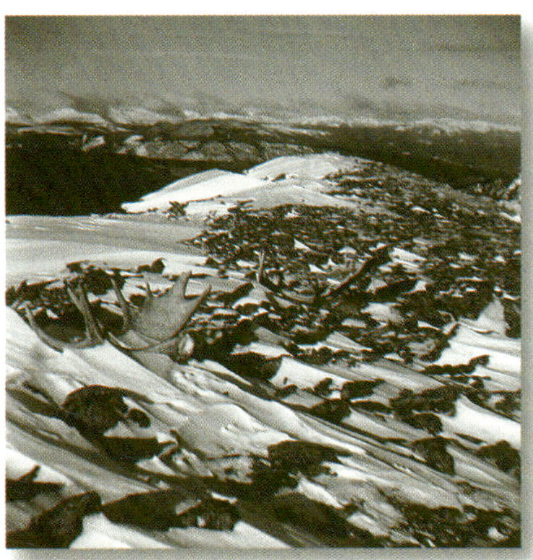

THE ICE-FREE CORRIDOR

On a map of western North America, archeologists have indicated a kind of passageway thought to have existed during the last great Ice Age. Looking closely at the archeological maps it is possible to calculate, roughly, where the Hinton Trail would later come to be. The ice-free corridor became the location for a modern, well-used trail. It was a habitat for various large animals edging their way to the grasslands and forests further south and became a migratory route for ancient hunters. The nomadic people of the Ice Age were likely drawn to Alaska from Siberia in search of large prey. These early hunters and gatherers left the north and pursued their quarry, gradually working their way south towards the heart of the continent.

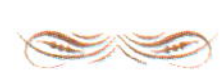

DRAWINGS: Scraping tool and arrowheads

PHOTO: Through a land of rock and wind...

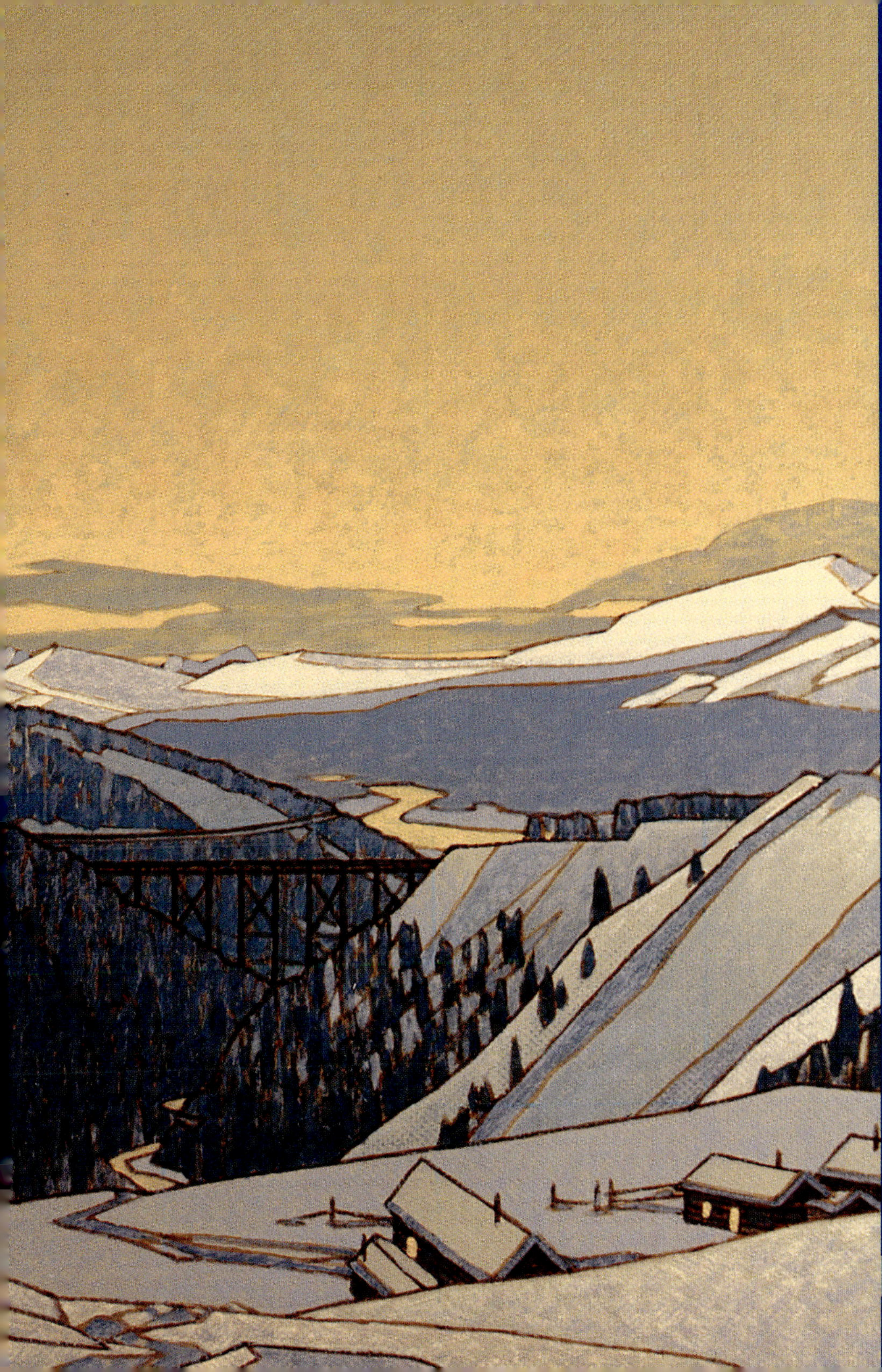

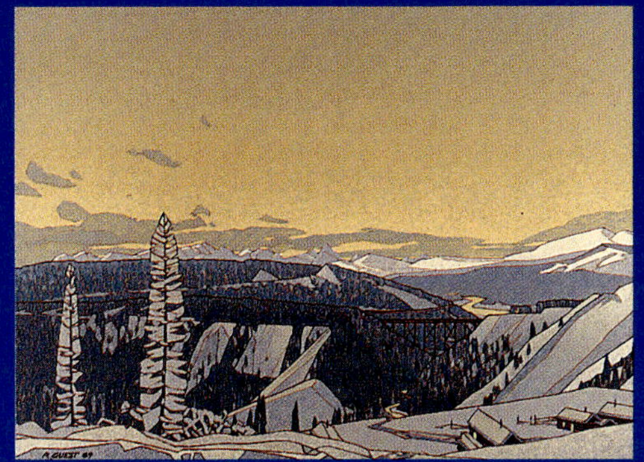

Athabasca Valley, Northwest of Hinton

"THE PATH, as seen on the globe, is the most direct possible. It lies up the eastern front of the Rocky Mountains, across Alaska, the Sea of Bering Strait and St. Lawrence Island, and the Stanavoi highlands. The bones of ten thousand species have marked it, and the Indian, or his ancestors, have left it strewn with his flints and camping sites."

D. Cushman, c.1966

Athabasca Crossing at Old Prairie Creek

In 1910 there was a short-lived, bustling railroad town named for the Prairie Creek, now called the Maskuta Creek. The town was situated close to the junction of the creek and the Athabasca River. Here there was a good ford, and traces of the old packtrail are still visible, heading off in a northwesterly direction from the far shore. The east branch of the Lower Trail (which pre-dated the railroad town) crossed here and was used for many years. When the river was in flood, or the ice was unstable during freeze-up, travellers would camp and wait, unwilling to risk their lives or lose their valuable horses.

Felix Plante's home cabin near Hinton

PRAIRIE CREEK AND THE RAIL

About 1910, tranquility was shattered when the age of railroads hit this part of the country in a feverish push towards the mountains. Both the Grand Trunk Pacific and its rival, the Canadian Northern, established rights-of-way, resulting in a period of growth and activity. Hundreds of construction workers appeared with heavy machinery and noisy camps. Within a year, a town had sprung up along the east side of Prairie Creek. It had all the boom town characteristics—rows of clay-plastered shacks, false-fronted stores, a hotel, barns for teams of horses, and scores of log cabins.

As soon as the construction period was over, the town began to disappear, and the railway workers moved on towards Tête Jaune Cache. As Prairie Creek faded into history, the town of Hinton became more important through the discovery of coal and other resources. It was named in honour of W. D. Hinton, a general manager of the Grand Trunk Pacific Railway.

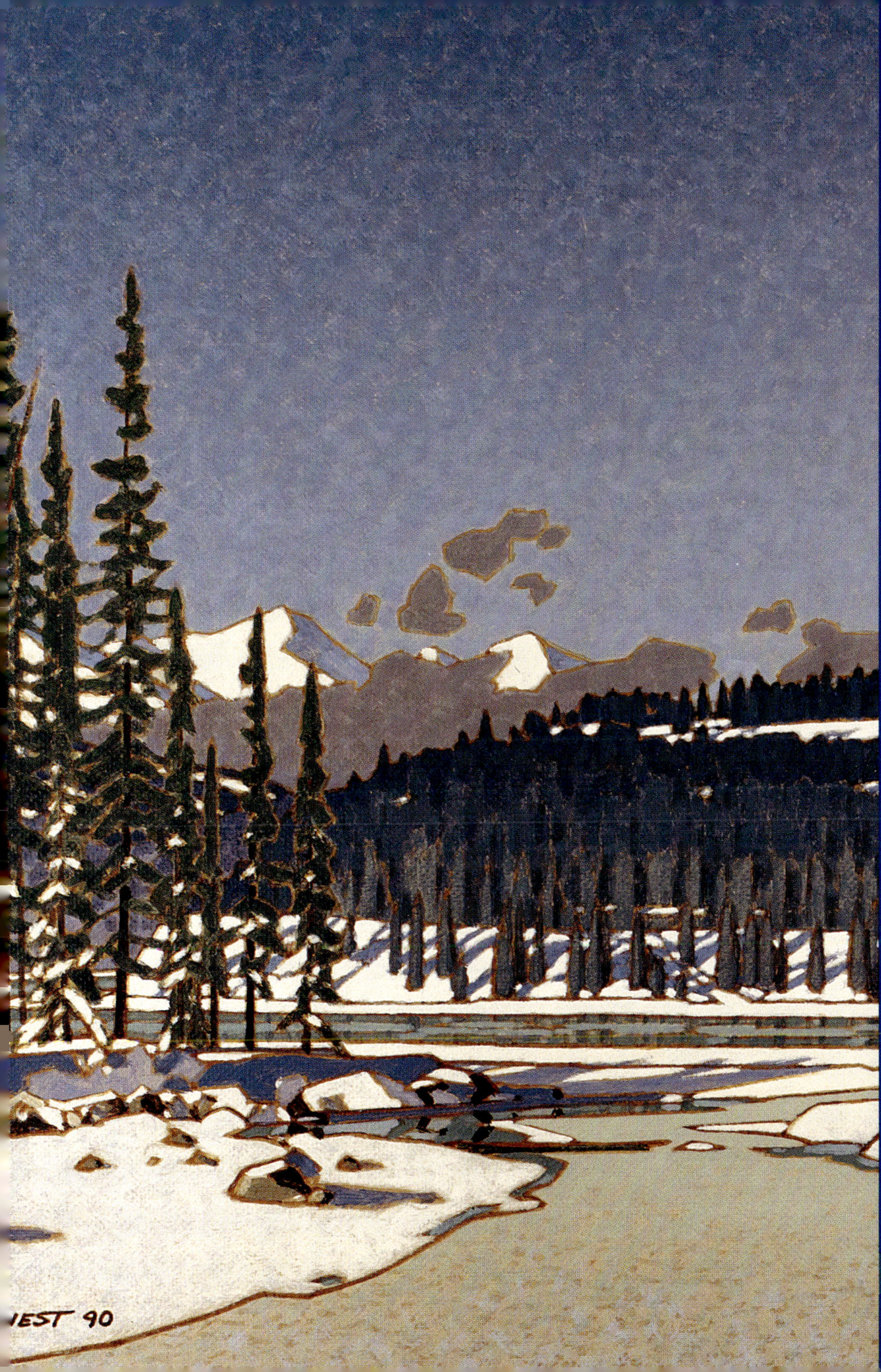

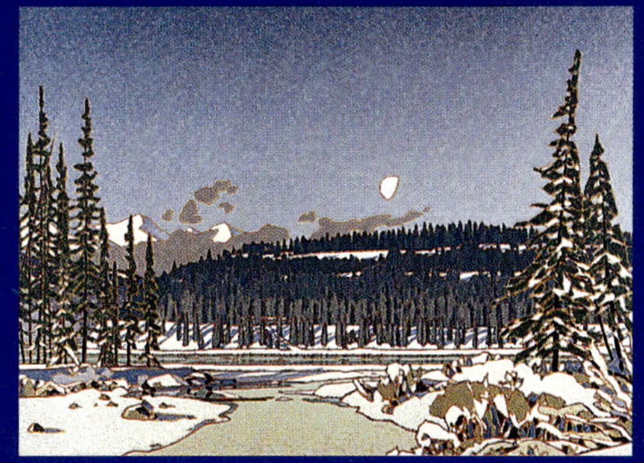

Athabasca Crossing at Old Prairie Creek

"I LEARNED *a lesson then that I never forgot. I looked down at the muddy water swirling all around me and I felt so dizzy that I almost fell out of the saddle. Then I focused my eyes on a point high on the opposite bank and I felt alright again and crossed without further incident."*

John Glenn, c.1920

Shower Clouds over Peppers Lake

The Peppers Lake shoreline runs approximately east and west. Grass and sedges grow in the muskeg-brown water. Through the years trappers have made their living around its forested shores, occasionally following the Wanyandi Trail over the height of land on its eastern edge—a part of the old Lower Trail. Some old maps show a "Winter Trail," where travellers crossed part of Peppers Lake on the ice when it was safe. The painting shows the lake in June, and the buffalo skull is one that Carl Luger found close to the lake some years ago.

TRAILBLAZING BUFFALO

According to some early traders, herds of buffalo were among the original trail makers. The large mammals roamed the prairies and foothills in huge herds, travelling great distances, leaving furrows that would stand the rigours of time. The winding trails, with a few dusting wallows, are still there. Many a buffalo trail was followed by early peoples, who made a change here, a shortcut there, according to their need. As proof of the ancient ownership of the trails, the occasional bleached buffalo skull, sometimes with horns attached, is found. People tracing the original trail from south of the Athabasca River up to the north country have reported finding these skulls. Like a visit out of time, the odd one appears in a washout, at a river landing, or even on a mountainside.

Ghosts of Buffalo Head Camp

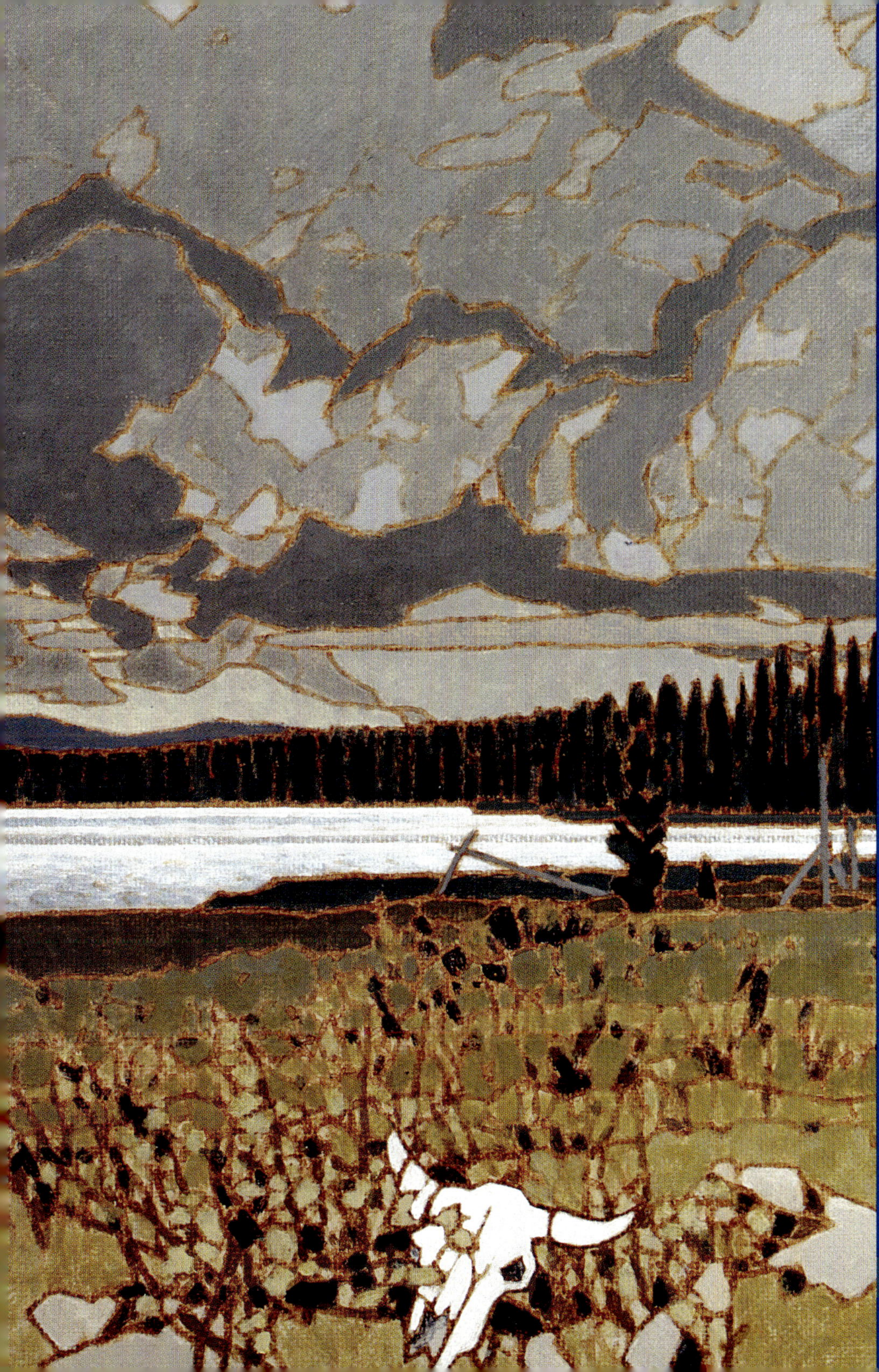

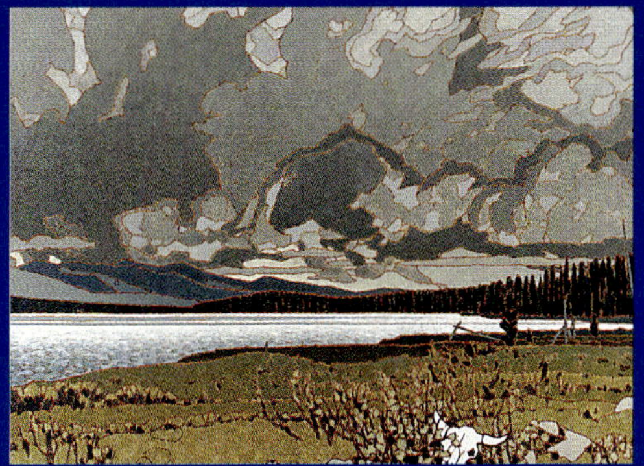

Shower Clouds over Peppers Lake

"THEN I remembered having noticed broad skulls in the vicinity, with the inner core of horns still attached. The outer horns would soon have been chewed off by porcupines."

John Glenn, c.1920

Athabasca River Crossing at Entrance

Because of its size and speed of current, many people thought the Athabasca the most dangerous of the rivers crossing the Trail. Apart from outfitters and native people, the early Forest Service was the largest group to use the ford at Entrance. They continued to use it even after a bridge was built downstream, perhaps because they didn't want skittish packhorses having to share the bridge with motorized traffic. Carl Luger crossed this ford many times and, although it was not too deep, one had to angle across the river on a submerged gravel bar in order to reach the landing on the far shore; otherwise horse and rider would drift downstream. The painting shows the Entrance crossing in June.

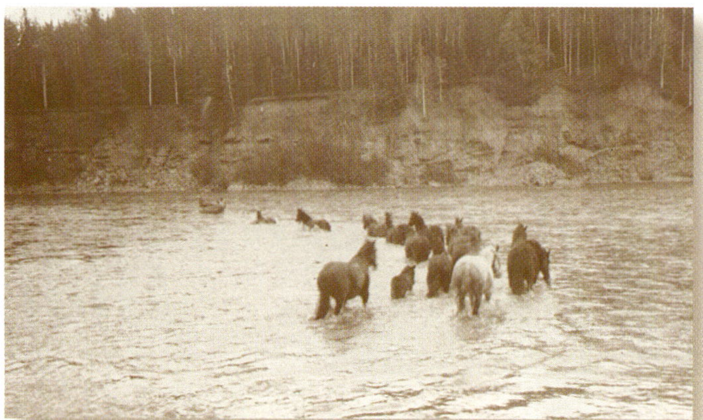

Horses crossing the Wapiti at Pipestone Creek, c.1950

THE ROLE OF ENTRANCE

The hamlet of Entrance on the north bank of the Athabasca River was well named—it was the last main railway stop before the entrance to Jasper National Park. Entrance was the early headquarters of the Athabasca Forest Reserve, which was under federal jurisdiction until 1930 when it was transferred to the government of Alberta. As a forestry centre, Entrance had ties that reached out over a wide area, extending north as far as Smoky River and to the British Columbia border, and was probably the most active forestry district in the entire province. Developers were interested in timber and watershed, and wildlife attracted hunters to the area, providing the forestry personnel responsible for wildlife protection with a year-round job. The men picked for that task were among the most able in the history of forestry.

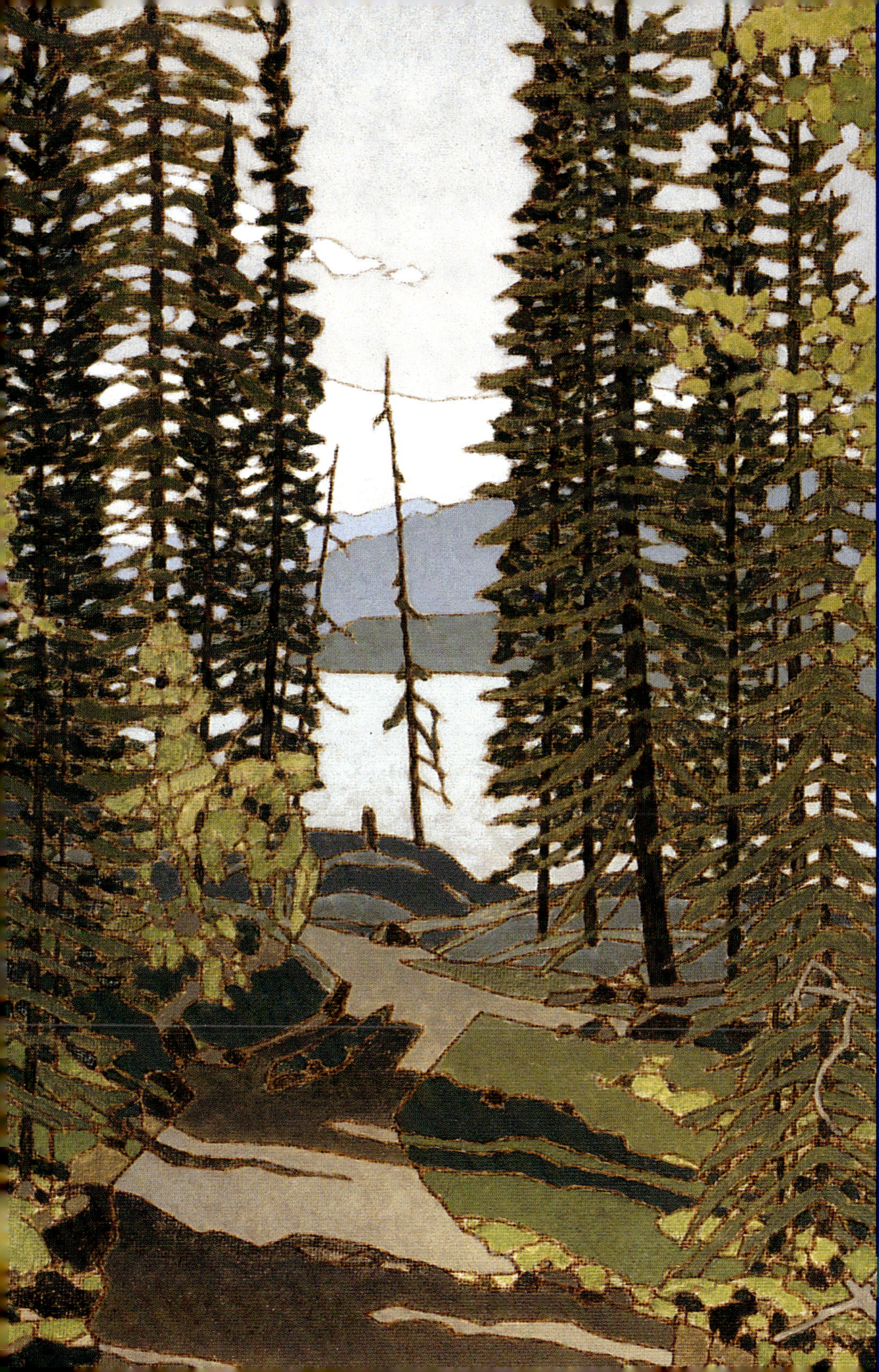

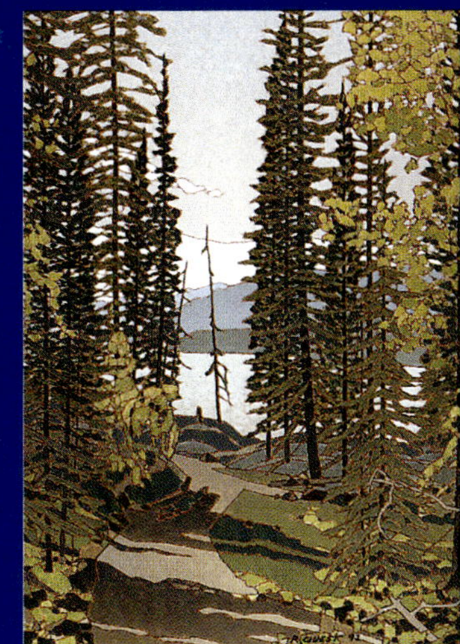

Athabasca River Crossing at Entrance

"IT WAS A *long swim and the current heavy, so that not a back was visible, their noses and ears being the only part of them above water. Slower and slower went the little procession till, one by one, we counted thirteen dark objects creeping up the bank on the far side."*

Mary T. S. Schaffer, 1911

Shand Harvey's Cabin, Old Entrance

Shand Harvey's last cabin was built on a semi-forested hillside close to old Entrance. It was a stone's throw away from the Athabasca River and from where the old packtrail went through to reach the ford. Having come into the country earlier as a surveyor on the 14th Baseline, Shand Harvey was a key figure in the days around 1909. Through his work for Forestry, he got to know the country better than anyone else of his time. He knew all the Indians from the Yellowhead Pass to the Smoky River, and was welcome in their homes. He travelled the old trails and is still remembered by some of the elders who went with him. His cabin still stands and is shown here with a log school, the first one built in the area, in the background. The time of year is late fall.

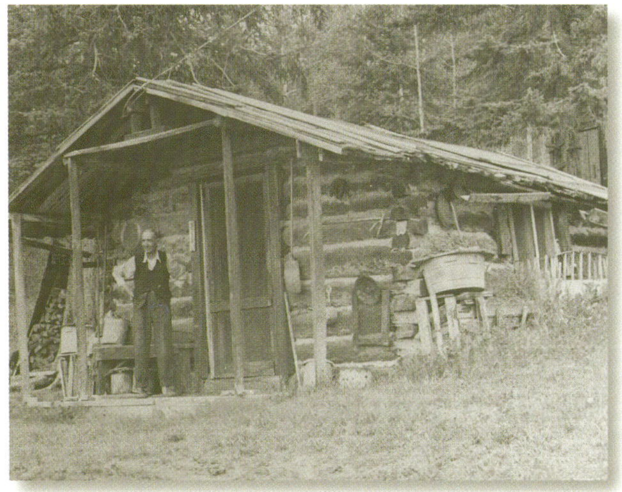

Shand's last home, a rugged log cabin, was built on the north side of the Athabasca River (1968).

◆

A CHANGE OF ENTRANCE

In its most active period the Entrance community had many buildings: a general store (owned by the Woodley brothers), a restaurant and poolroom, a train station, the first log school in the district, and a number of trappers' shacks. There were forestry buildings such as the Superintendent's house and a ranger's cabin with barn and cache, contained by an attractive fence around the property. It was a popular spot, often admired and photographed by people travelling through by train.

This all changed in 1926 when the Canadian National Railway abandoned its tracks and moved to the south side of the Athabasca River. Being associated with the name of Entrance had been very profitable, especially for outfitters and the guiding business, and when the railroad transfer was made, the name of Entrance went with it. A small stopping place called Dike became "new" Entrance.

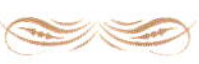

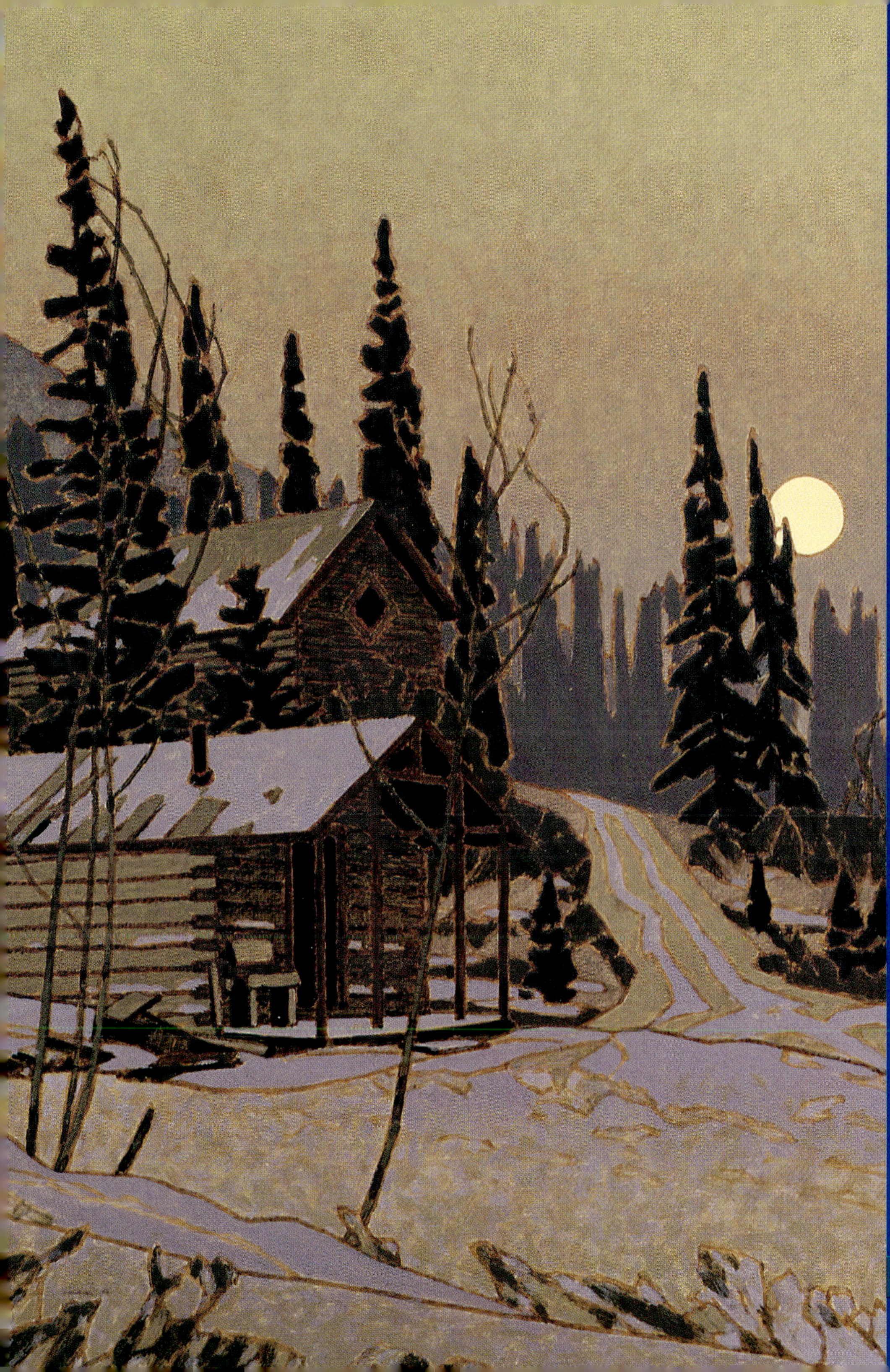

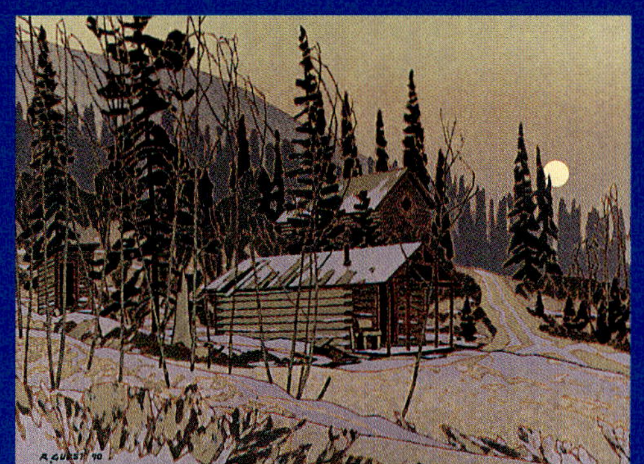

Shand Harvey's Cabin, Old Entrance

"On his way around from one trap to another, and from one cabin to another, [Shand] blazed trees–both sides of the tree, for he knew that someday he might want to reverse his line of travel.

And then, high on a tree nearby he set about making a cache where his supplies would be secure from wandering wolves, marauding bear, or meandering mice."

J. G. MacGregor, 1962

First Athabasca Lookout in Early Winter

In the 1920s the government established some of the first fire lookouts in west-central Alberta. The painting is a reconstruction and shows the type of structure made, in those years, entirely of wood. The lookout cabin was situated on the summit of a high hill between the east and west branches of the Hinton Trail as it approached the Athabasca River. The cabin, built about 1926, is on stilts, overlooking Brûle Lake and the entrance to Jasper National Park. The logs and lumber needed for construction were taken to the site by horses, and it was one of the earliest lookouts to be connected to the first Forestry telephone line. The painting shows the building on a cold evening after the first snowfall in the high country, looking as if it was only recently abandoned, with its door, and some of its window shutters, left open.

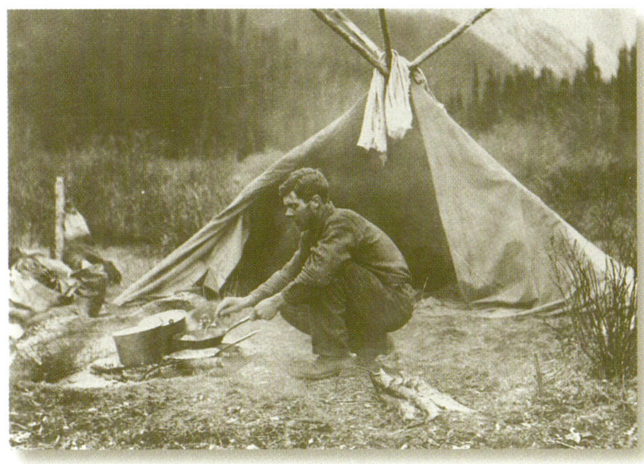

A lone forester makes use of his cooking skills in a fly-camp around 1920.

THE EARLY TRADING POSTS

The earliest trading post in the Athabasca valley was one built by William Henry in 1811. He was employed by David Thompson who represented the North West Company. In the 1850s, the important trading post on the Athabasca was the Hudson's Bay Company's Jasper House. But starvation threatened and the post was abandoned. This was surprising since Jasper House was one of the more profitable locations.

In 1858 Henry John Moberly, a chief factor for the Hudson's Bay Company, received permission to reopen the post. Henry and his wife, Suzan Cardinal, gathered together some forty-odd horses, a cook, a French-Canadian wrangler, and six young Iroquois. He had been to the area and decided to try an overland trip instead of relying on river travel. They set out from Lac Ste. Anne on October 20th and arrived at Jasper House about the middle of November. Shortly after their arrival they began work to restore the dilapidated buildings before cold weather set in. Henry and Suzan began a long line of Moberlys, starting with their two sons, Ewan and John.

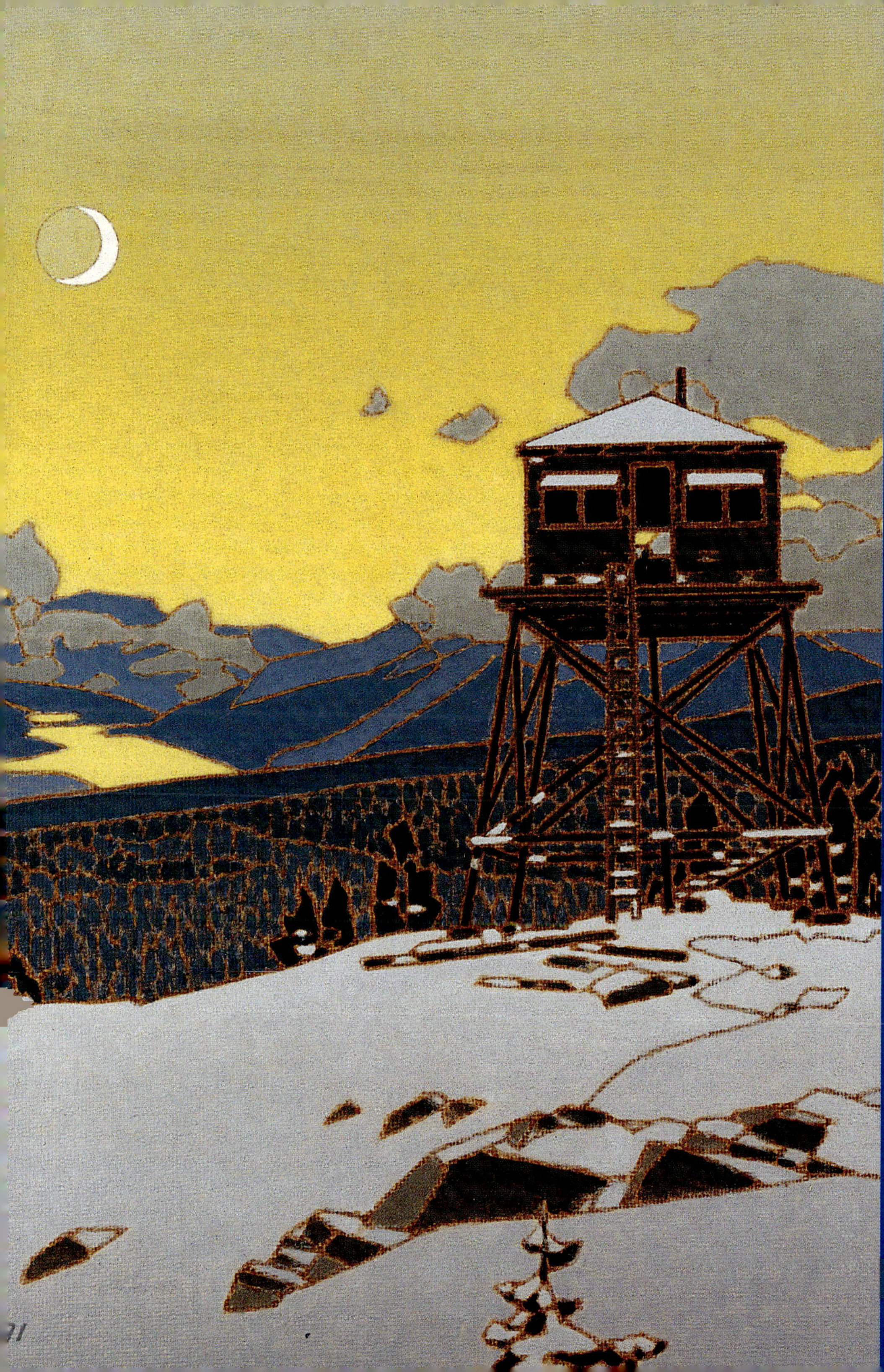

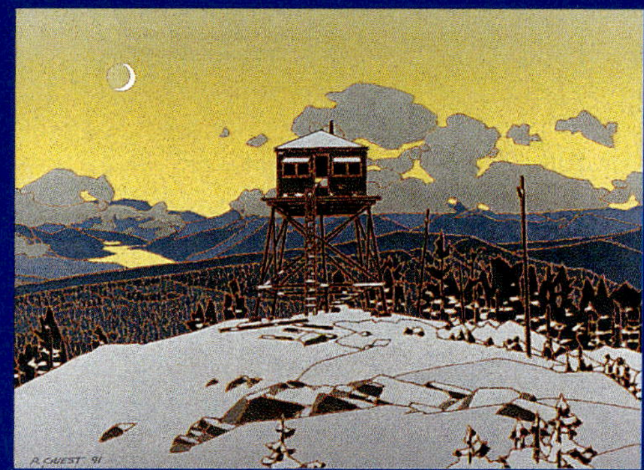

First Athabasca Lookout in Early Winter

"EVERYTHING *was covered with a fresh fall of snow, the spruce trees bending under the heavy load. The Athabasca was almost frozen, just a narrow stream of dark water flowing swiftly between the ice banks. Then up over the heavy bank of clouds came the sun, flooding the gigantic peaks with light, till the whole range shone and glittered like a dazzling chain of jewels. The mountains have many moods, but never have I seen them more beautiful than on that morning."*

J. B. Bickersteth, 1911

Old Sundance Tipis, Full Moon

The large group of Sundance tipis at Jarvis Lake differed from the usual tipi structures. These were erected from poplar saplings and were built for a religious ceremony by a band of Salteaux Indians some time ago. This area was previously known as Fish Lake Flats and was a traditional camping spot for people travelling over the old Trail. Near the tipi structures were a number of willow sweat lodges and the charred remains of old campfires. The painting shows how the tipis looked on a night in early August. When the I visited the spot the moon was full, adding a mysterious atmosphere.

SCOUTING WILES

Early trailblazers made lines over the landscape in all directions, and eventually these became part of a trail network. Their paths often took them through potentially dangerous areas. Those who had the task of assessing travelling conditions and trouble spots ahead of the others, the scouts, needed to avoid swampy places, soap holes, box canyons, heavy brush or deadfall, dangerous rocks, and spots where there was poor visibility. While on the lookout for game, there was always the chance of surprising a mother grizzly with cubs.

A dangerous river would have meant making a long detour to find a safer crossing, where the current was not so swift and the rapids not so deep. The balance between safety and reaching their destination in good time always had to be weighed.

Sweat lodges, Fish Lake Flats

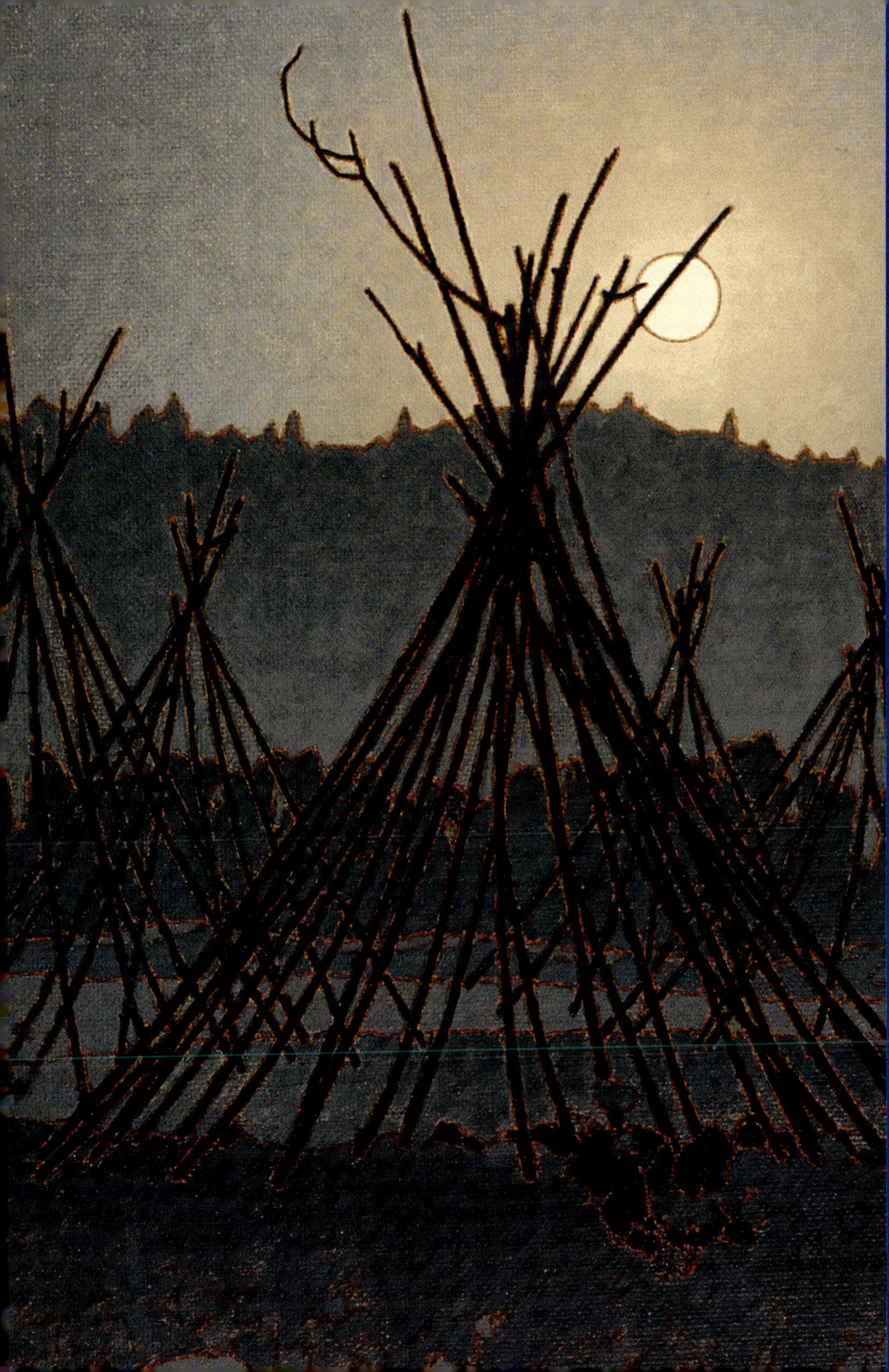

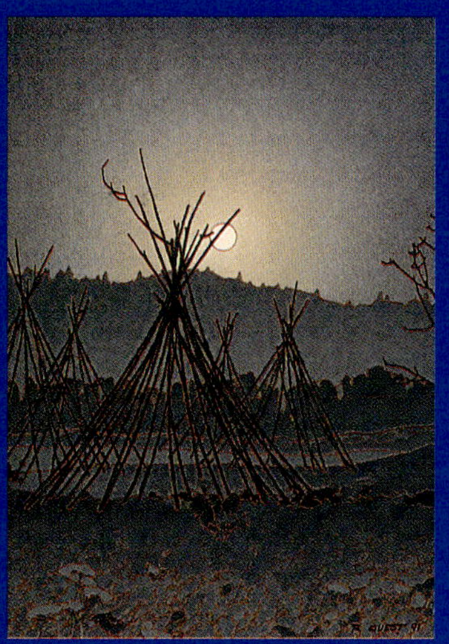

Old Sundance Tipis, Full Moon

"He believes profoundly in silence–the sign of perfect equilibrium. Silence is the absolute poise or balance of body, mind and spirit. The man who preserves his selfhood, ever calm and unshaken by the storms of existence–not a leaf, as it were, astir on the tree; not a ripple upon the surface of a shining pool - his, in the mind of the unlettered sage, is the ideal attitude and conduct of life."

Ernest Thompson Seton, 1911

Sundance Tipis, Red Dawn

Some of the same Sundance tipis shown in the previous painting are shown here, at the break of day when the first shock of brilliant red appeared along the horizon to the northeast. It was approaching 5:30 a.m., and the call of a solitary raven broke the silence. The dark silhouettes of the tipis made a special impact seen against the raw colours and strange pattern in the sky. It was an unexpected reward for waiting in the area for much of the night.

◆

LOW IMPACT TRAILING

It has been pointed out that, unlike white people, the Indians made trails without chopping down trees or moving obstacles out of the way. They preferred to go around them, which was less bother and seemed more in harmony with the environment. Their cayuses, raised in the wilds, were rugged and well adapted to this kind of trail making. Most Indian trails saw their heaviest traffic during the summer and fall when conditions were suitable for moving families.

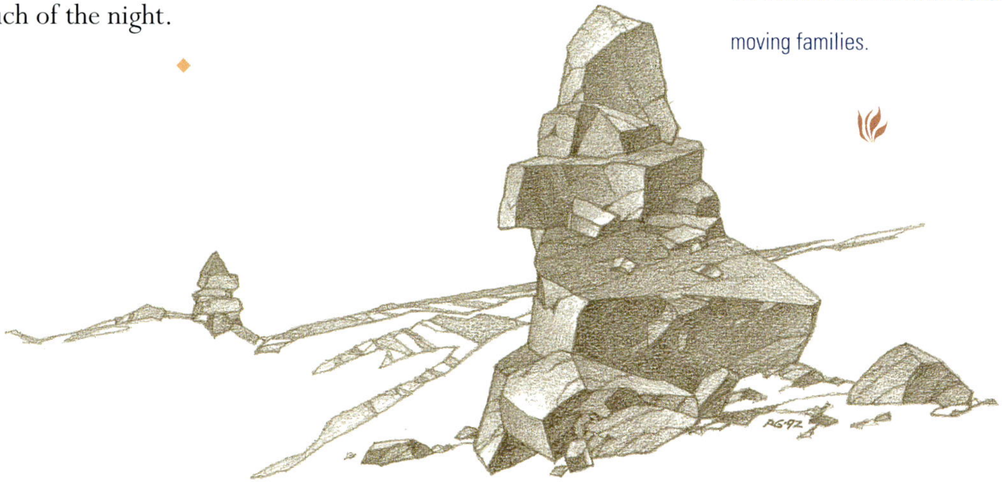

Stone markers for early hunters

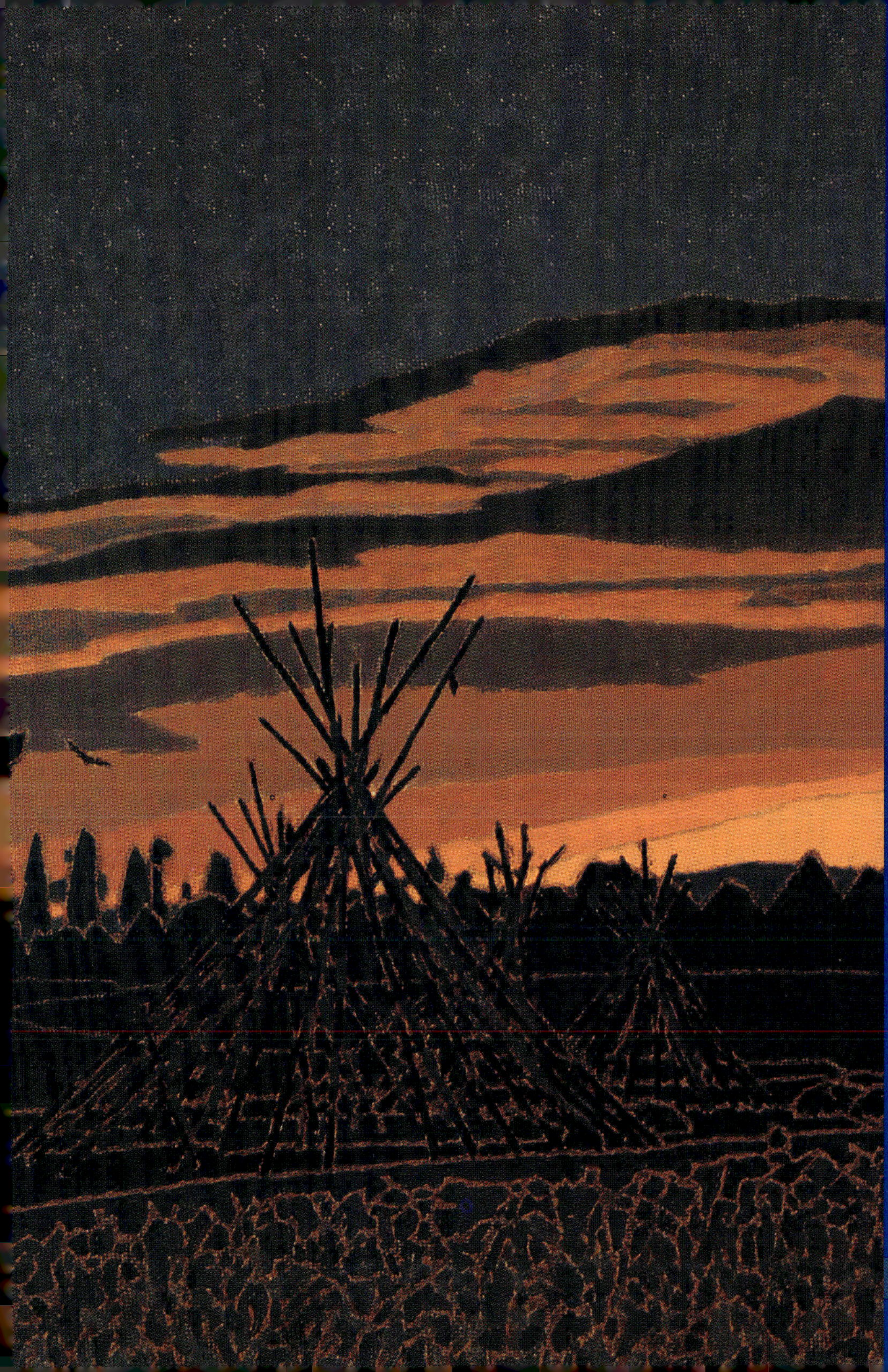

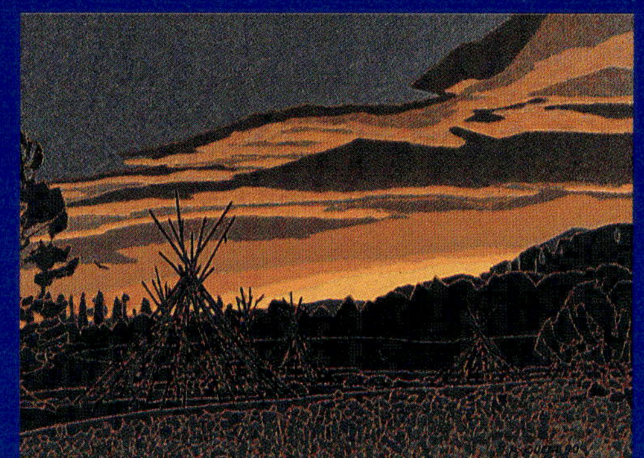
Sundance Tipis, Red Dawn

"If you ask him,
'What is silence?'
he will answer, 'It is the great mystery! The holy silence is His voice!' If you ask, 'What are the fruits of silence?' he will say, 'They are self-control, true courage or endurance, patience, dignity and reverence. Silence is the cornerstone of character.'"

Ernest Thompson Seton, 1911

Fish Lake Flats Graveyard, Moonlight

South of Jarvis Lake, partly hidden on flats covered with willows and poplar trees, is a graveyard. These are the graves of natives—men, women, and children—who once camped in the area and followed the old packtrails. Most of the spirit houses at Fish Lake Flats are the old style, but a few could be as recent as 1950. There are about 50 graves, all contained by a fence made of long rails that seems to try to keep out the surrounding forest. It was a night in late summer. From the eastern horizon a full moon rose above the hill and gave an eerie bluish light to the entire valley. Everything was still.

◆

Ceremonial cloth tied around trees, Fish Lake Flats

THE SPIRIT HOUSE

There are Indian graveyards at various locations throughout the foothills; a number of them are close to the Hinton Trail. Many of the old-style burial grounds include structures commonly referred to as "spirit houses." Most of these wooden shelters look like small, A-frame huts, and were meant to protect the remains of loved ones and items they might need in the next world. The spirit houses were also meant to provide a refuge for the soul. They had a purpose in both a physical and spiritual sense, and their origins date back to the early 1800s.

Spirit houses likely had their beginning with one or more of the Athapascan groups, like the Sekani and Beaver Indians of northeastern British Columbia. The traditions of these groups, especially their mortuary rites, have left their mark in western Alberta where tribal territories overlapped today's provincial boundaries.

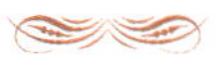

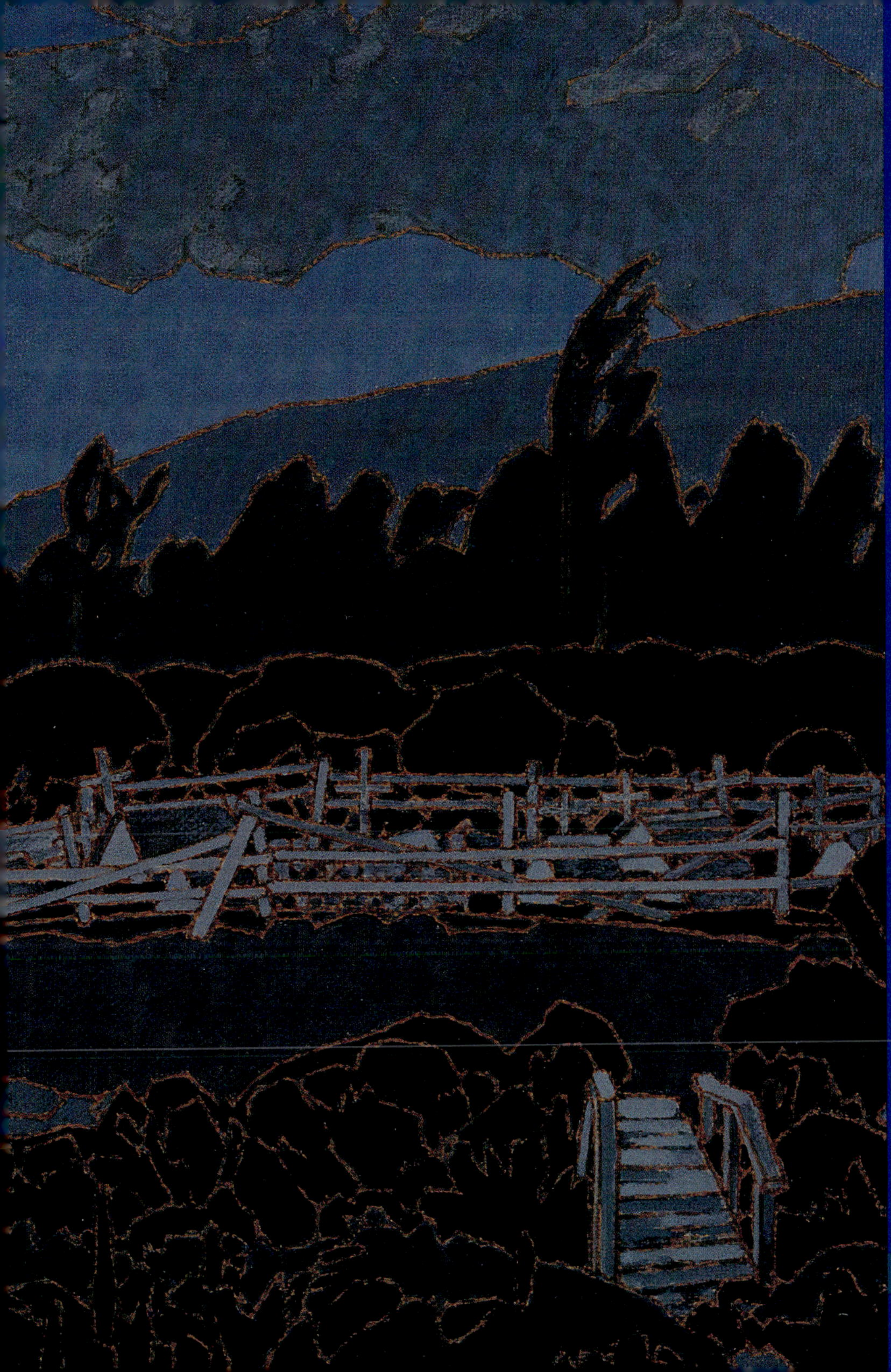

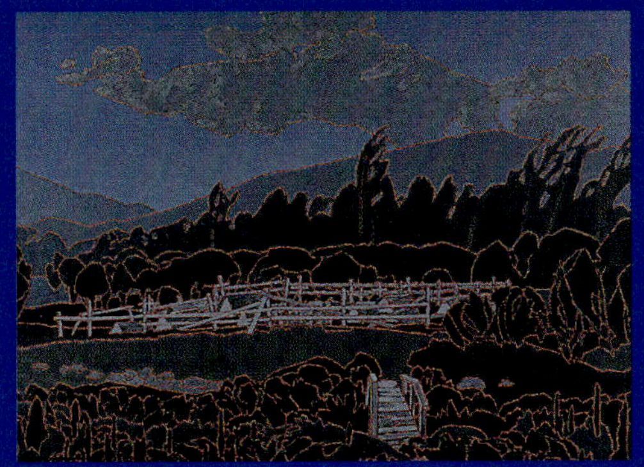

Fish Lake Flats Graveyard, Moonlight

"I saw some kind of fence just within range of the firelight and assumed that some prospector had built a smudge for his horses as I did at Grande Cache. Next morning I was in for a shock. What I figured out to be a smudge turned out to be an Indian grave. The customary roof was missing and in its place a few rocks were mounded up, with a wooden cross, badly rotted, lying on top. I lost no time in getting my bedding away from there."

John Glenn, c.1920

Summer Night at Jarvis Lake

It was the end of a hot day. The last light in the western sky was getting dim towards midnight, and the silhouetted forms around the shores of Jarvis Lake became very dark, almost black. This lake, along the old Lower Trail, was not far from old Entrance, and has always been a popular spot for the people of the Trail. Its original name, Fish Lake, was quite appropriate; over the years, travellers could catch fresh fish at almost any time of year—a welcome change from their otherwise moosemeat diet. There was always a good supply of firewood and shelter for camping on the flats, particularly at the southwest end of the lake. The main packtrail kept close to the west shore of the lake, and the meadows provided excellent grazing for horses.

◆

Rowboat on the shore, November

JASPER PARK EXODUS

When Jasper Park was established, a number of prominent Metis families were asked to leave the homes they'd made along the Athabasca River. Their forebears had come from eastern Canada, and some were of Iroquois and French extraction. On January 4, 1910, a parks official from Ottawa came to the area and, after two meetings with the Metis, settled the terms to remove them from the proposed national park. The thought of leaving Jasper was not to their liking, but the cash and the prospect of being able to make a better living were attractive, and they accepted the terms.

In the spring the move was made. John Moberly took a choice quarter-section close to Prairie Creek, where his descendants still own property. His son, Ewan Moberly, and Adam Joachim went as far away as Grande Cache. They took the old Forestry trail from Entrance and cleared it to move livestock, wagons, sleighs, ploughs, and other things the new settlers needed. This was thereafter known as the Moberly Trail.

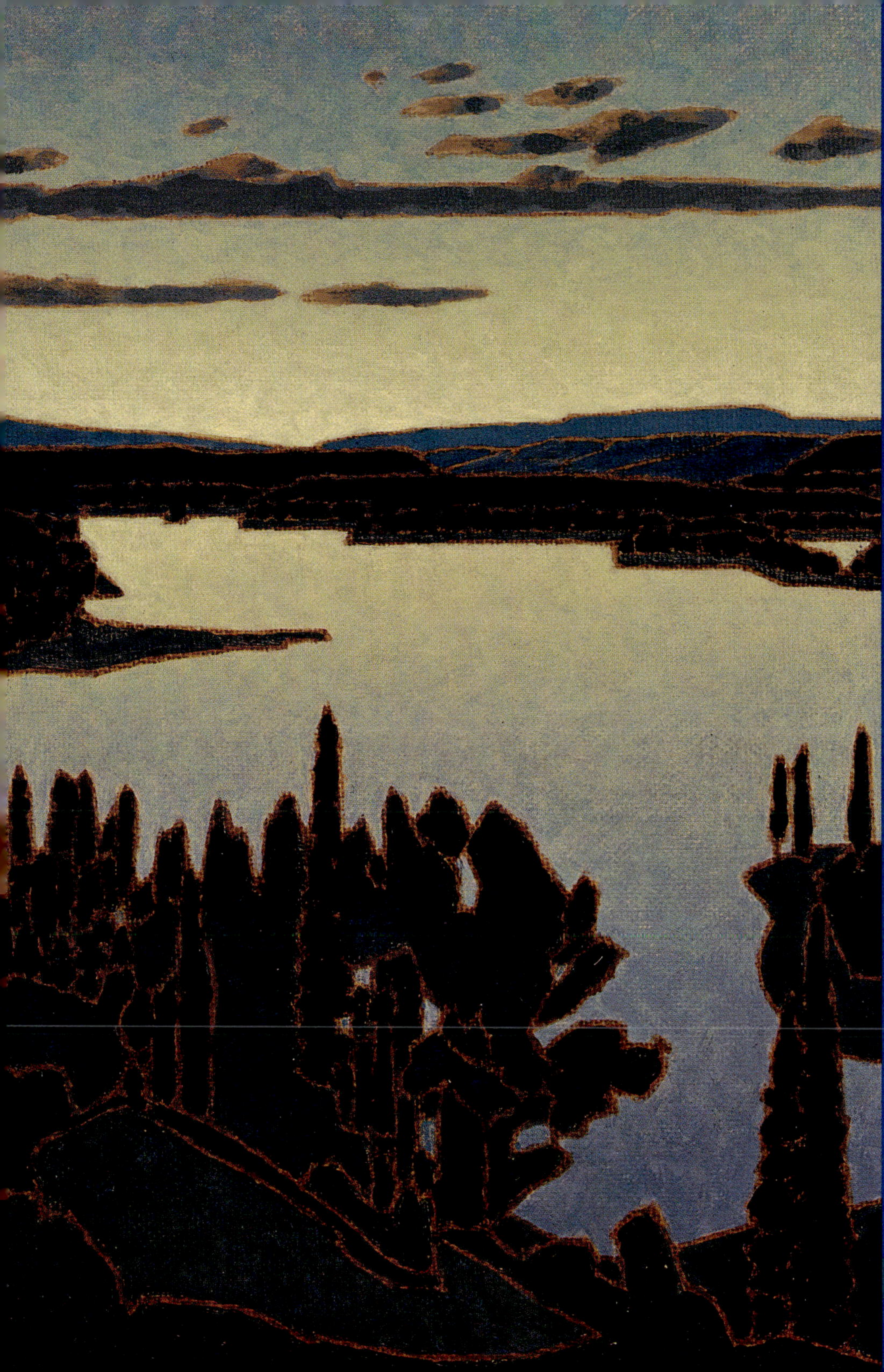

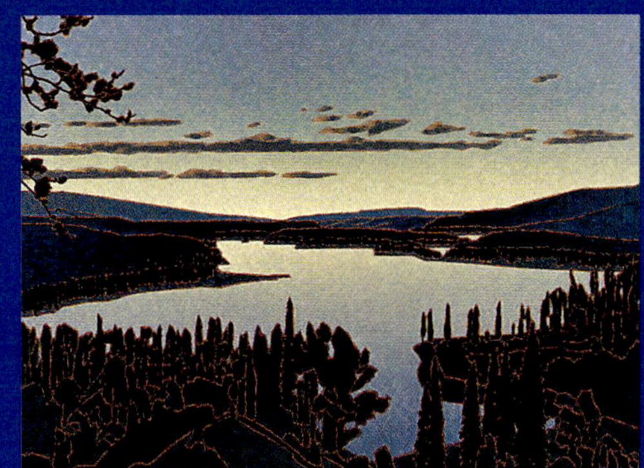

Summer Night at Jarvis Lake

"The campfire crackled, on the soft breeze came the distant tinkle of horse-bells, a mosquito hummed, and a night hawk with his shrill cry swept past, the moon's rays filtered through the spruce bows, the fire died down and the camp slept. And they ask if one grows lonely. Lonely? How could one, when all nature sings the evening hymn."

Mary T. S. Schaffer, 1911

Crossing on the Wildhay River

In some of the finest mountain and foothill country, the Wildhay River flows to the northeast. After the spring runoff the water clears to a turquoise colour, like other mountain streams whose origins are the great icefields of the Continental Divide. The river flows through prime wildlife habitat. Historically, trapping and hunting have been the main attractions of the area, with many local native and other people using the Lower Trail for access into it. Although the Wildhay, or the "Hay" as it is sometimes called, looks pastoral and harmless in midsummer, it has been the site of drowning accidents when waters were high and horses were swept off their feet. Like most mountain rivers it can change almost overnight.

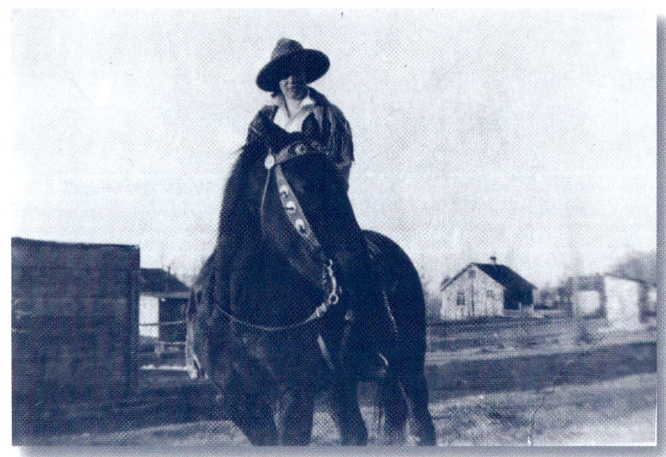

Emma Nickerson was in her element at the local rodeo.

EMMA NICKERSON WAS UNSINKABLE!

Emma Nickerson was quite an impressive figure in the Hinton area. She was an outdoorswoman who, with her husband Nick, started a guiding business for hunters in 1929 which lasted for 29 years. Emma was one of the very few women to hold both a guiding and an outfitter license. She was frequently a winner at local rodeos, starring in such events as the half-mile relay race and steer riding. But most of all, it was her skill with a gravel truck that brought her fame. She was likely Alberta's first successful woman truck driver. Once, when giving a group of native people a ride in the back of her gravel truck, she accidentally tripped the unloading gear, dumping the whole gang, grannies, children and all, on the ground. They loved it, and asked her to do it again.

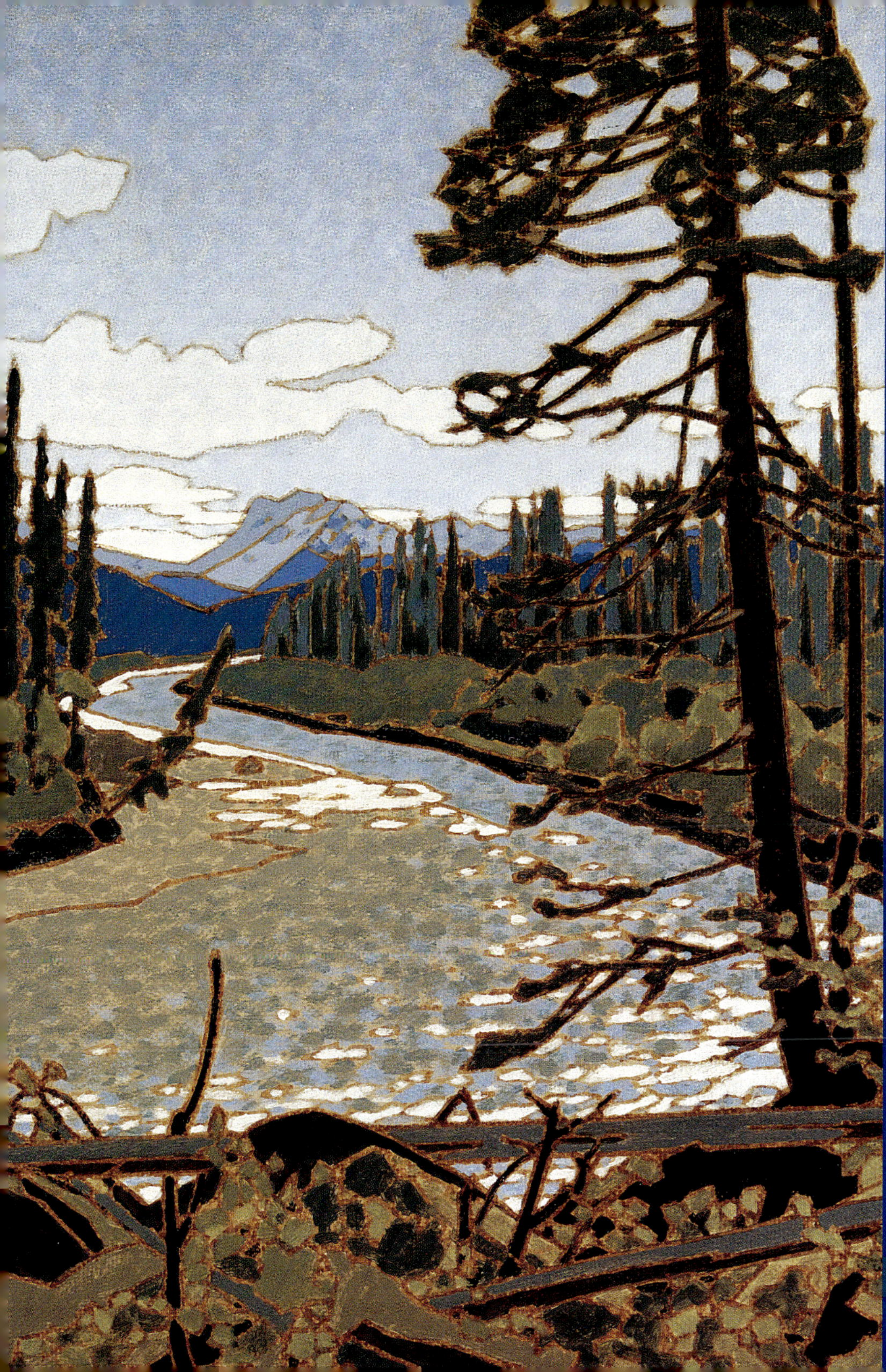

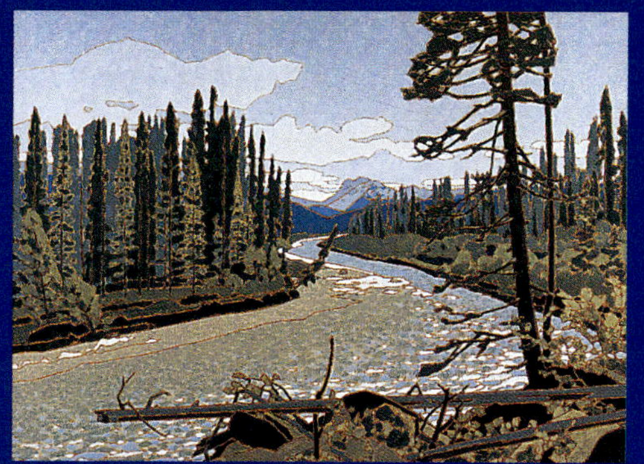

Crossing on the Wildhay River

"GIVING THE old fellow his head, and planting my feet firmly down in the stirrups to prevent their natural tendency to come to the surface and float in front of me, I abandoned life, fright, everything, and watched in numbness that angry flood."

Mary T. S. Schaffer, 1911

Telephone Line on Old Lower Trail

The first telephone line was set up along the Lower Trail. It was a Forestry project started about 1920, roughly the same time that Ludwig Hoff was clearing the first horsetrail from Grande Cache to the Athabasca River. The objective at that time was to have a line of communication between Forestry headquarters at old Entrance and a distant ranger cabin at Muskeg River. After months of clearing a six-foot swath through the bush, with crews working with axes in all kinds of weather, the project was completed. And what a feat it must have been! Quite often the telephone line ran parallel to the packtrail as shown in the painting. The view is from a spot on the top of the hill on the east side of the Berland River. It was early June, and among the lodgepole pines I could smell and see the Labrador Tea, dotted with cream-coloured blossoms.

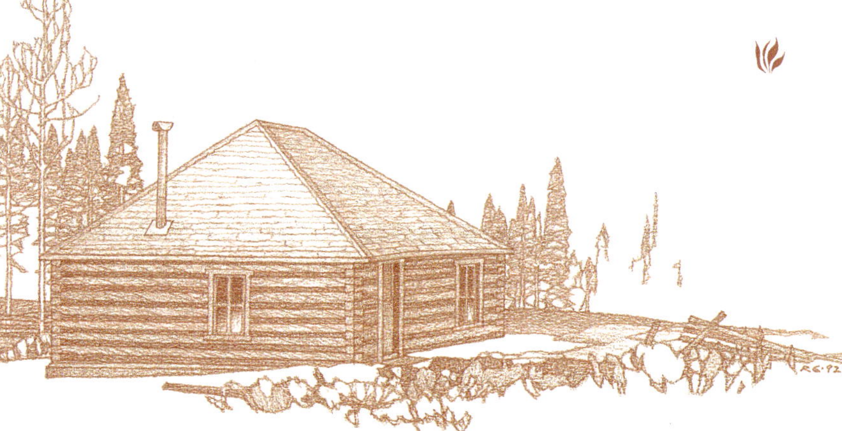

Moberly Creek ranger station

PUSHING THE LINE THROUGH

For the ranger, duties were a year-round commitment. As well as trying to keep an eye on the forests, he was expected to maintain campsites for big game hunters, conduct wildlife counts, and act as game warden. During the mid-1920s, in addition to his other duties, he had to organize the crews putting the first telephone line through from Entrance to the ranger station at Muskeg River. This was referred to as Mile 60, being approximately sixty miles northwest of Entrance. The project involved local residents, one of whom was Felix Plante of the Hinton area. The following men became known for their contribution to the formative years of Forestry: James Shand Harvey, Ludwig Hoff, Stan Clark, Bill Smith, and John Glenn.

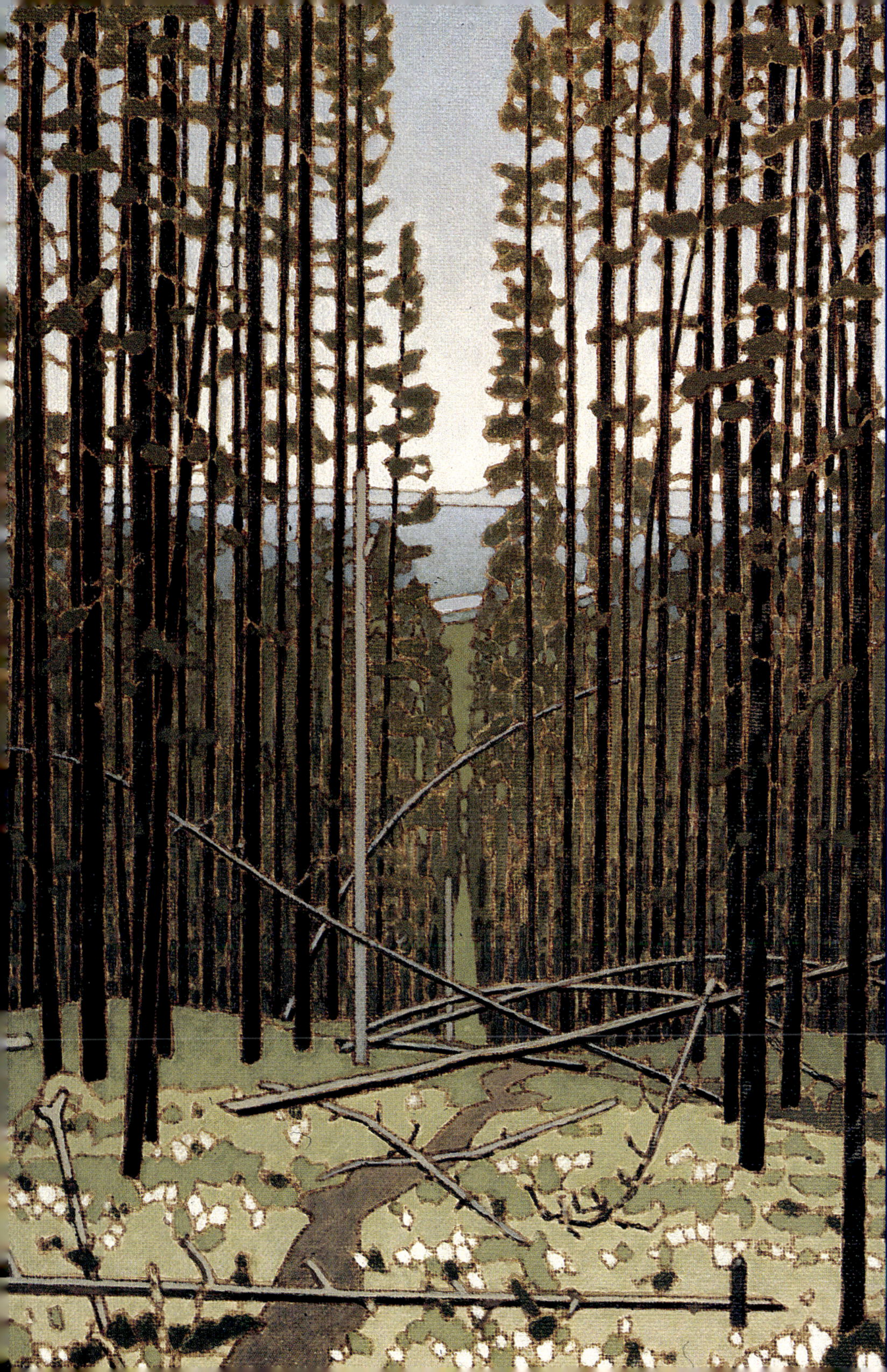

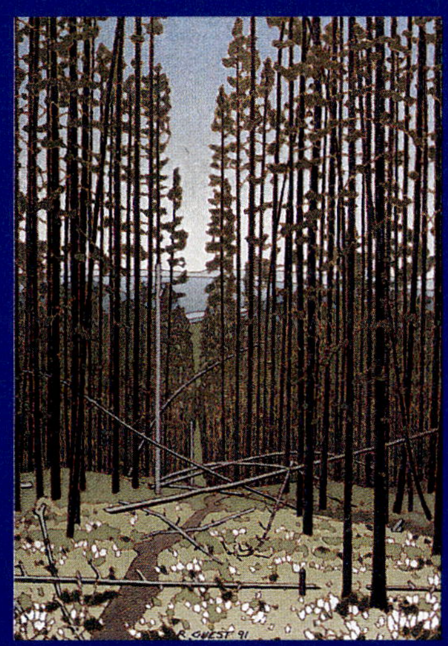

Telephone Line on Old Lower Trail

"[Ludwig Hoff's] cabin was about a quarter of a mile distant and it always amused me to visit, as it was built on a sloping hillside. He had not gone to the trouble of levelling the foundation, with the result that he appeared to be walking uphill no matter what he was doing. If he had ever fallen out of bed he would have ended up against the stove or the door at the lower end."

John Glenn, c.1920

Main Baptiste Cabin, Cabin Creek

One of the original Forestry cabins can still be seen along the Lower Trail. This sturdy log building is an example of the type built in the Athabasca Forest Reserve during the 1920s. It is situated on Cabin Creek and now serves mainly as a base for a local trapper during the winter months. Although its appearance has been altered with the addition of a porch on the front and a storage shed on one side, the building has not been changed much over the years. The Baptiste Cabin overlooks a stretch of hay meadows along the creekbed, forested foothills, and, further west, the snowcapped Rocky Mountains. This is a late-spring view.

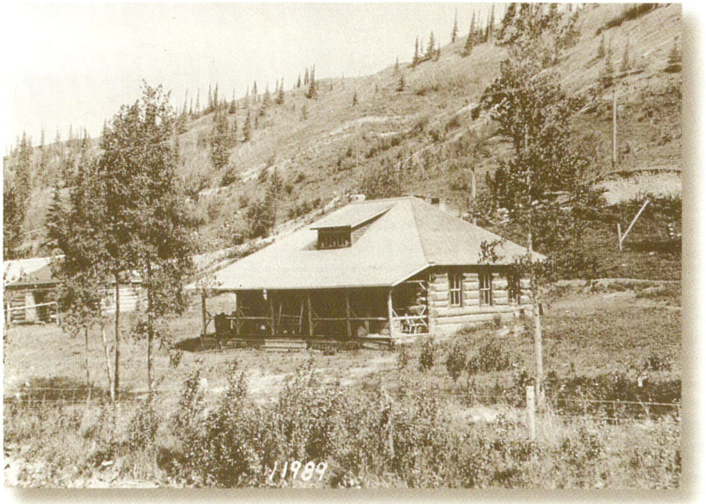

An early Forestry Superintendent's house in 1917

THE ATHABASCA FOREST RESERVE

The Athabasca Forest Reserve was 4,000 square miles in area, from Prairie Creek to the 15th base line in the north and to the British Columbia border in the west. James Shand Harvey was hired as one of the first rangers in 1912, and his duty was to patrol the Rock Lake and Grande Cache district. Only a few trails were passable then, and there were no forestry cabins at all. By the 1920s there had been changes. A network of bush trails had been opened for packhorses through the headwaters of Sheep Creek and the Sulphur and Smoky Rivers, extending east to the vicinity of Grande Cache. These trails tied in with older ones, such as the Hinton Trail, coming down from the north. A number of stop-over cabins for the rangers had been built. The cabins were usually about 20 miles apart—the average distance a forest ranger was expected to ride in a day, weather permitting.

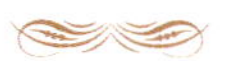

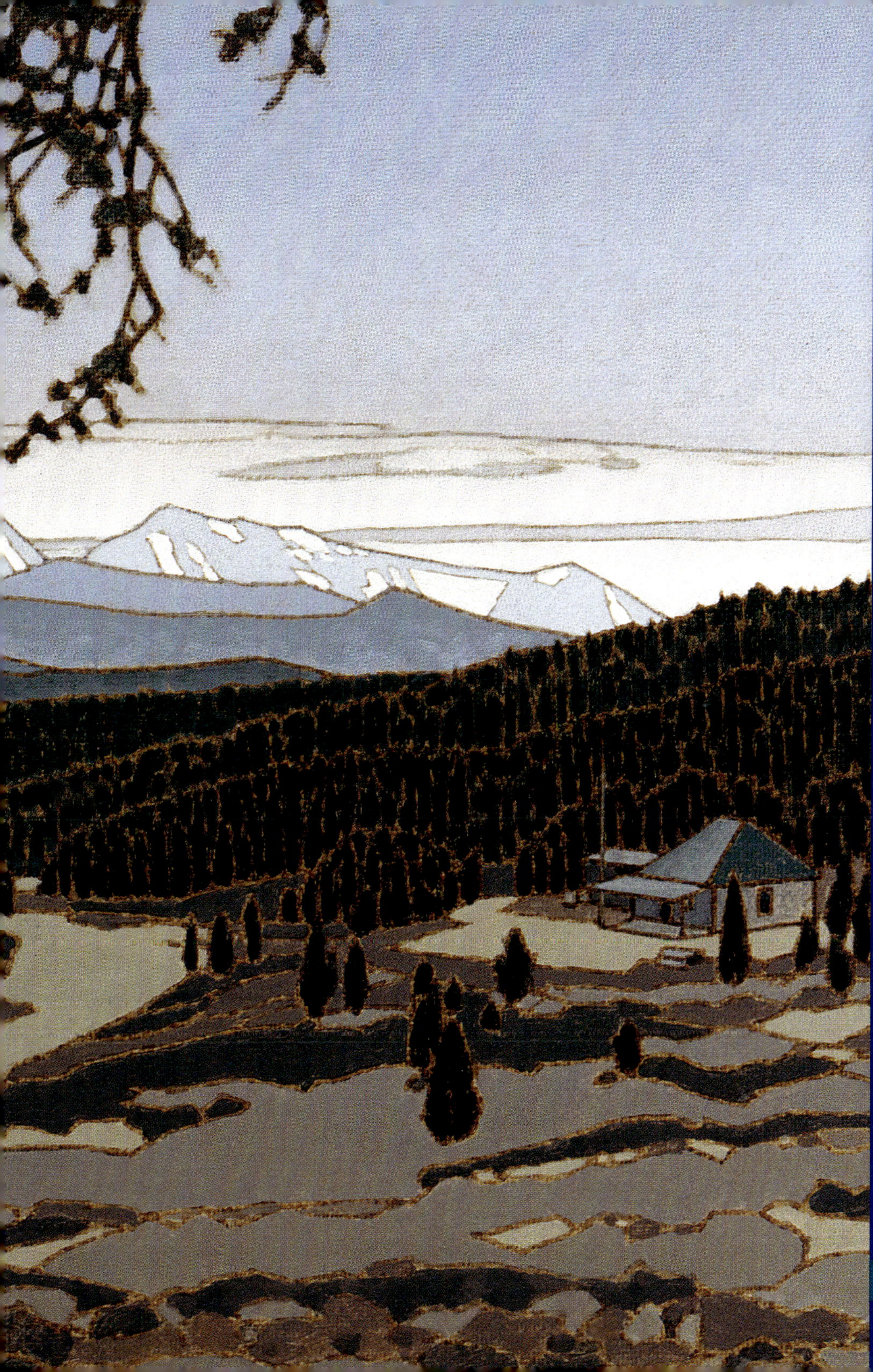

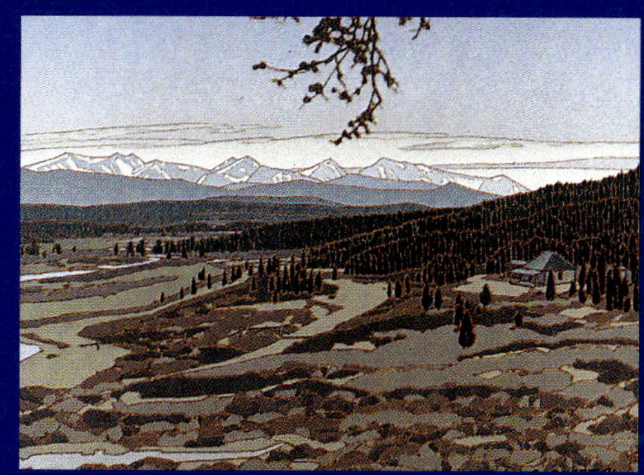

Main Baptiste Cabin, Cabin Creek

"ACTION was [Curly Phillips's] antidote to loneliness. In the cabin he always had a dozen things waiting to be done and his utter fearlessness of the wilds helped him disregard the shrieking wind, the howling wolves, or the sharp crack of timber split in the cold. On one occasion at least, kept in by a blizzard, Curly had finished all his repairs, cooking, washing and sewing, and was reduced to rereading old newspapers trying to memorize all the church notices and want ads."

W. C. Taylor, 1984

Downstream from Berland River Crossing

The river known as the Big Berland runs through one of the most scenic spots accessible between Grande Cache and Entrance. By midsummer, when the spring runoff from the mountains had cleared and the water level had dropped, crossing with horses was no problem. Likely the best ford the old Trail crossed was close to the bridge now on Highway 40. The view for the painting is downriver from the bridge, facing north. Woodland caribou live in this area, with its timbered foothills and open river flats, and they migrate back and forth, depending on the season. Native trappers and hunters have long preferred this kind of country, and the original Indian trails were maintained for access by the early Forestry Service.

By midsummer the river water clears to blue-green.

Rifle and caribou gunrack

THE EVOLUTION OF HIGHWAY 40

Part of the Trail that wasn't phased out was the section called the Lower Trail, going northwest from Entrance. Looking back, one can see how this original pack-trail evolved over the years. It began as an Indian trail, winding its narrow path across country between the Athabasca and Smoky Rivers. Later, Forestry widened and cleared it for wagons and sleighs, and then, about the time oil was discovered in the Muskeg River area, it was upgraded for vehicles. Finally, when the town of Grande Cache was established, and the mine opened, the road was paved. It is known today as Highway 40. There were the inevitable minor changes along the way, such as straightening sections and bypassing swamps, but generally the highway has kept to the trail route.

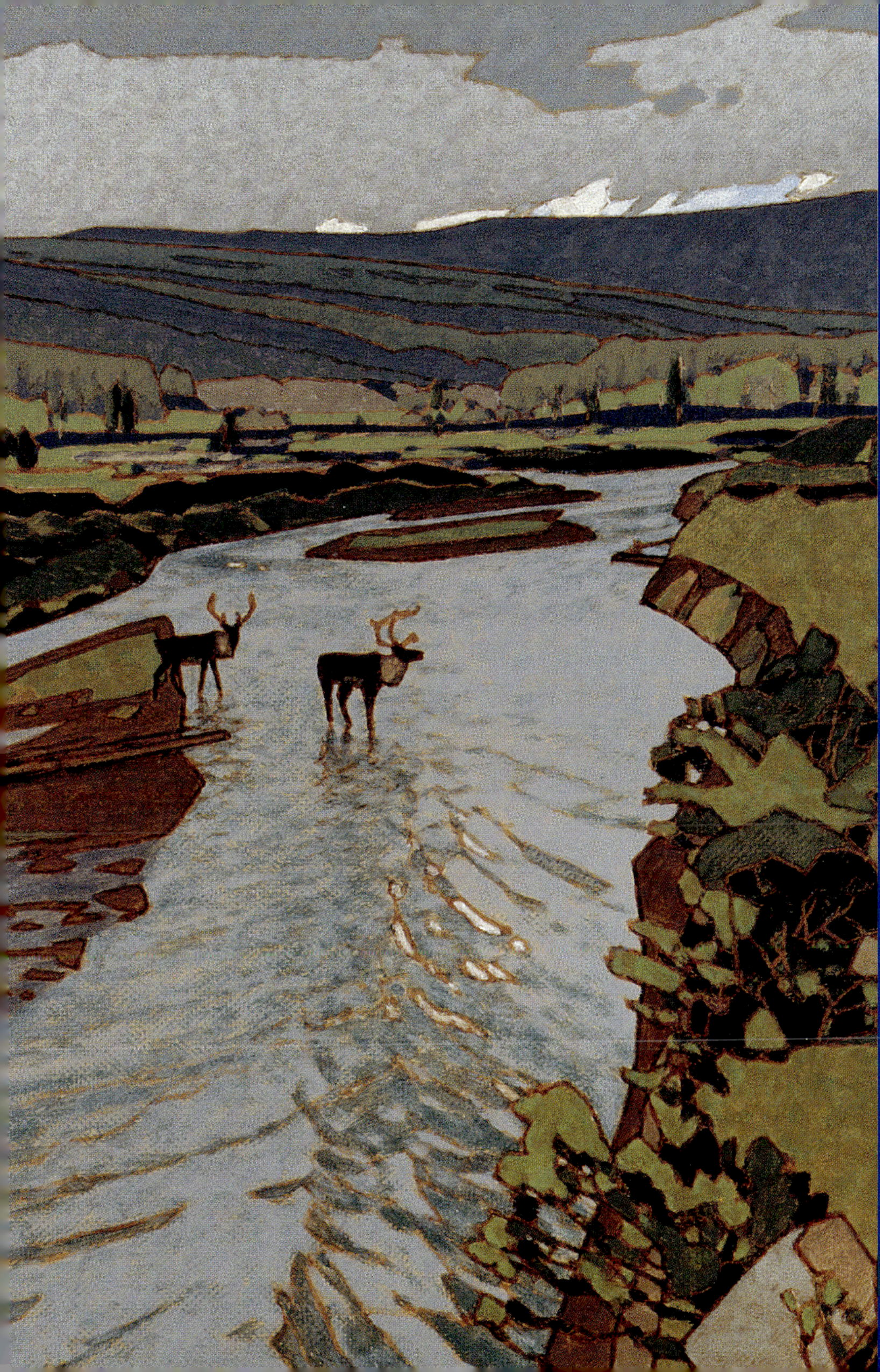

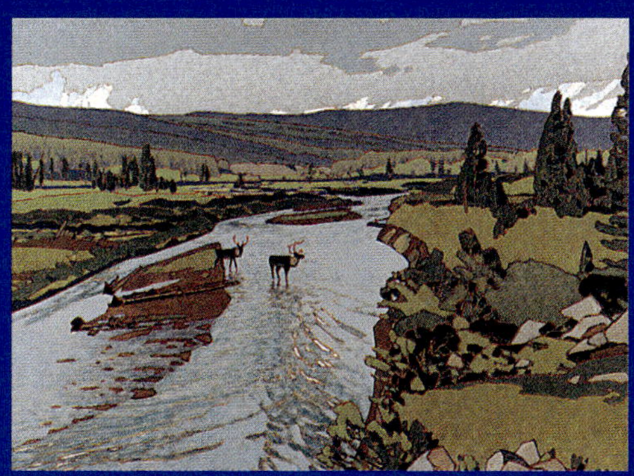

Downstream from Berland River Crossing

"Mr. Stauffer, who lives at Prairie Creek, has thoroughly informed himself as to the merits of the route. The road is constantly travelled winter and summer by trappers and packers, who take supplies into the headwaters of the Smoky and to the Peace River. Mr. Stauffer claims a man can travel over the road any time, dry shod, on foot."

Edmonton Bulletin, 1910

Location of Pierre Grey's Trading Post

The Pierre Greys Lakes were named after Pierre Gris, commonly known as Pierre Grey, a pioneer trader of the Grande Cache area. He had a homestead at Lake Isle, east of Hinton, and he established a successful trading post in 1889, west of the lakes that bear his name. He dealt with trappers, mostly native, over a wide area north and west of his holdings. Like other freetraders of his day, he avoided the Hudson's Bay Company, preferring to sell fur directly to the buyers in Edmonton. Near the old Lower Trail, a group of log cabins and a few scattered graves mark the spot where Pierre Grey's post was located, but, victims of time, many have fallen in. The painting shows the spot in mid-September.

◆

PIERRE GREY, TRADER OF THE LAKES

Of the various fur traders in the west at the time, Pierre Grey was one of the more successful. He came into the country before there was much competition and soon developed a good relationship with trappers over a wide area north and west of Hinton. An example of his success was the winter of 1921–22, when he took 100 horses, laden with furs, to sell in Edmonton. Reportedly, 26 horses carried nothing but valuable marten pelts. His success enabled him and his wife to take in a number of homeless native children. He was a shrewd businessman, not particularly liked by the Hudson's Bay Company. Although there is no record of Grey taking the Hinton Trail north, he had many occasions to travel the southern portion of it on his way to Edmonton.

Stretched hide of a black bear

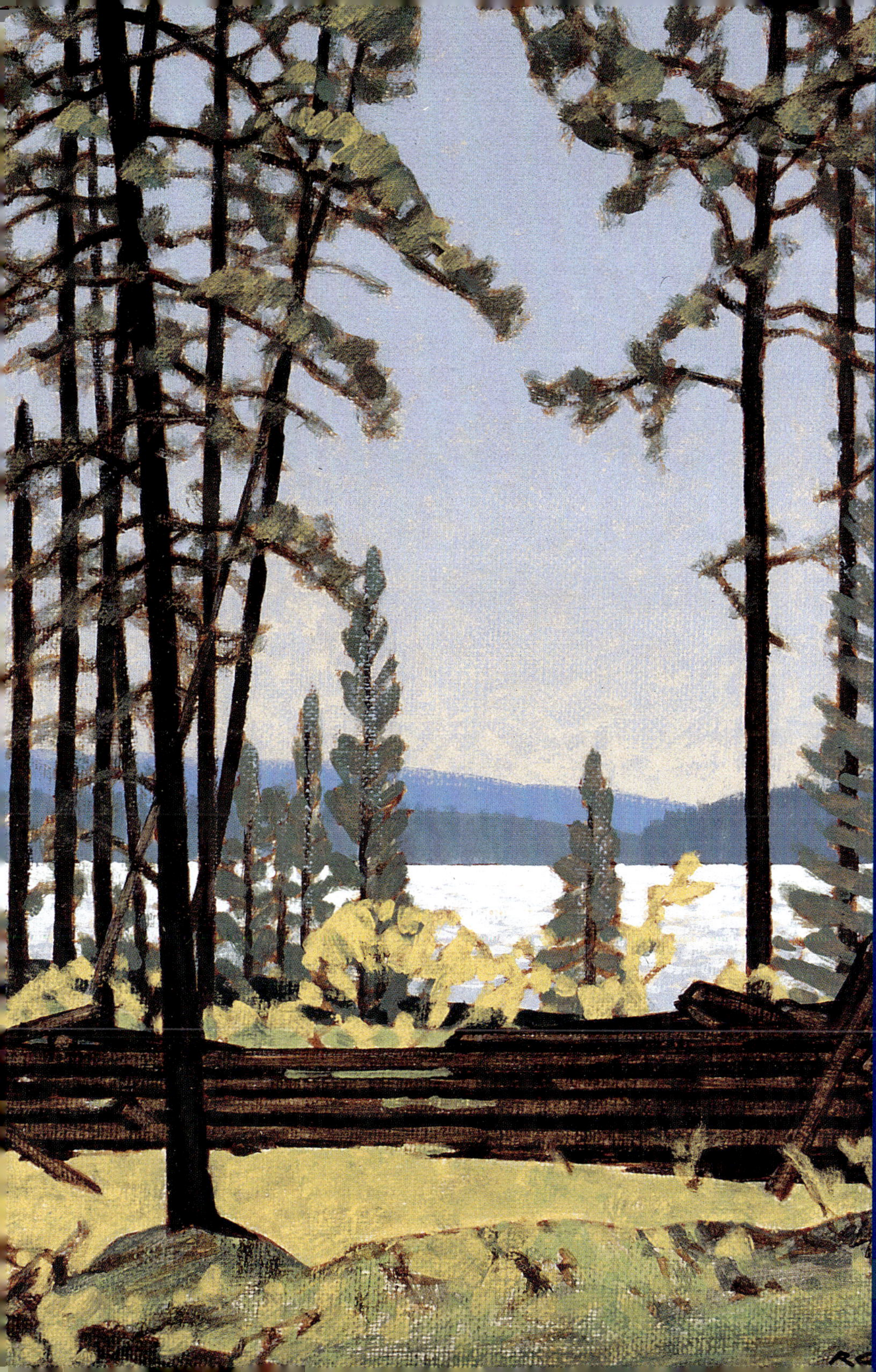

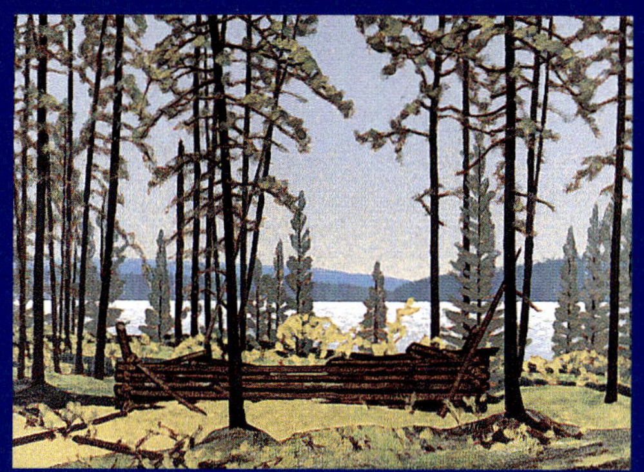

Location of Pierre Grey's Trading Post

"With willing ears we listened to the tales brought in by hunters and trappers, those men of this land who are the true pioneers of the country in spite of the fact that they have written nothing and are but little known."

Mary T. S. Schaffer, 1911

Approaching Thunderstorm at Pierre Greys Lakes

This thunderstorm was observed at Pierre Greys Lakes, but not the lake where the trading post was. The five lakes, spread out in different directions, are all surrounded by lodgepole pine and spruce, and caribou moss covers much of the forest floor. The lakes are close to the original packtrail. In summer, canoeing and fishing have been the main attraction and, in winter, there is ice fishing if the snow and ice are not too thick. The Pierre Greys Lakes have more than their share of stories of violence, death, injury, and incidents alluding to the supernatural. Witnessing the eerie atmosphere just before a storm breaks makes such tales seem quite believable. I painted this in early summer.

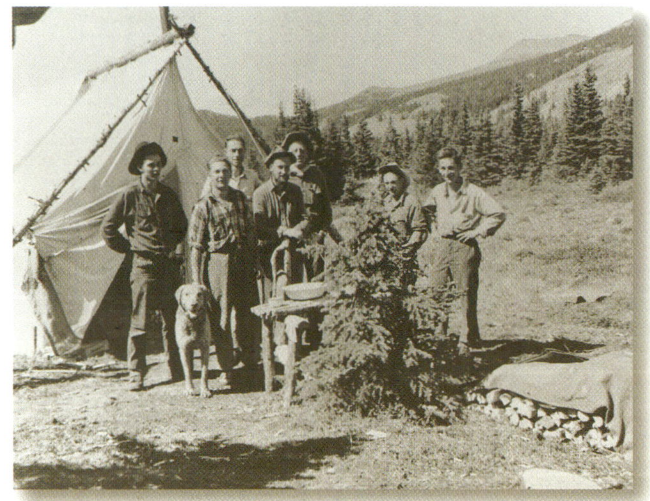

In the early 1950s Dr. Irish (third from left) and his crew surveyed much of the high country.

DR. IRISH AND THE GEOLOGICAL SURVEY

Dr. E. J. W. Irish made a significant contribution to the history of the area. In the late 1940s, Dr. Irish was a leading figure in the Geological Survey of Canada, and represented the men and women who took part in field work in those days. For a number of years Dr. Irish, with his crew and the necessary wrangler, packer, and cook, combed the foothills of the front range through much of what is now Willmore Wilderness Park. He gathered scientific descriptions of the rock, soils, and minerals of that area. His detailed maps featured such things as strata, main trenches, and faults, and he also noted trails and stopping places. This kind of information was useful to early gas and oil exploration programs. In 1949 the first oilwell was drilled near Muskeg River. Because roads were non-existent beyond Grande Cache, Dr. Irish, like others, had to make use of the old trails to reach his study area, which went back as far as the Continental Divide.

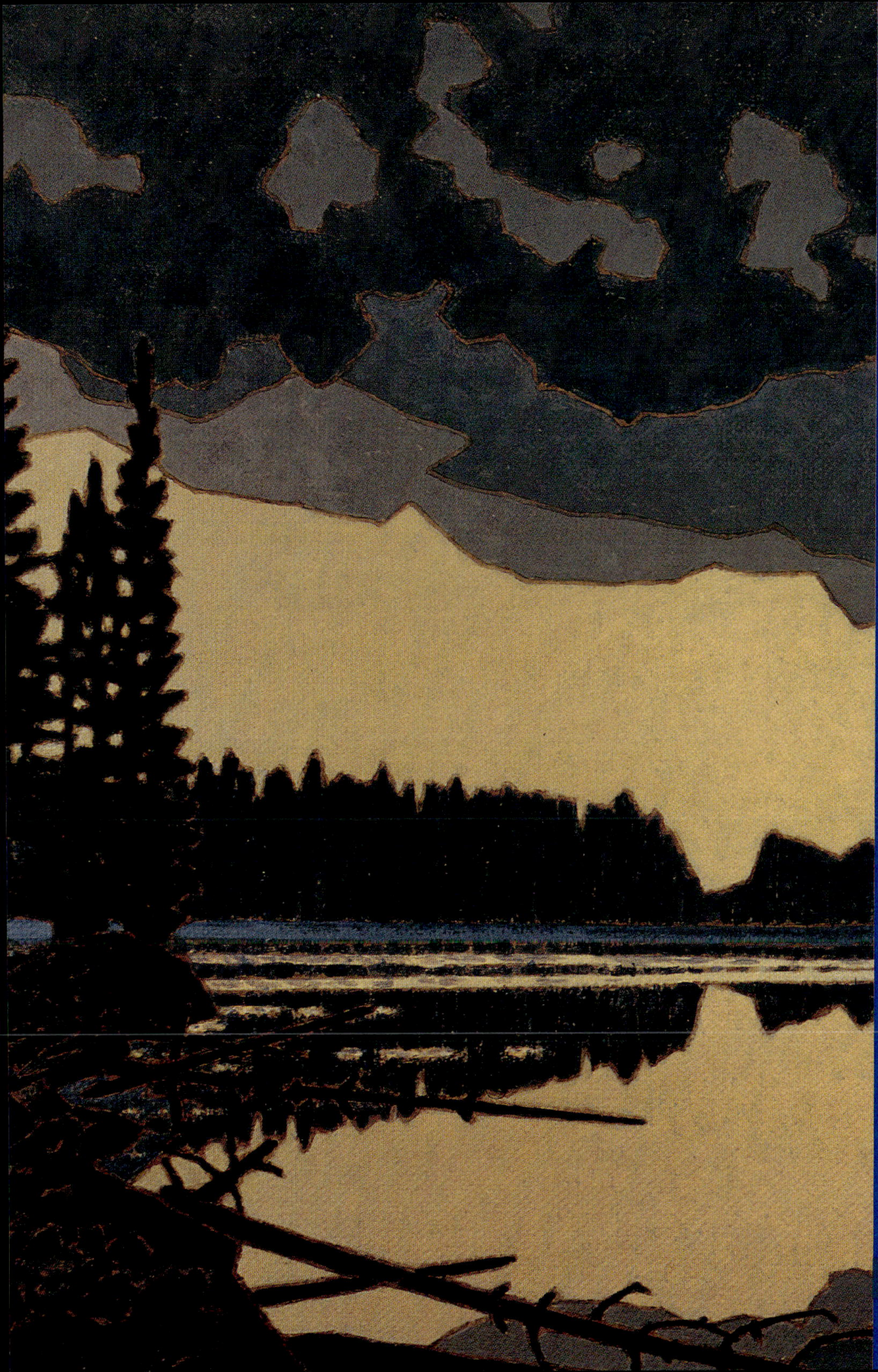

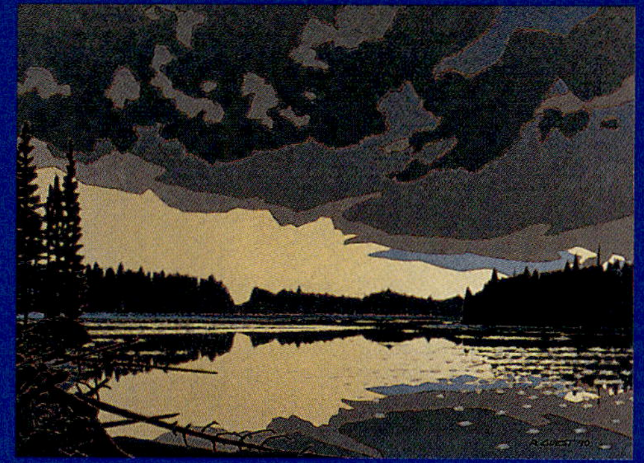

Approaching Thunderstorm at Pierre Greys Lakes

"SOME TIME *during the night I was awakened by a terrific crash. The wind had blown down an old dry snag which in turn had smashed the ridge pole of our tent. In all other camps I had made double sure that all dry snags likely to fall on the tents were taken down but on this occasion lack of time had prevented us from doing so."*

John Glenn, c.1920

View from the Falls on Muskeg River

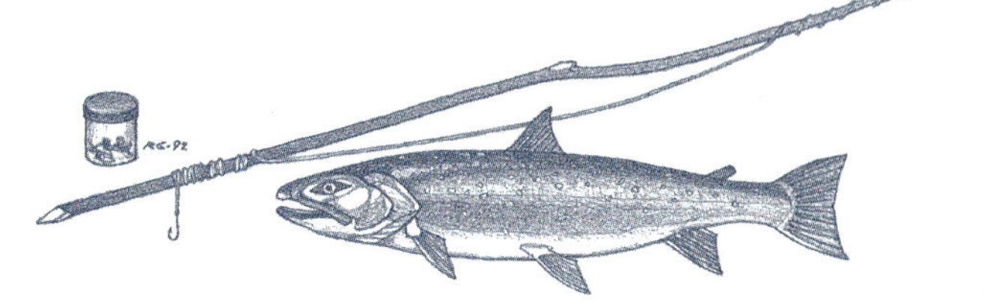

Of the many landmarks in the Grande Cache area, the tumbling, roaring falls on the Muskeg River stand out. In the past, travellers left the packtrail above to try their luck in the deep pools. In times of need, fresh trout was a wonderful change from a diet of dried meat. In places, the rock canyons rise at least 100 feet above the river, making the bottom of the falls area dark, even on a bright, sunny day. The falls were observed in early June.

JOHN PATTON AND THE SEARCH FOR OIL

Oil exploration was a major development in the 1950s. Among others, John Patton was there to take part in it. In 1954, as a geologist, he made a trip into the foothills area between Hinton and the Smoky River, near Grande Cache. He was always one to enjoy a little adventure, but he had no way of knowing what he was in for as he and his crew set out along the old road northwest of Entrance. Bridges on the only road had been washed out by flooding—vehicles were out of the question and the crew had to rely on packhorses. A few balky ones, unpredictable when fording swollen creeks and rivers, added spice to the trip. During his study of fossil beds and outcrops, he reached some of the highest ground along the Smoky River. It all made for a very challenging summer.

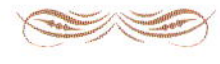

Ammonites and a Shell Fossil

TOP: The endangered dolly varden, Muskeg River

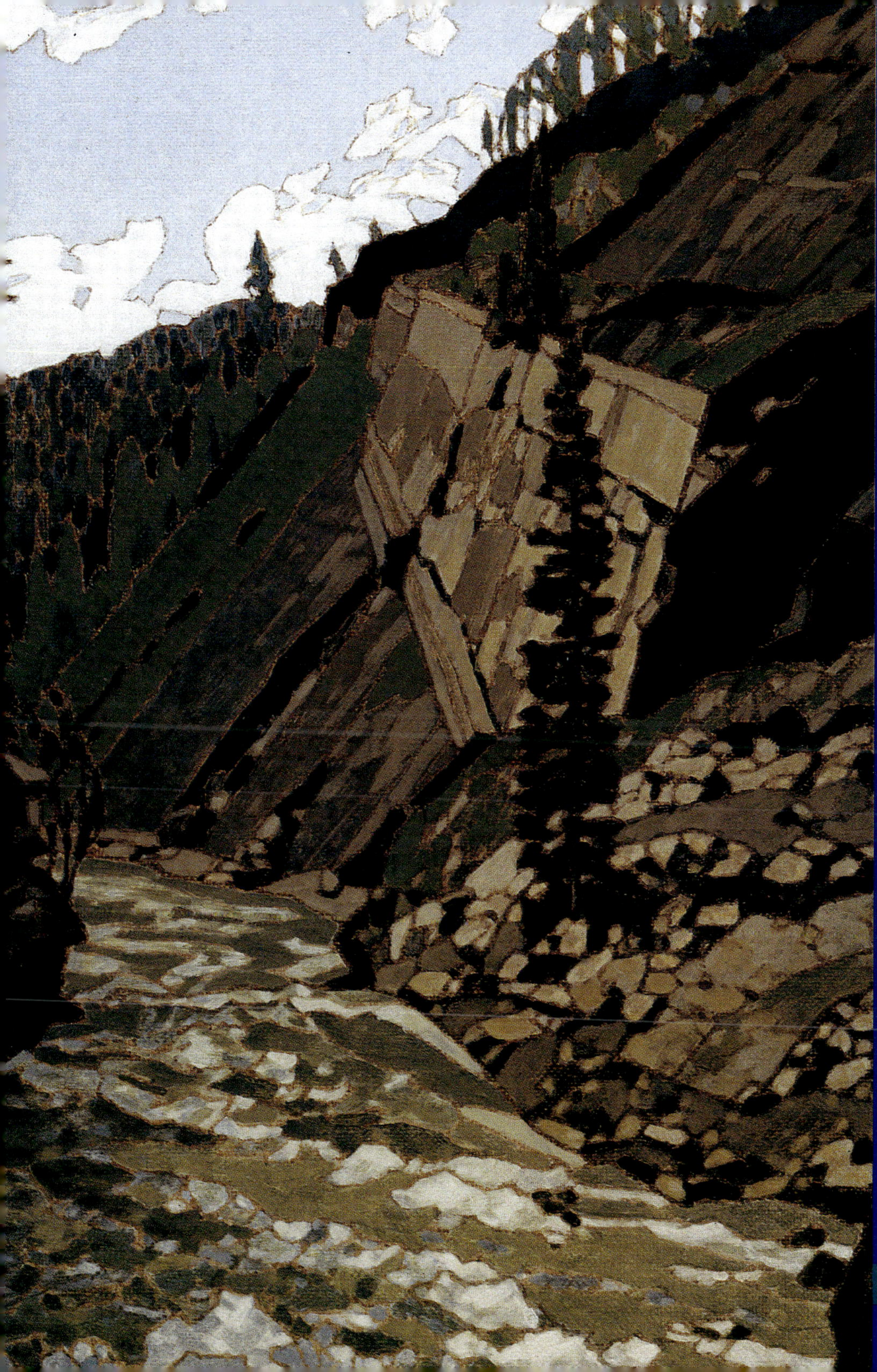

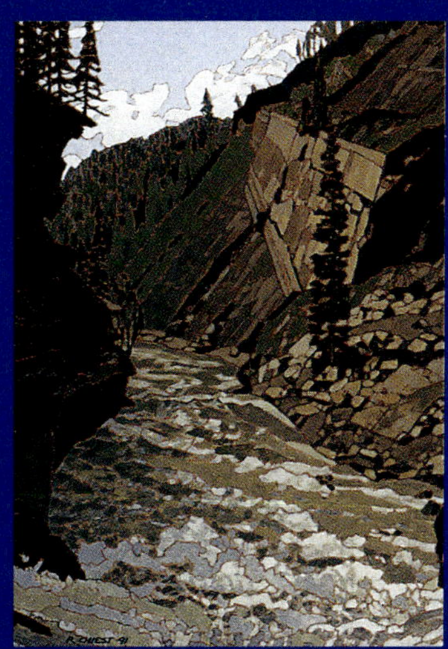

View from the Falls on Muskeg River

"ONE NEVER *wants to take those large rivers which are fed by the great icefields, other than seriously…it is then that you think of your guide's words of caution, 'If your horse rolls over, get out of your saddle, cling to his mane, tail, or anything you can get a hold of, but don't let go of him altogether! He may get out, you never will alone.'"*

Mary T. S. Schaffer, 1911

Oldest Cabin on McDonald's Flats

Some travellers on the old Trail took the shortcut across McDonald's Flats, a link between Daniel's Flats on the Smoky River and the Muskeg Stopping Place. Those who took it missed seeing the lakes of Grande Cache valley, but it was an interesting trip nevertheless. The McDonald families who lived on the flats had built log cabins, raised horses and cattle, and lived well. Most of the flats were accessible by packhorse, although a rough wagon trail was used for awhile. When Grande Cache became a company town in the 1960s, the residents of McDonald's Flats decided to move closer to civilization. Nowadays, only three forlorn cabins remain, along with some old corrals and a small Indian graveyard at the far end of the hay meadows. The drawing was done in late fall.

MY TRIP TO THE CABIN

It was a one-room building where a family had been raised. There were metal bedsteads, shelves still holding a few cans, and a cookstove off to one side with a few parts missing. Along the walls, a few old shirts still hung from nails, as though waiting for their owners to return. A pair of boots lay in a dark corner where they had been kicked for the last time. There was no sign of recent visitors. About the only suggestion of life was a packrat's nest on one of the shelves, but we didn't see the rat. There were also two good-sized bee hives—fortunately both abandoned at that time of year.

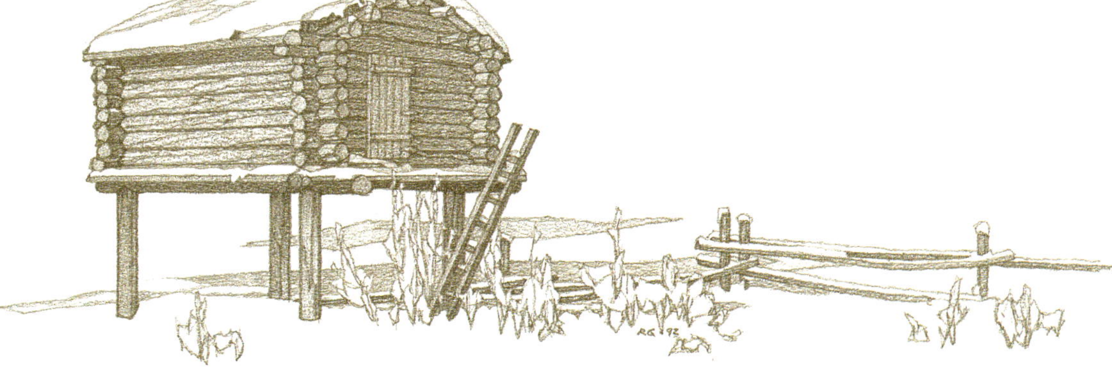

Food cache—the lower type

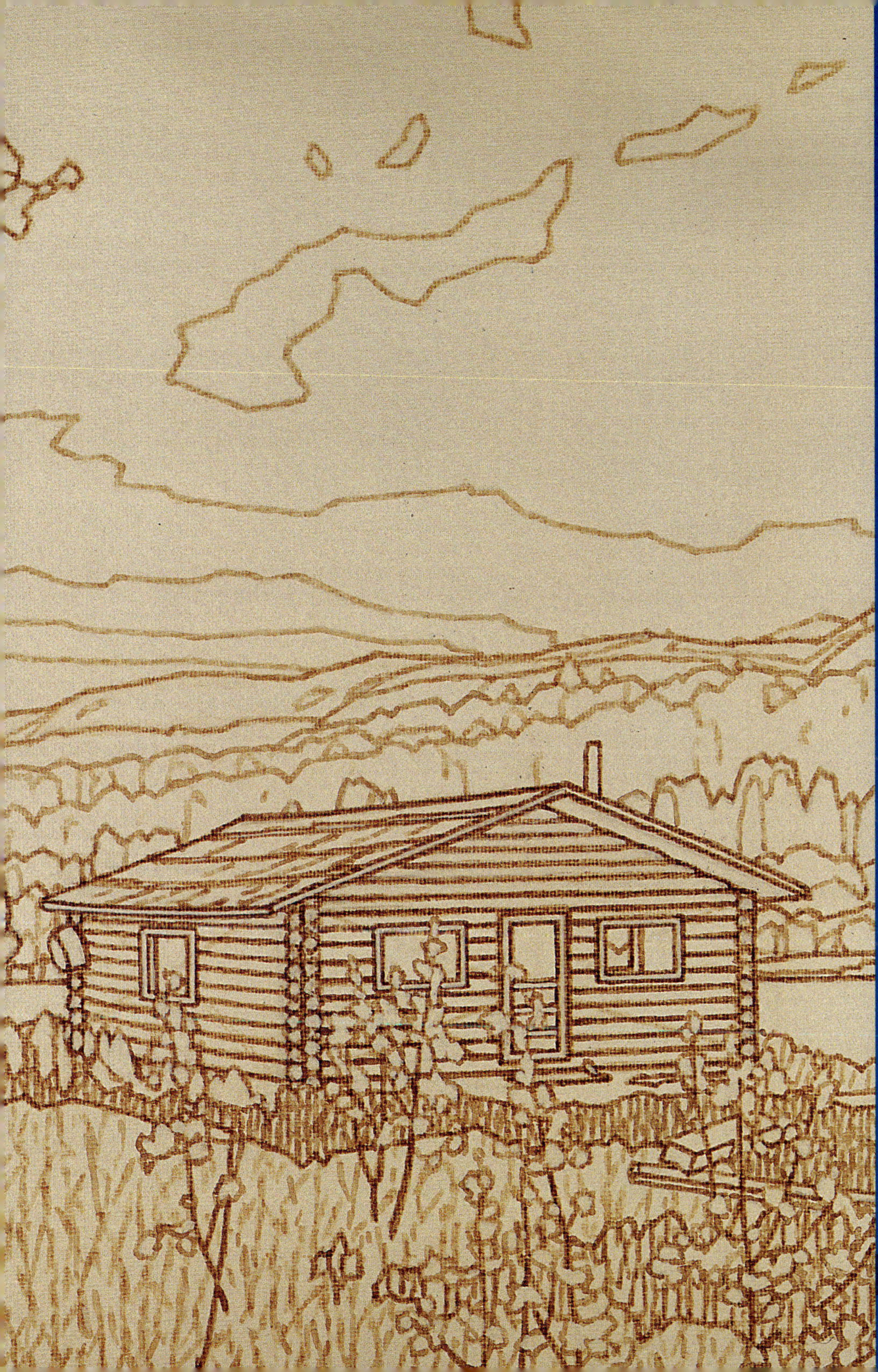

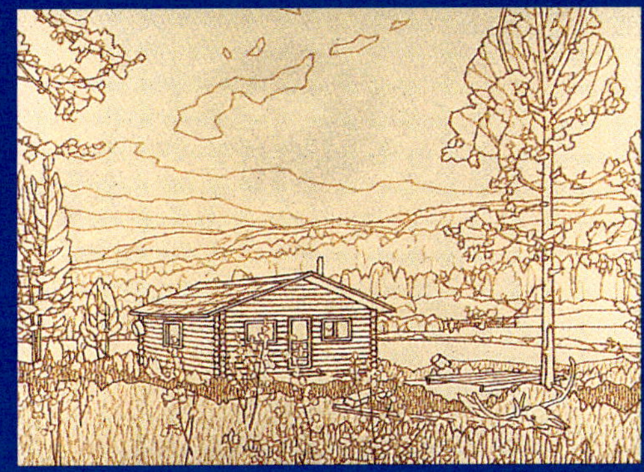

Oldest Cabin on McDonald's Flats

THE OLDEST *cabin at McDonald's Flats was said to be haunted. Some of the natives thought it might be a 'wendigo,' a malevolent, wailing wind spirit. The log building is situated about 250 yards from a burial ground, across the meadow to the northeast. From here, the 'Woman of the Seven Graves' is thought to come forth at night and frighten anyone in the building.*

Local Legend

Muskeg Stopping Place on a Rainy Evening

One of the best places to stop along the old road between Hinton and Grande Cache was the Muskeg Stopping Place. It was handy in times of emergency, and served as a link with the outside world. Initially, this spot along the Lower Trail, close to a small river, was little more than a good campground with grass and water for livestock. But through the years a settlement began to emerge with cabins, a ranger station, and a trading store that served a wide area. A very popular rodeo was held there annually. In later years, the store owner set up an ambulance service to the nearest hospital, in Hinton. This small settlement was often referred to as "Mile 60" because it was at the north end of the first telephone line connected with Forestry headquarters at old Entrance. The painting is a reconstruction; the buildings were torn down some years ago.

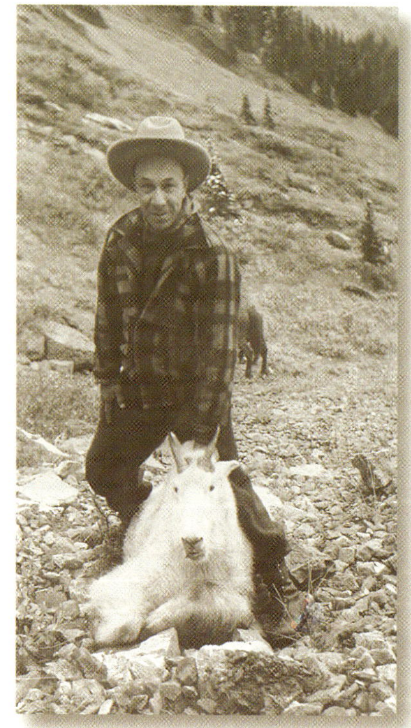

Felix Plante worked with the early Forest Service as a trailblazer and carpenter.

MEMOIRS OF FELIX

Felix Plante, born in 1893 at Lac Ste. Anne, moved west at an early age. With his father, who used to haul freight to and from the Peace River country in 1909–10, Felix, at 17 years of age, had an opportunity to visit the spot where the city of Grande Prairie stands today. He remembered there were only two families there then, the Fergusons and the Sinclairs. For many years, Felix and his wife Caroline (Moberly) had a trapline near the Wild Hay River. He also spent a number of years employed in the national park, working for Fred Brewster. Later on he bought his own outfit and settled in the Entrance area where he lived the rest of his days. More than anyone else, Felix is credited with having cut the first telephone line through from Muskeg to Entrance.

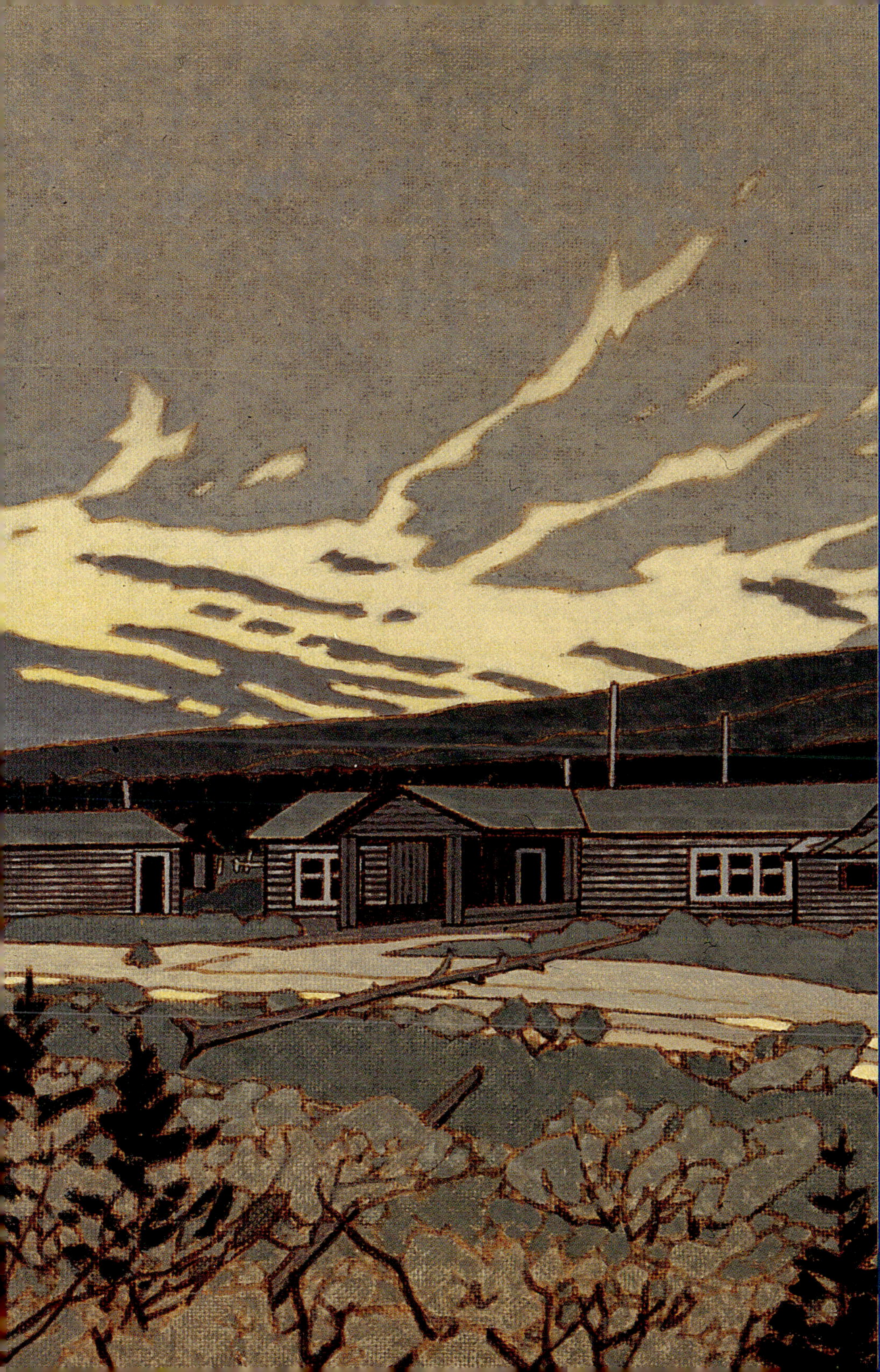

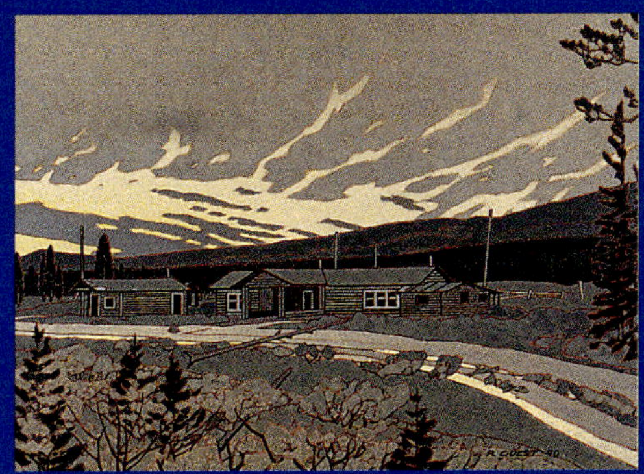

Muskeg Stopping Place on a Rainy Evening

In the store at Muskeg, Charlie had a system of account books, one for each native family. This was based on a system of credit and barter as the natives at that time had little use for money.

From Charlie and Jean Fox

Indian Graveyard at Muskeg River

Years ago this quiet spot, overlooking the Muskeg River, was set aside by the natives as a graveyard. It was close to the old packtrail, on a small knoll with the foothills and mountains rising in the southwest. In some ways it is similar to other burial grounds, with a group of wooden spirit houses carefully arranged with carved crosses at the west end of each grave. A rail fence was built to keep grazing animals out. Members of the same family were likely buried here, and they are believed to be victims of a flu epidemic. The painting shows the graveyard in October, with a half-moon above the horizon.

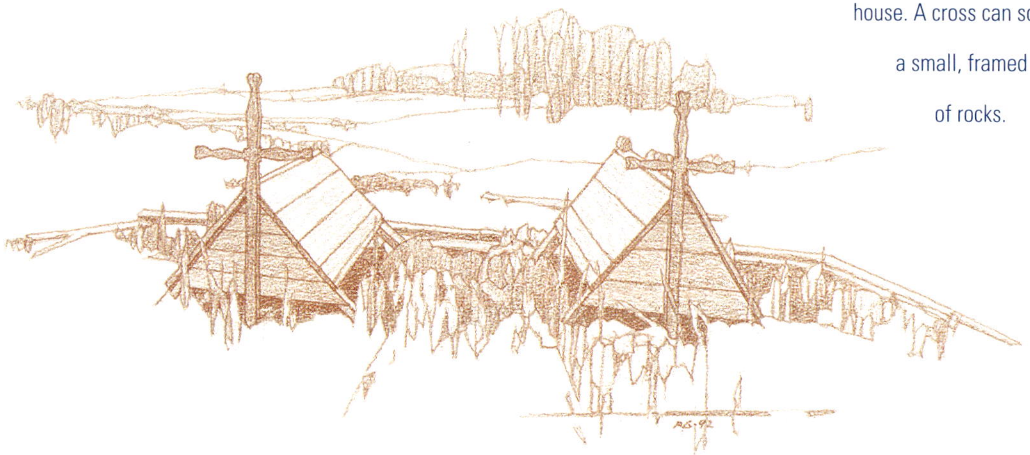

Indian graves, headwaters of Nose Creek

GRAVE POSITIONS

It seems to have been customary to align native graves along an east-west axis. In earlier times, the head of the interred was placed at the east end of the grave. This was so the wandering spirit, which left the body during the night, would see its own shadow cast on the grave when the sun came up, and would re-enter the body. But this tradition seems to have been altered, possibly by early missionaries who wished to change certain "pagan" beliefs. The head position was switched to the west end of the grave. Throughout the area I have noticed there are few exceptions to the cross being at the west end of the spirit house. A cross can sometimes be found at the west end of a small, framed enclosure, or fixed in an arrangement of rocks.

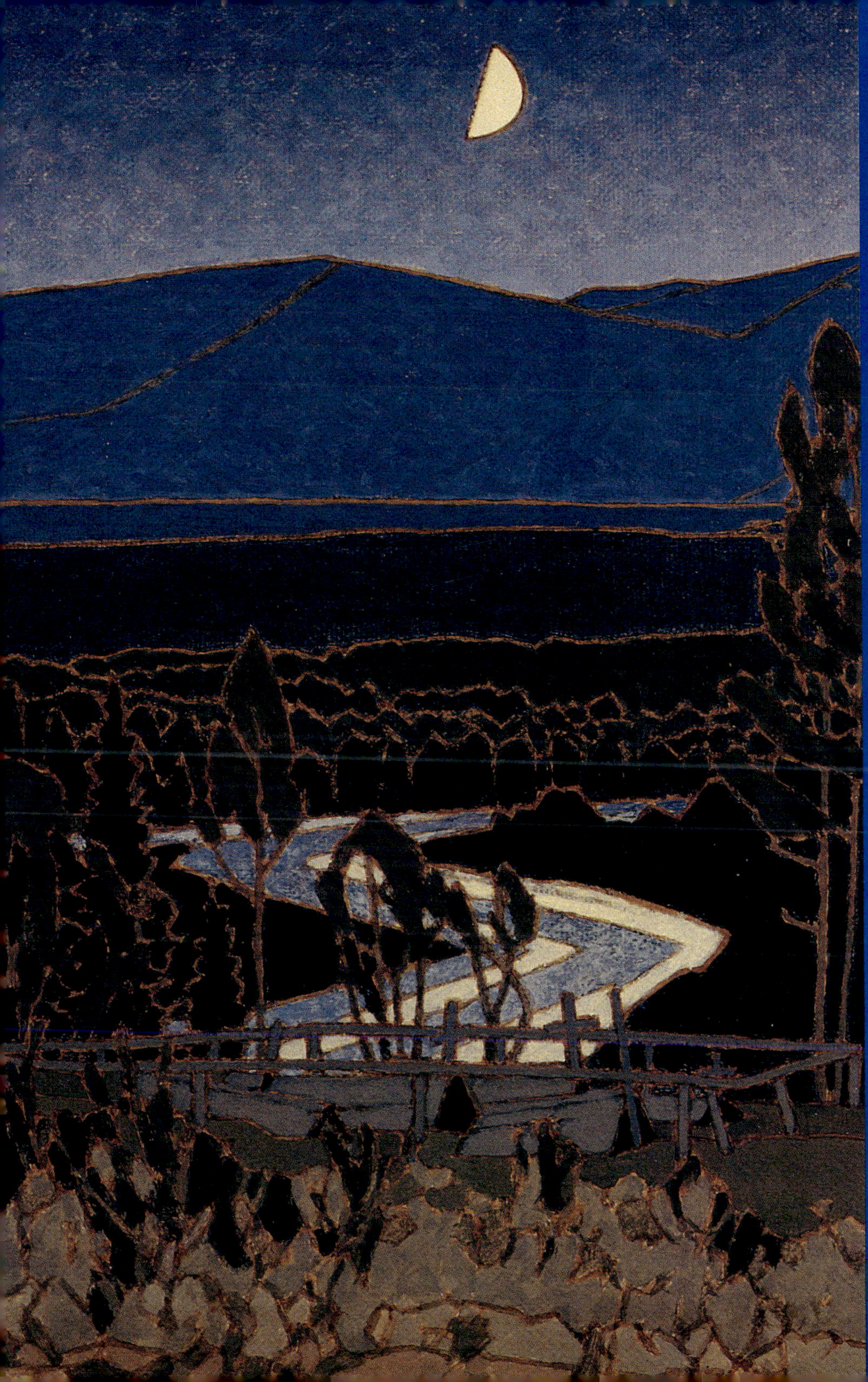

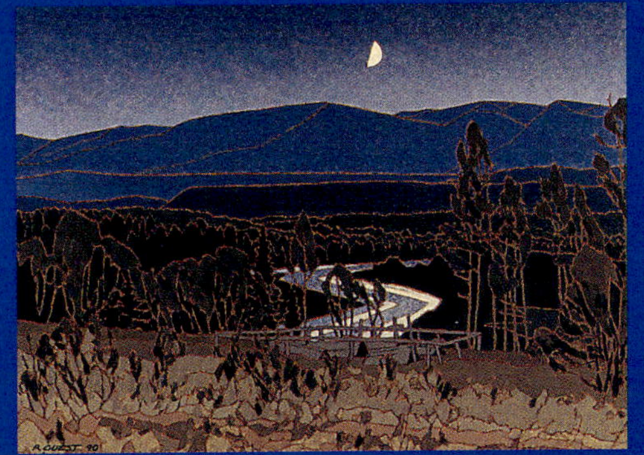
Indian Graveyard at Muskeg River

"On a gravelly knoll above the stream Shand and the other man scratched graves out of the frozen gravel. With bowed heads the men listened as, amidst the anguished wail of Indian women, Adam Joachim consigned the victims to their eternal rest. As the gravel was heaped up, the pine trees sighed and swayed before the wintry wind–the clean wind that had swept away the scourge. In a few days Shand and the men had fashioned the little roofs that made the graves of the natives–the roof that symbolized loving kindness and protection from the evils that beset man here and hereafter..."

J. G. MacGregor, 1962

Forest Trail near Mason Creek

It is difficult to estimate how many miles of packtrail went through mixed woods forest. This type of forest was the most common from south of Nose Mountain all the way to Hinton, covering a vast area of the foothills. People on horseback preferred lodgepole stands over dark spruce because visibility was better, and the logs of the tall, slender pines had many uses in camp. The ground in lodgepole stands was usually drier, with a carpet of reindeer moss, and huckleberries provided a delicacy throughout August and September. Over years of heavy use the packtrail wore down, exposing the roots, and axe blazes can be found on some of the older trees. The height of some blazes indicates that the Trail was also used in winter when the snow was deep.

◆

PRACTICAL KNOWLEDGE

Some trails were developed for local use, perhaps to a favourite hunting area or, in season, to the most likely spot to find blueberries or saskatoons. Side trails could lead to a shrine or a family graveyard off the beaten track. There is a difference between trails used by horses and those used by wild animals, and knowing the difference could save someone from becoming hopelessly lost. One of the things to watch for was the way tree roots became exposed. If many of the roots had the bark knocked off, it was likely done by horses' hooves. Wild ungulates such as moose or elk tend to lift their feet higher.

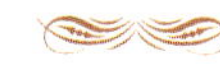

Old Campsite with lodgepoles

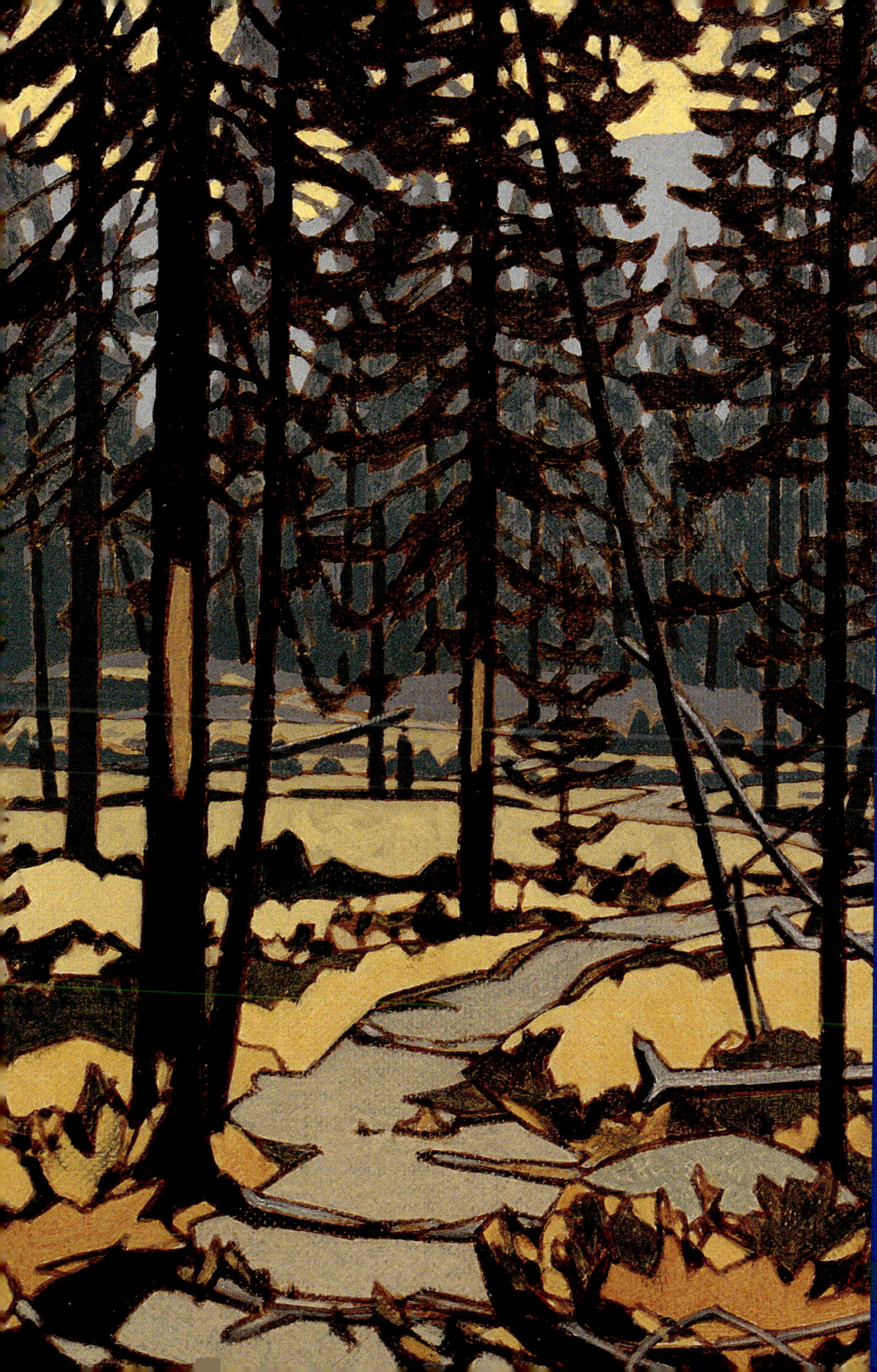

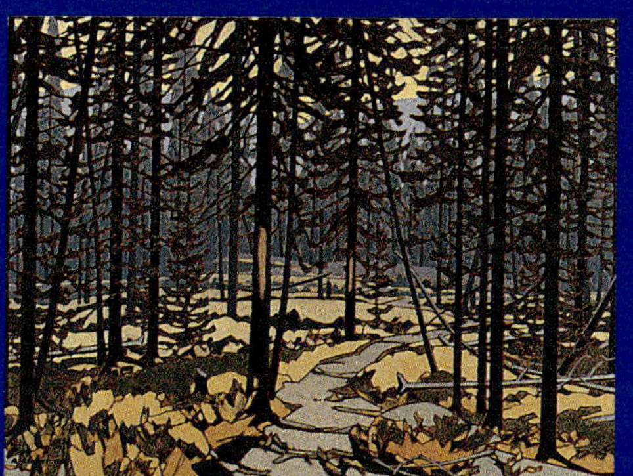

Forest Trail near Mason Creek

"IMAGINE a string of Indian ponies, stretching perhaps nearly half a mile–some with packs on their backs, and some carrying the squaws and children–the men leading them or walking by their side. The squaws were dressed in red and other bright-coloured blankets–their babies either slung on their backs behind, or propped up on the saddle in front. The pack ponies were heavily laden with tents and clothes and camping utensils. Most of the women carried their husband's guns slung on their shoulder as well as the babies!"

J. B. Bickersteth, 1911

Metis Log Church at Susa Creek

About 1930, a small church was built along Susa Creek, almost right on the old packtrail. Possibly the earliest Roman Catholic church in the Grande Cache area, it was made of logs and lumber prepared on the spot. It was designed for a small congregation and there was a room in the back where a travelling priest would stay. With the church was a separate bell-stand, and in a meadow to the west, not very far away, was a cemetery. This church, Our Lady of the Rockies, was not only a place of worship, but also served as a community centre, and is likely the only one of its kind still standing. In recent years a larger church has been built close by. It was a bright, sunny afternoon in late May.

◆

Jack pine by the trail

THE NATURE OF BELIEF

When the Metis people left Jasper Park they brought their religion with them to the new settlement in the Grande Cache valley. This was in 1910 and their religion was Roman Catholic. It was a faith that served most of the elders for as long as they lived, and they handed down the teachings of the church to their children and grandchildren.

Probably the best-known priest who travelled from Edmonton to the Grande Cache area was Father Rheaume. He visited Susa Creek and points along the Smoky River for many years, starting about 1947. This gentle cleric is remembered and loved by all those who got to know him. Nowadays it is obvious from the wooden crosses on Indian graves that Christianity touched the lives of these people.

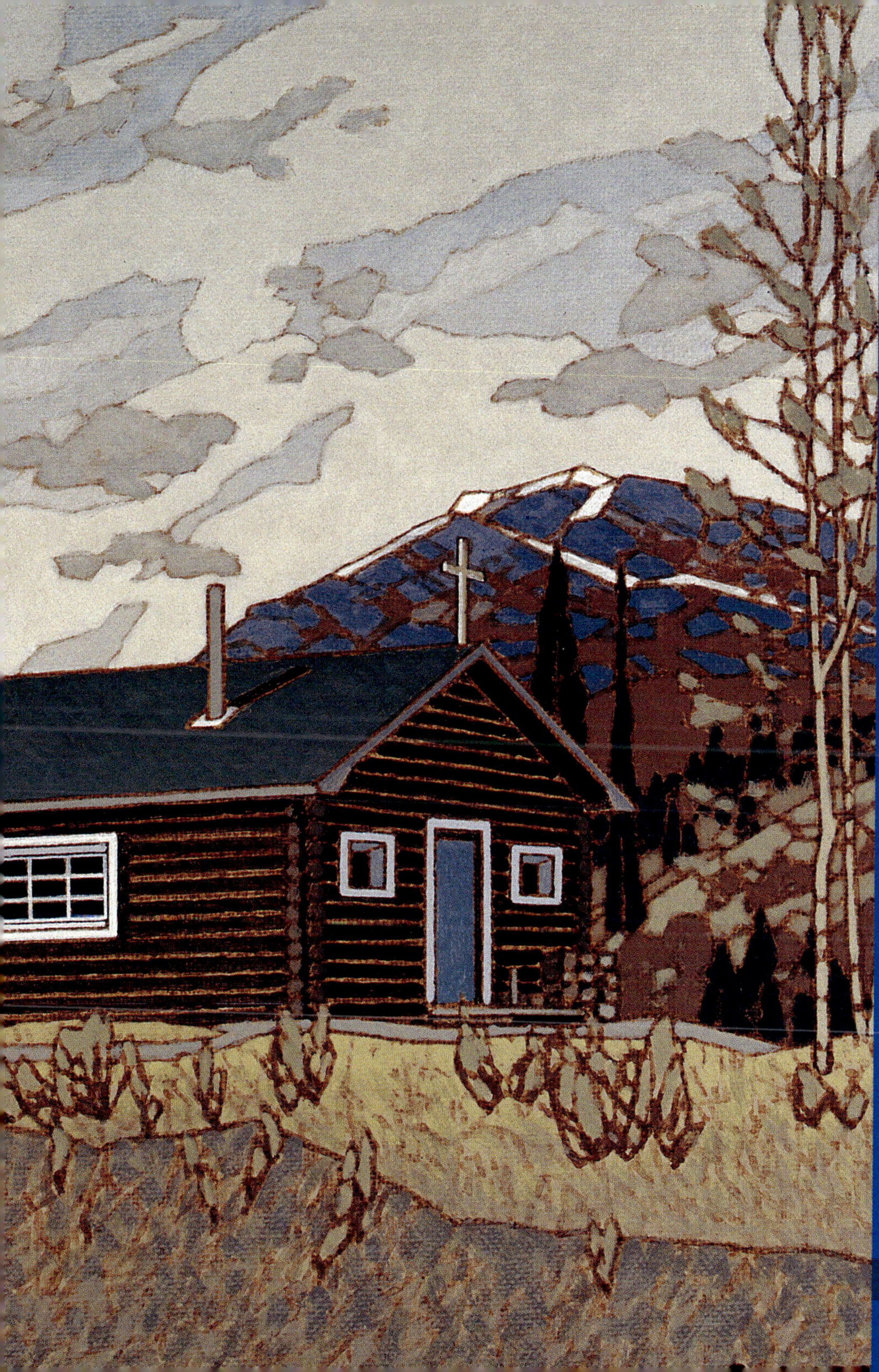

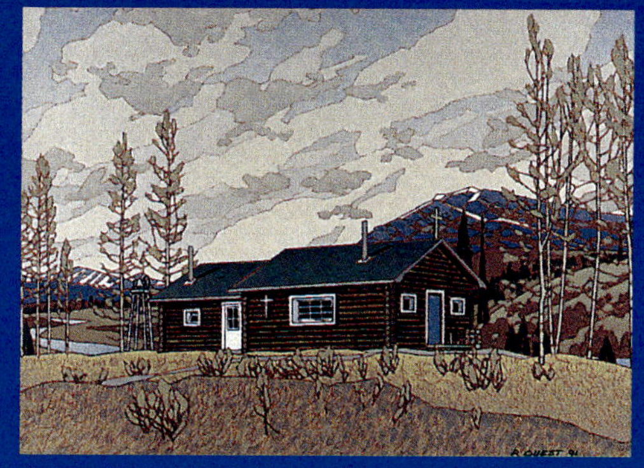

Metis Log Church at Susa Creek

"ONE GREAT *difference in our ways is that like the early Christians, the Indian was a socialist. The tribe owned the ground, the rivers and the game; only personal property was owned by the individual, and even that, it was considered a shame to greatly increase. For they held that greed grew into crime, and much property made men forget the poor."*

Ernest Thompson Seton, 1911

Grande Cache Valley, View Southwest

Grande Cache valley marked the halfway point between Lake Saskatoon and Hinton. Not far from the present site of Grande Cache, the main trail, generally referred to as the Jasper-Hinton Trail, divided in two. One branch, called the Mountain Trail, went south through the mountains, ending in Jasper Park. The other crossed the foothills toward Hinton and was known as the Lower Trail. Over the years, the valley became home to several native families who raised horses and cattle, and were employed by big-game hunters, outfitters, and the Forestry Department. In more recent times, the extraction of natural resources such as coal and timber has provided a livelihood for many of the same residents. Outdoor recreation has become an industry, providing such activities as trail rides, skiing, camping, and backpacking. This scene was observed in mid-October, when there was a dusting of new snow in the high country.

VALLEY OF PLENTY

The first residents were the Iroquois, and possibly Stoneys, who from time to time came over the old Trail. The Grande Cache area, with its picturesque setting, was a choice hunting area with a variety of big game animals and excellent fishing in the many streams, rivers, and lakes. It was a peaceful, scenic valley often blessed with chinook winds during the long winters. This made survival easier especially for those who, in later years, would try to raise livestock. For a long time this semi-alpine valley was bypassed by modern civilization. Many preferred it that way.

Carl Luger's cache on the Smoky

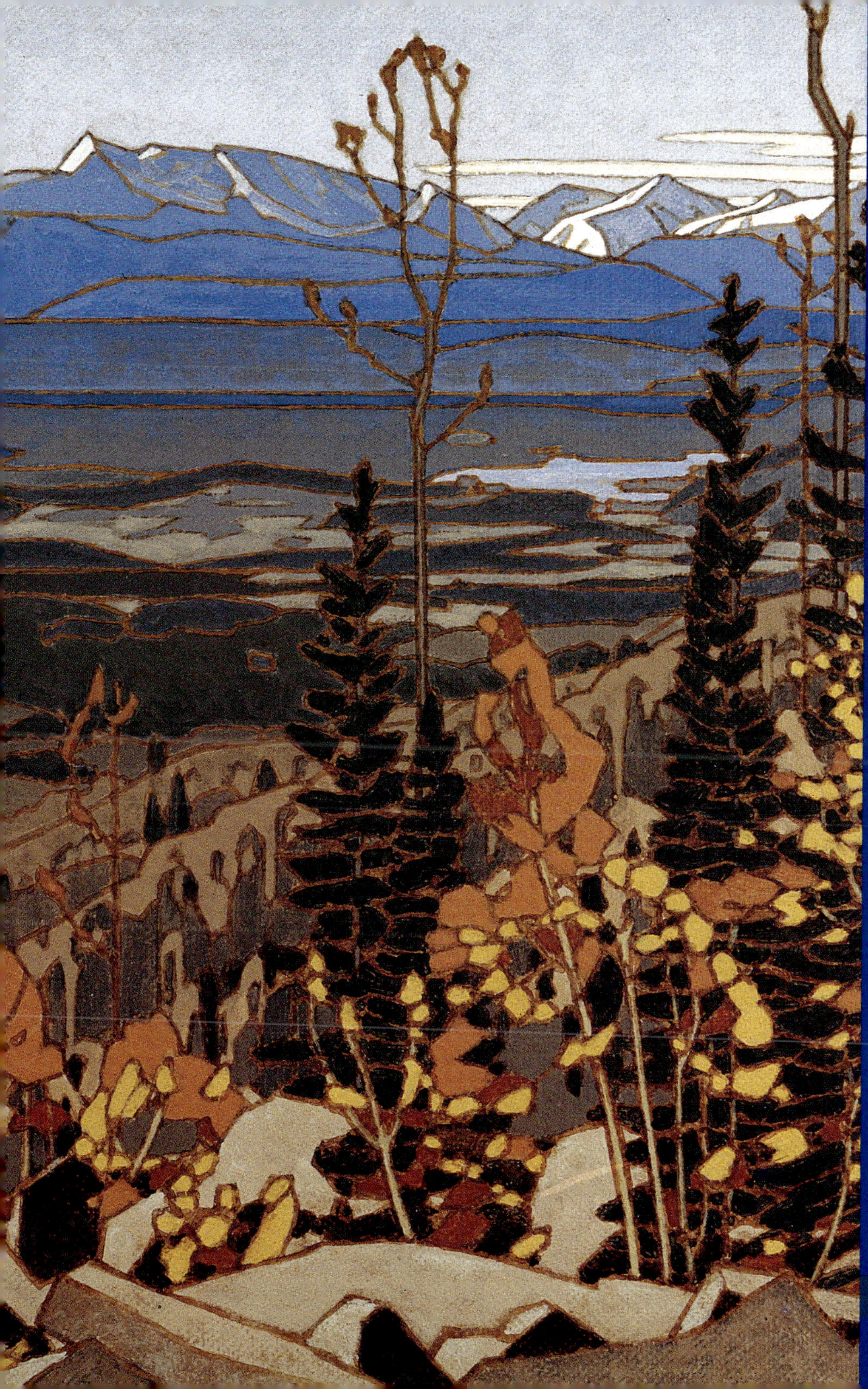

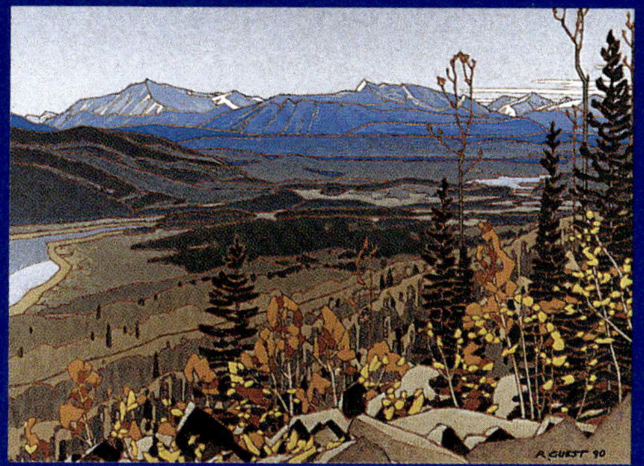

Grande Cache Valley, View Southwest

"THERE IS *a valley on the upper Smoky full of warm springs and covered with luxurious grass. Snow never lies to any depth on the rich soil.... [T]his spot doubtless will be a favorite resort and, if I am any prophet, a veritable garden. I have a theory that coal beds have been smoldering beneath it for ages, and that the smoke issuing from the banks of the Smoky and to which it owes its name comes from fissures in the earth. The scenery all about is magnificent."*

Henry John Moberly, 1885

Location of Trading Post at Victor Lake

Of several trading posts known to have existed along the Hinton Trail, the one at Grande Cache was likely the earliest. Shortly after 1910, Ewan Moberly built a store there, close to the shores of Victor Lake. It was here that, in the winter of 1914, the North-West Mounted Police stopped for supplies before returning up the Trail to the Peace River country with Asa Hunting and Mildred Shaw (see p. 52). Moberly died during the flu epidemic of 1919 but the store appears to have served the area until the early 1930s. By 1935, another post opened at approximately the same spot, owned by Fletcher Smith and operated by Sam and Betty Unruh. Later the Unruhs operated Fletcher's second post at Sheep Creek, one day's walk farther north. These two trading posts lasted about seven years and were eventually closed because of food rationing during World War II. The painting shows the location of the post as it is today, on a winter's evening. Mount Louis is in the background.

THE ONE-WAY PACK SLEIGH

In 1938, a special freighting toboggan was built for use on the narrow Trail. It was commissioned by Fletcher Smith and built by George Pandachuk of Elmworth. Its construction was heavy, designed to haul furs and freight from Hinton over the Lower Trail. One night, on reaching the Athabasca valley near Hinton, Sam and Betty Unruh ran into severely cold weather, about 40° below zero. They were taken in by Emma Nickerson, and their frost-covered horses were cared for. The Unruhs later picked up the sleigh at the Hinton railway station and set out on their return trip to Grande Cache. As they approached Muskeg, chinook conditions made it heavy going and one of their horses had to be replaced, but eventually they reached Victor Lake. They realized the special sleigh was not suitable for chinook conditions, and it was never used again.

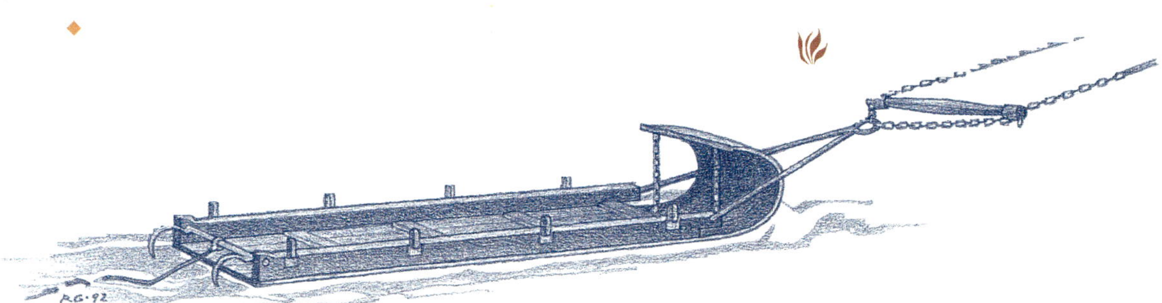

The ill-fated toboggan

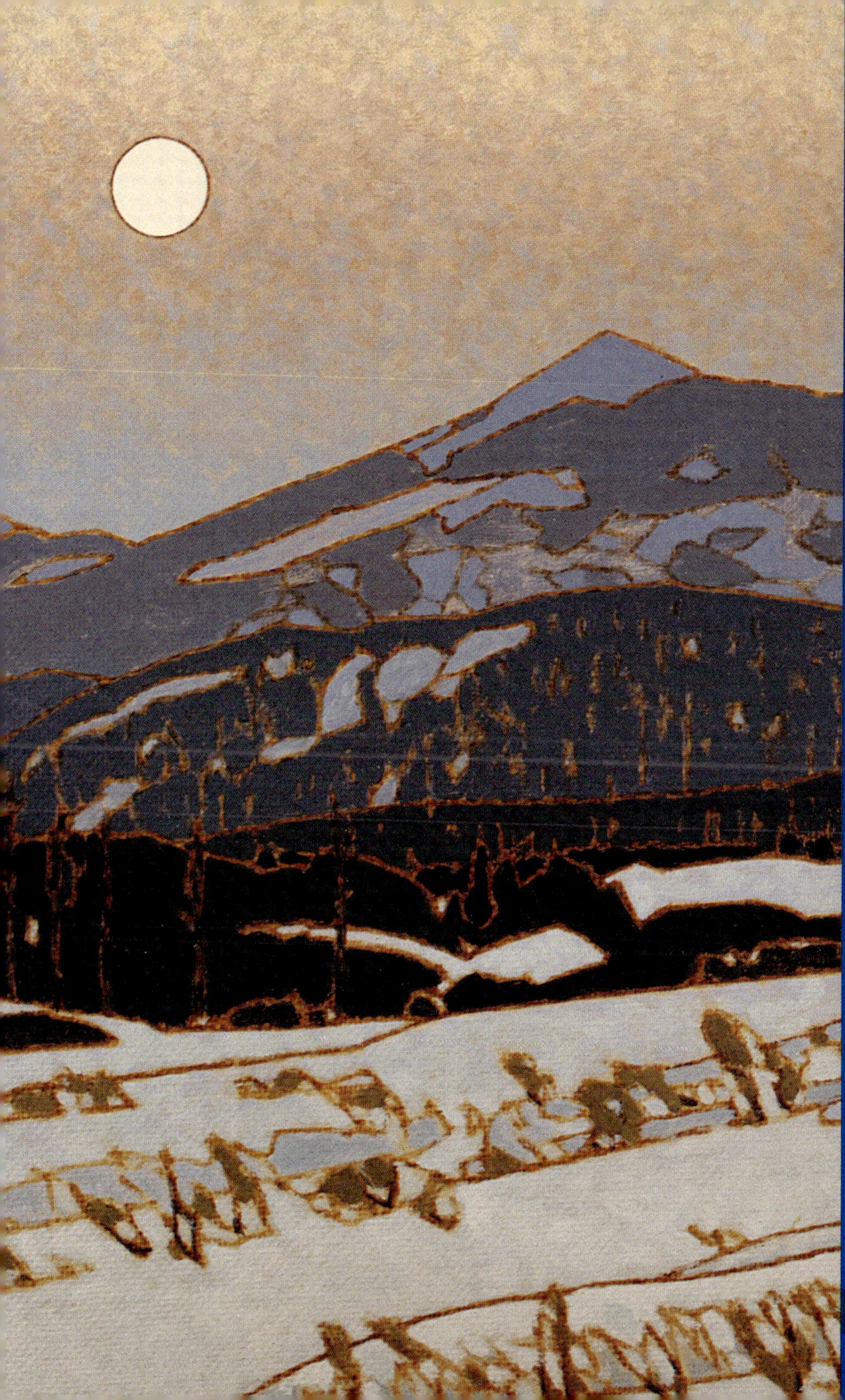

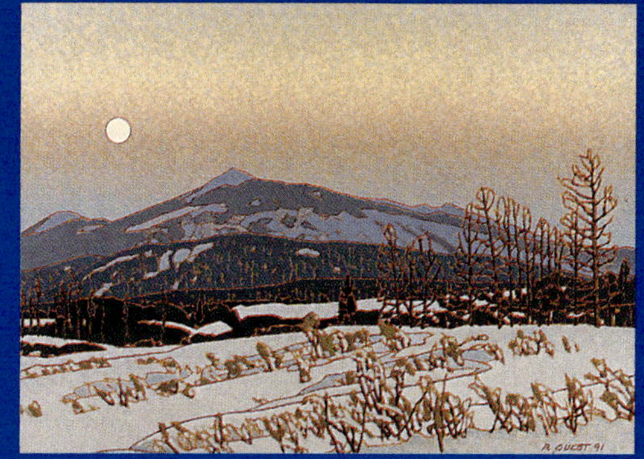

Location of Trading Post at Victor Lake

AT SAM and Betty's trading posts the native children often got candy. It came in 100 lb. lots (four 25 lb. wooden boxes). The Indians brought in furs, moccasins, and other things to trade, but no cash was given, only goods in exchange. And, when somebody died leaving an unpaid debt, the others would get together and cover it.

From Sam and Betty Unruh

Medicines for the trading posts were such things as: aspirin, the tonic 'Beef Iron and Wine', Dodd's Kidney Pills, a ration of 6 bottles of whiskey, iodine, Strepticide, and Vaseline.

From Evelyn Rose (née Smith)

Smoky River Crossing at Grande Cache

Among the different crossings on the Smoky River, the one nearest the town of Grande Cache was likely the best known. It was from there the main trail made a connection with the trading post at Victor Lake. The ford was used for many years, approached with apprehension by the people travelling the Trail. The Smoky is a dangerous river to cross, due to its swift current and a riverbed that changes from time to time. The water never clears, making it impossible to avoid deep holes, and people crossing with horses were wise to hire local Indians as guides. The river was named partly because of its smoky colour. In earlier times there were underground fires caused by burning coal seams, and this gave a smoky haze to the surrounding country. Over the years there have been drowning accidents at most of the crossings on the Smoky.

◆

Log raft and gravel bar

GETTING YOUR FEET WET

Even though the Hinton Trail crossed 11 rivers and more than the same number of creeks between Hinton and the Lake Saskatoon plains, it was not known to the canoeist. Unlike other routes in western Canada, the 200-mile Trail crossed the rivers rather than followed them, keeping parallel to the eastern slopes of the Rockies. Rafts and rowboats were used for some of the river crossings. Most of the time travellers had a string of packhorses with them, and when the water was high it was better to unpack the animals and transport the loads across by raft.

Both Paul Marshall and Carl Luger have had experiences with rafts that were difficult to handle and could be very dangerous. According to Paul, "Once you got on one, it was sometimes darned hard to get off again." Carl added, "One could end up a long way downriver with a lot of back-tracking to do—even on the same side you just left." It was often a better idea to stay with the horses.

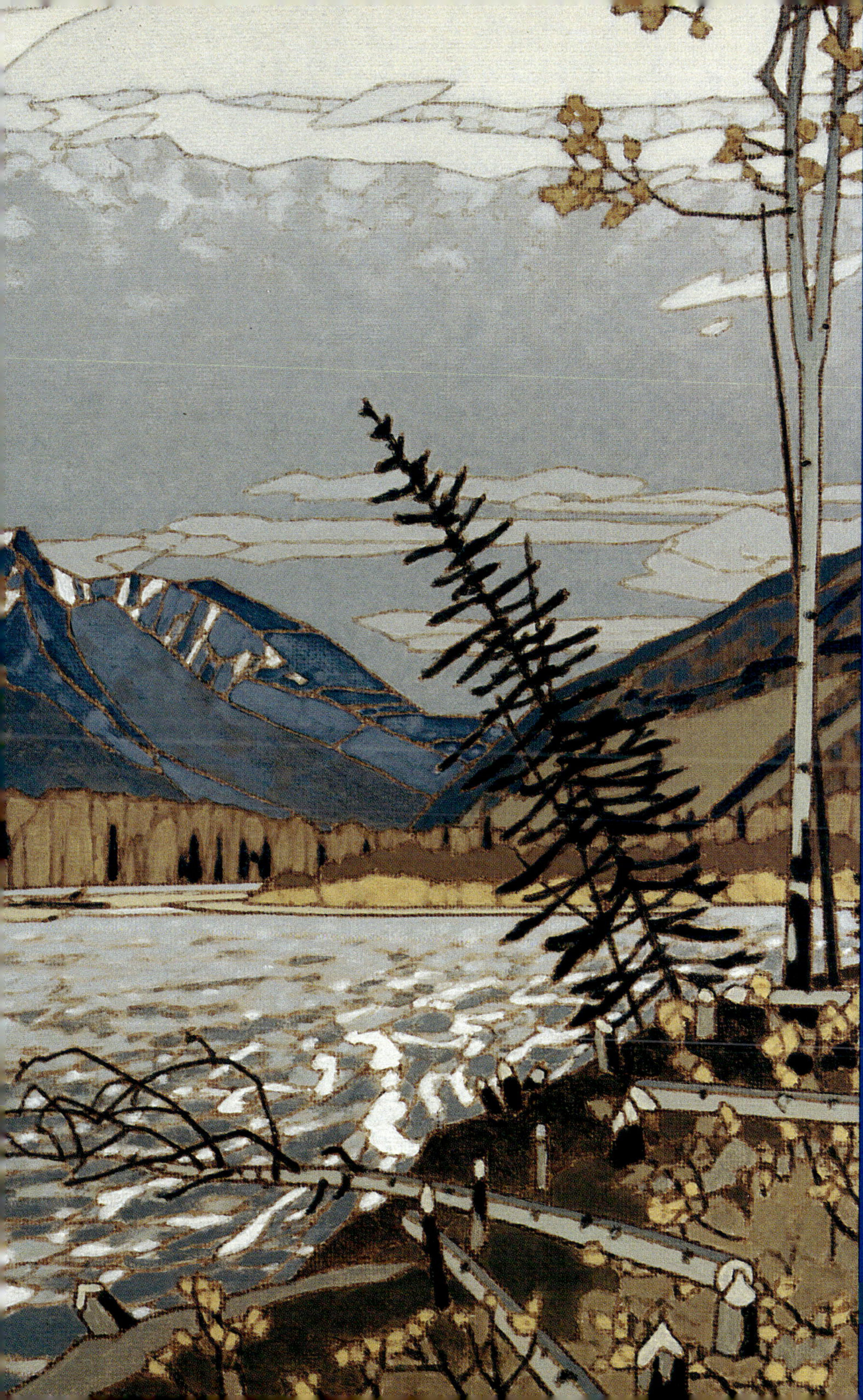

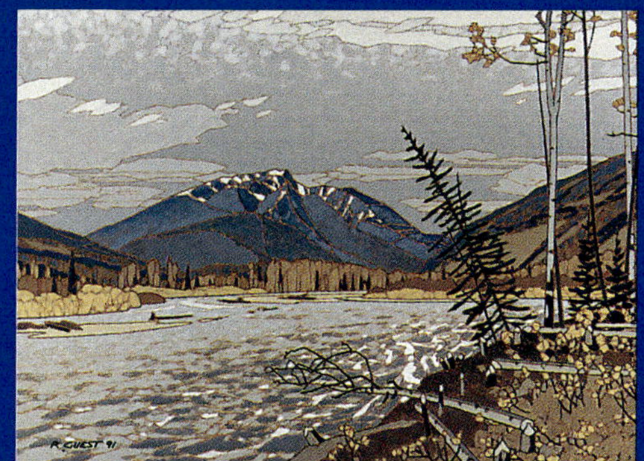

Smoky River Crossing at Grande Cache

"We constructed a small sturdy raft and fashioned a paddle to go with it. Harold never hesitated a minute but grabbed the paddle, stepped aboard and shoved off. The small craft bobbed like a cork when he steered the raft into mid-stream and was hit by the full current. Naturally he drifted a long way down-stream with the whole crew running along the bank trying to keep abreast of him, but I don't know what we could have done if anything had gone wrong. Just before he hit the bank he made a mighty jump and landed safely."

John Glenn, c.1920

Asa Hunting's Campsite on the Muddywater

The Shaw abduction case drew more attention to the Hinton Trail than anything else. In the summer of 1913, Asa Hunting and the underage Mildred Shaw left the Redwillow area and travelled south over the old packtrail as far as Grande Cache. The weather held until December, but by January there was a change for the worse, with snow and cold weather making travel with horses difficult. Evidently, the trapper and the girl set up a winter camp along the Muddywater River close to where it joins the Smoky, although the exact spot is not known. It was most likely on the west side of the river in a stand of spruce trees. Their shelter was a wickiup, a kind of tipi made of logs, bark, and pieces of canvas and moss. The painting was completed from sketches done after a 45-mile walk along the Smoky River valley, and shows the Muddywater River in the late evening.

THE DESPERATE CASE OF ASA AND MILDRED

Asa Hunting was a seasoned trapper who could survive in the outdoors any time of the year and it took the North-West Mounted Police months to catch up with him. He was out on his trapline and Mildred was alone when the police arrived. On his return Asa was arrested and plans were made to break camp as soon as possible. It was a long, cold trip north to the Peace River country, with snow almost up to the horse's bellies. On January 26, 1914, Asa Hunting appeared for a preliminary hearing at Lake Saskatoon, and was charged with the abduction of Mildred Shaw. He was transferred to the District Court at Grouard to be incarcerated during the time of the trial. He was acquitted mainly on the testimony of Mildred, who claimed she was not abducted but went of her own accord. The two were eventually married and the story had a happy ending.

A horizontal wickiup constructed by Alex Moberly

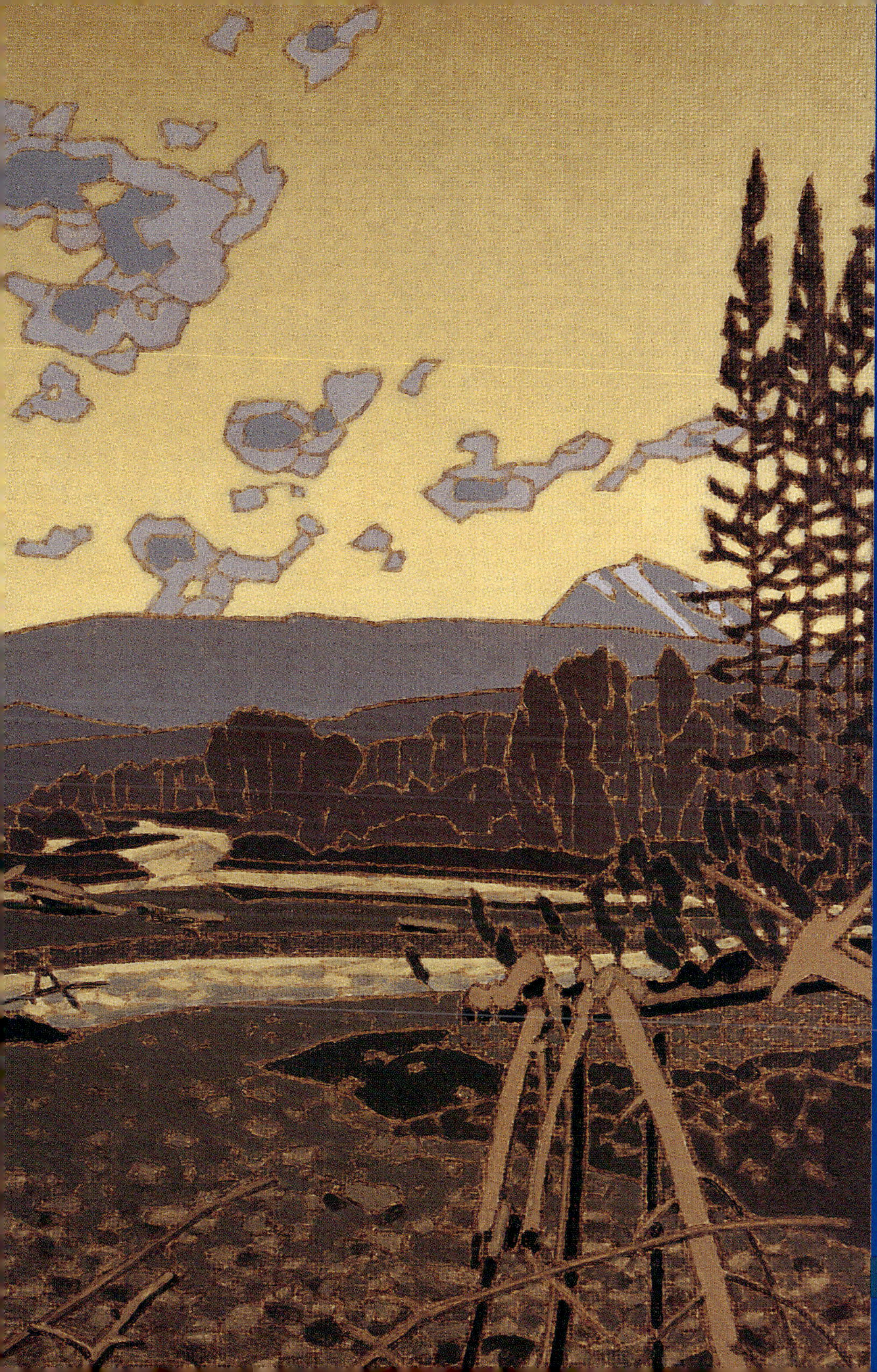

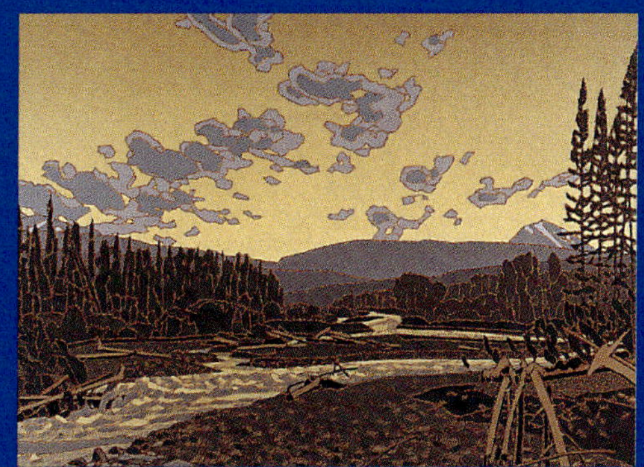

Asa Hunting's Campsite on the Muddywater

"The mission on which they went was to arrest Asa Hunting who according to reports is guilty...of inducing to leave home a young girl of 15 by the name of Shaw. Much anxiety is felt as to the safety of the party as they only had a month's rations with them, and from reports brought in by some breeds who were trapping in that district it is feared they have met with foul play."

Grande Prairie Herald, December 3, 1913

Wanyandi Cabins on the Smoky

The packtrail followed the western edge of Wanyandi Flats. At this point on the Smoky River, the Trail crossed from Sheep Creek to join up with the section along the east bank of the Muskeg River. This was another ford that was tricky at times, depending on the season. The actual flats were large and partly covered by stands of poplar and alder, and open meadows used for grazing. It was here that Daniel Wanyandi, after whom the flats were named, built cabins, planted a garden, and raised a family. Besides being in the guiding business the Wanyandis were known for the excellent livestock they raised, sometimes taking cattle to market over the Trail to the Peace River country. Eventually a small area was set aside for a graveyard west of the fences and buildings. The painting shows some of the original cabins, with a glimpse through the trees of the mighty Smoky as it flows quietly past. It was midsummer.

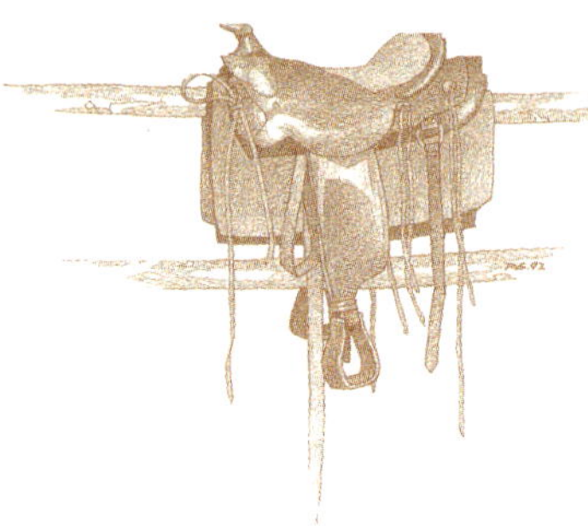

THE HORSE TRADE

There was a demand for horses at a time when "horsepower" meant the real thing. The settlers had a lot of new ground to break on flat plains extending north and west almost as far as the mountains. Charlie Fox thought the horses raised by Daniel Wanyandi were outstanding. Evidently the trouble of raising them was worth it; horses brought a very good price. Horses were being brought north over the Hinton Trail, but crossing the Smoky was always very dangerous. At least one occasion resulted in tragedy. An ex-ranger by the name of Harvey was taking horses to the Peace River country when a young man drowned.

DRAWING: Tom Brown's saddle

PHOTO: Cattle raised on the Smoky River, c.1940

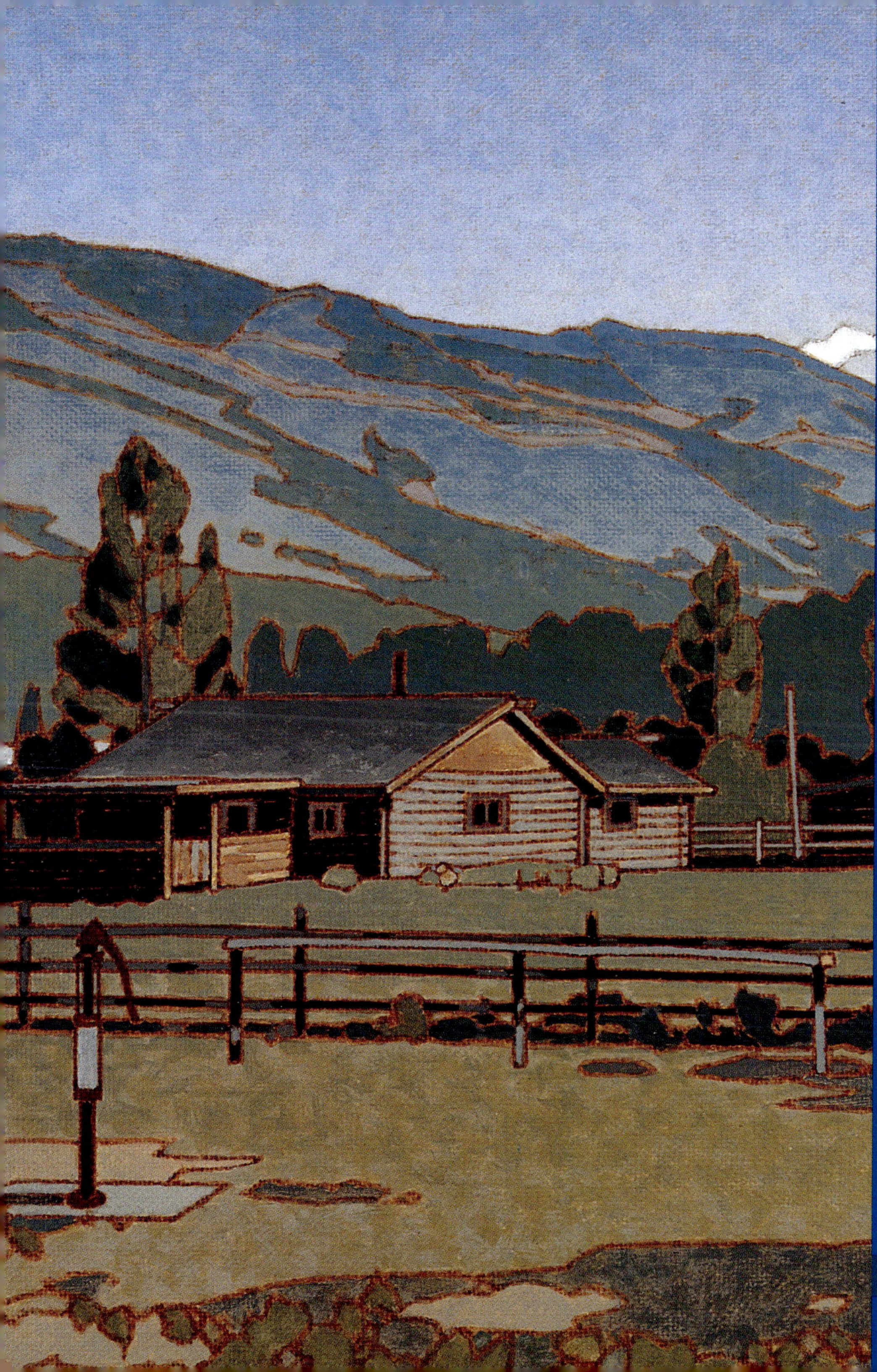

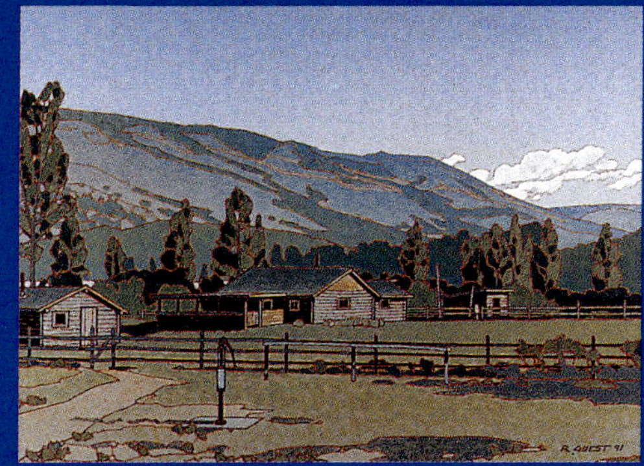

Wanyandi Cabins on the Smoky

"HE HAD *with him a lad of eighteen or so. Not being familiar with the ford on the Big Smoky, he had attempted to cross at the eddy...It was alright to swim horses here when they were unpacked but foolhardy to do so when they bore loads or riders. It seems the lad got into serious difficulty and he got out of the saddle and attempted to swim himself. When he looked back Harvey noticed the empty saddle but there was no sign of the rider. We found the horse later...which was pretty nervous and hard to catch."*

John Glenn, c.1920

Smoky River and Sheep Creek Junction

Through the years there were at least five places along the Smoky River where the Trail crossed. Some were more accessible than others and considered safer, depending on conditions and the time of year. This afforded travellers a bit of choice as the river was changeable. One of the safer fords was at the mouth of Sheep Creek. This was near the Unruhs' second trading post and, under normal conditions, packhorses could make the crossing without difficulty. Sometimes a rowboat was cached on a riverbank and used to ferry supplies and travellers, making it safer for horses to swim. The spot was visited on a chilly, windy day in October, and there was a feeling of frost in the air.

As a team, Sam and Betty Unruh (shown here in 1938) ran two trading posts for seven winters.

SAM AND BETTY HIT THE TRAIL

Sam and Betty Unruh travelled the Hinton Trail from about 1934 to 1941. Twice a year the couple made the long trip back and forth on horseback. When the Unruhs opened the trading posts at Victor Lake and Sheep Creek, they renovated cabins that had already been used. The one at Sheep Creek had been the old home of Solomon Karakonti and they had to set up two tents inside because the sod roof leaked every time it rained.

The Unruhs' adventures came to an end when war-time food rationing made trade in foodstuffs difficult and reduced the profit margin. At the outbreak of the war many young Metis left the Grande Cache area to join up, and there were too few trappers to supply enough fur to keep the trading posts going. Sad to leave the trading posts and their many friends in the Grande Cache valley, the Unruhs headed their horses back home for the last time.

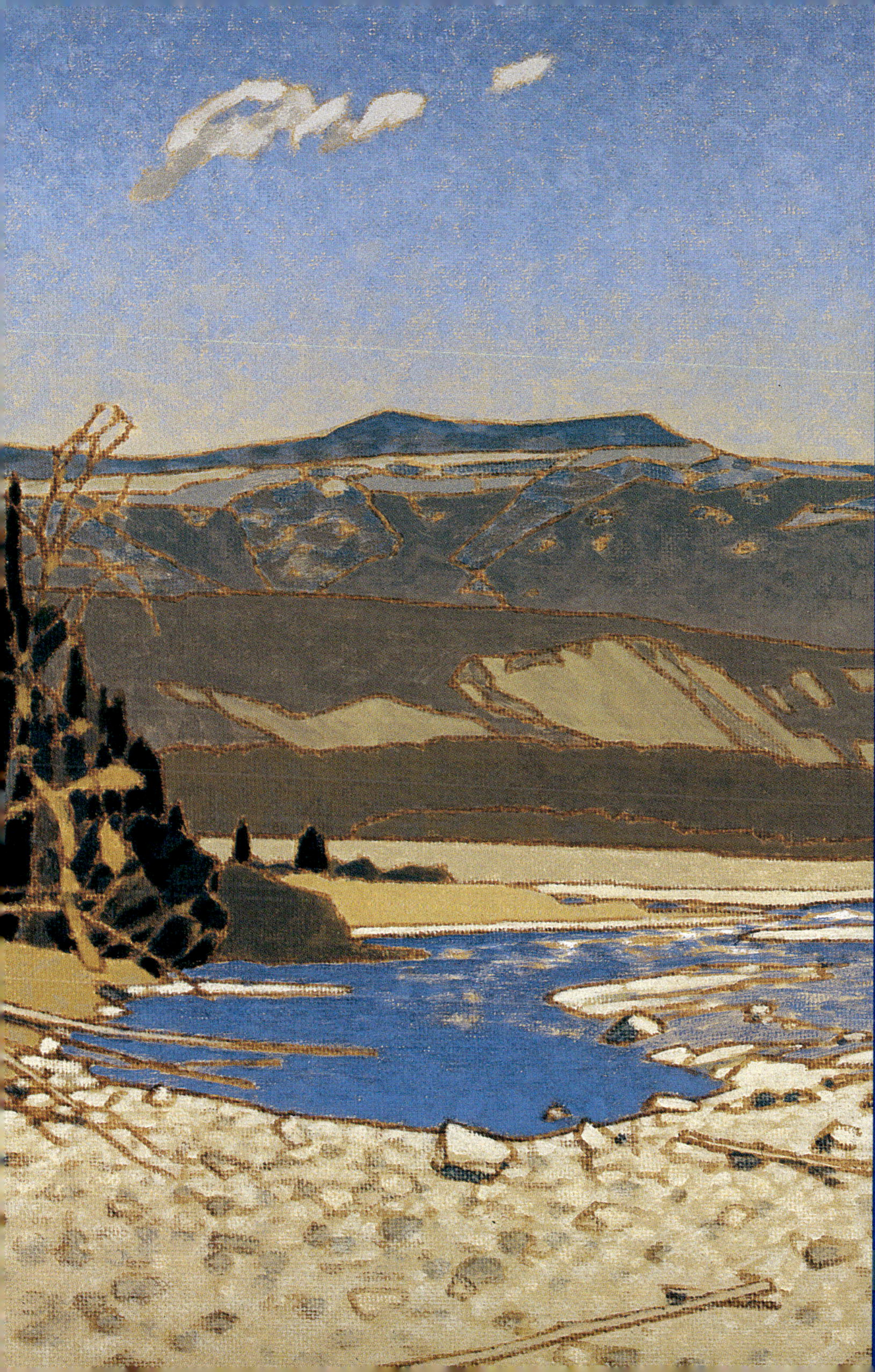

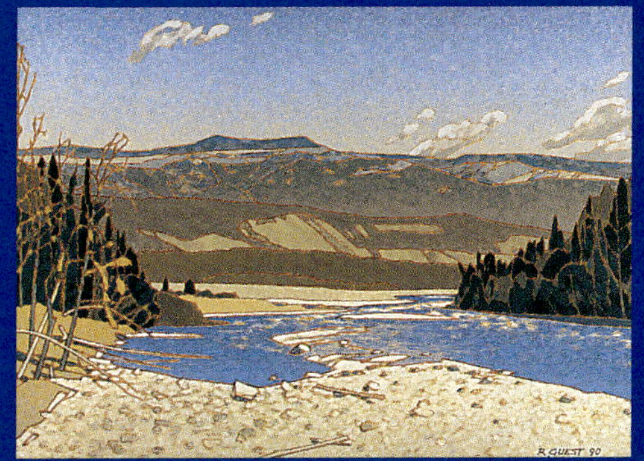

Smoky River and Sheep Creek Junction

"Smoky River is difficult and dangerous to cross. The river is swift and can be forded only where horses can obtain good footing. Like all glacier-fed streams, the water is so charged with silt that the bottom is seldom visible. In addition, the position of sand and gravel bars changes from year to year. It is advisable, therefore, for travellers who are not familiar with the crossings to obtain help from the Indians of the district."

Dr. E. J. W. Irish, 1992

Along Sheep Creek in Late Spring

One branch of the Trail went over a pass and came down on Sheep Creek. The creekbed had steep banks and the stream was fast-moving, with only a few places fit for crossing. So the packtrail made a ford, climbing the opposite bank which was quite steep, and headed in an easterly direction. The headwaters of Sheep Creek provide some of the best habitat for big horn sheep and mountain goats, and many big-game hunters were attracted to the area. Today much of this high country along Sheep Creek is within the boundary of Willmore Wilderness Park, and travelling is by horseback, or on foot, only. This view was to the west and it was late spring.

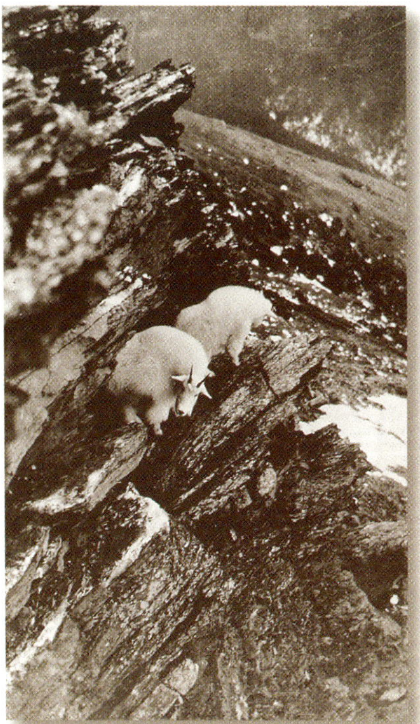

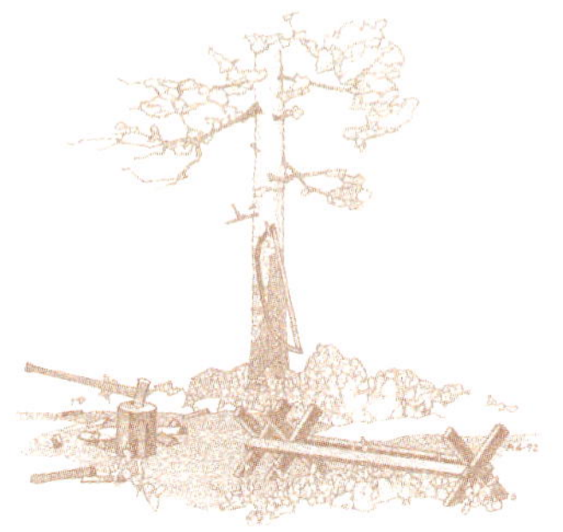

THE DUTIES OF FORESTRY

In the early settlement period the Forestry Service had the biggest impact on territory not served by the railroad. Once away from the main line along the Athabasca valley, transportation seems to have been by packhorse or wagon in the summer, and dogteam in the winter. It was Forestry that cleared and improved the existing trails, and had the responsibility of cutting new ones through endless miles of spruce and pine forest, muskeg, and over some of the passes of the front range. Besides trying to keep trails clear of such obstacles as brush and deadfall, it was also the duty of the forest ranger to see that bridges were built over the more troublesome creeks. Logs were cut and trimmed to lay corduroy over low wet spots. In some areas, like today's Willmore Park, the corduroy roads were so well constructed that sections have been used by hunters and hikers almost to the present day.

PHOTO: Mountain goats on a cliff

DRAWING: Tools for getting firewood

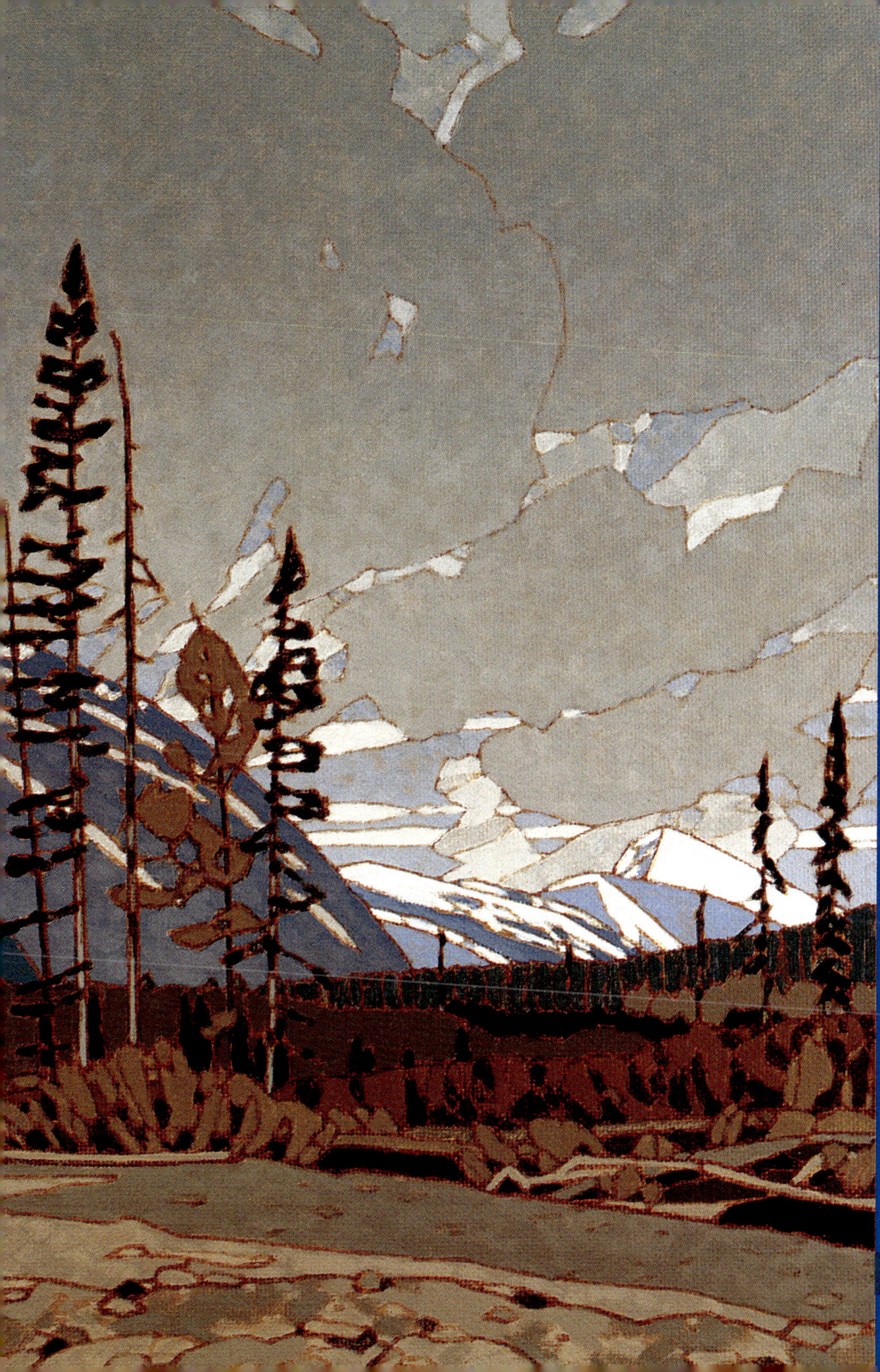

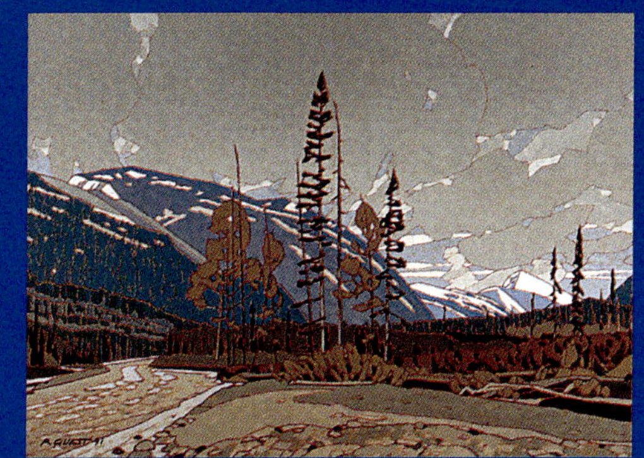

Along Sheep Creek in Late Spring

"We turned in our saddles to look with pride on the sight so glorifying to a trailer, sixteen perfectly packed horses slowly advancing, sixteen white pack-mantles moving deliberately among the trees."

Mary T. S. Schaffer, 1911

La Force Creek Trail

The section of packtrail that went up La Force Creek was likely the most isolated of the entire Trail. Some old-timers think it was the original trail. From where it divided near the mouth of Copton Creek, with one branch heading uphill and the other staying low, it was a long and rugged stretch to the banks of the Smoky. At the highest point the La Force Creek Trail went over "Windfall Hill." The low trail, following the creek, was preferred to the uplands, especially during winter. A few scattered campsites can still be found where people or trappers stopped on their way through, probably in the 1950s. The area is almost inaccessible, except by helicopter. The painting shows a frozen beaver pond in early December.

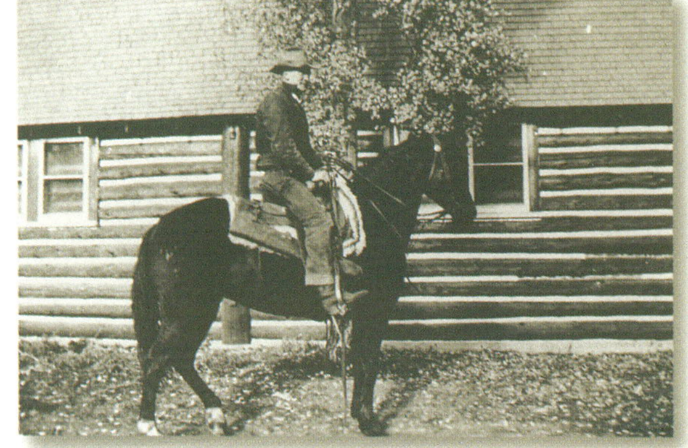

CARL AND ART

Carl Luger arrived in the Hinton area in 1937. Carl obtained his guiding license before enlisting in the RCAF in 1943. On his return he bought his own outfit and never looked back. In a typical year he had three seasons to prepare for: he guided trail rides to Maligne Lake during the summer, hunting parties each fall, and in the winter he went logging and spent time on his trapline.

Art Allen also covered the foothills north and west of Hinton during the years 1926 to 1958. Art liked the Narroway River west of Nose Mountain and he went through that area with hunting parties, and on collecting trips for museums with the Hargreaves brothers. He also did some unusual carpentry work, building cabins along the hiking and riding trails in Jasper Park. One season Carl and Art teamed up for a long walk to the upper reaches of the Smoky River where they did some trapping, sometimes walking up to 30 miles a day if conditions were good.

Carl was a guide, a successful trapper, and he worked for the oil companies.

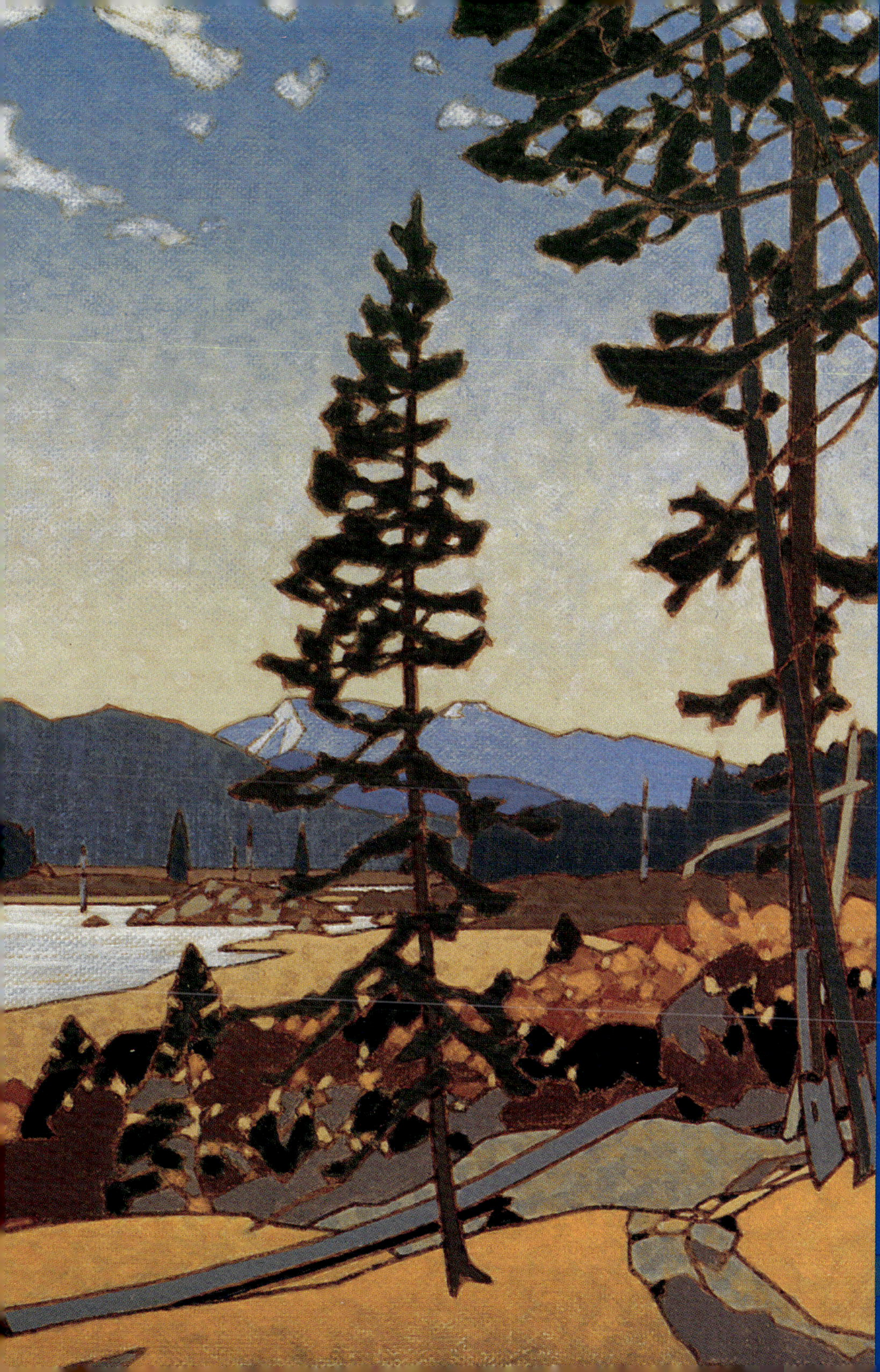

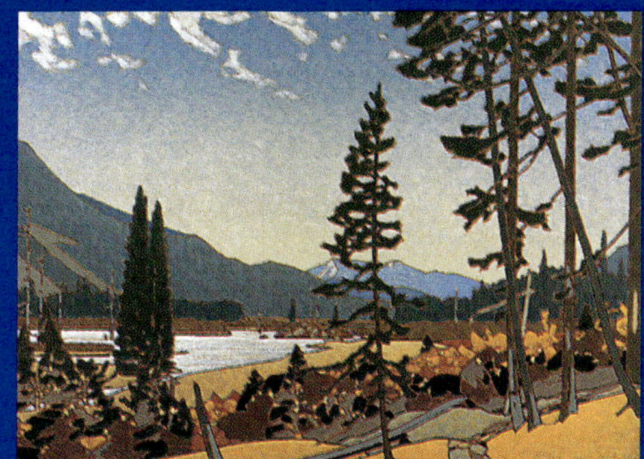

La Force Creek Trail

WALTER TOLD about the time a cougar almost got his dog. He fired his .22 rifle. There was quite a commotion and the cougar ran away, leaping a frozen creek with ease. But his dog was not so good at long jumps, and tried to chase it, falling flat on the ice.

From Walter Delorme

Beaverdam Creek along the Eastern Slopes

One of the finest areas for big-game hunting in the foothills is the Beaverdam Creek area, a side trail of the one heading north. Here, ideal wildlife habitat has been relatively inaccessible, except by packhorse, and remains unchanged. The area is also considered prime watershed, where the snowfields of the front range become the source of numerous streams and creeks, all flowing to the north and east, eventually ending up in one of the main rivers such as the Kakwa or the Smoky. The location in the painting is above the water divide where the weather can change quickly, taking hunters and travellers by surprise. Sudden snowstorms have had tragic results, especially in the late fall when they swoop down without warning. Probably the best game there is the lordly moose, and their large antlers and bleached bones can be found in many spots.

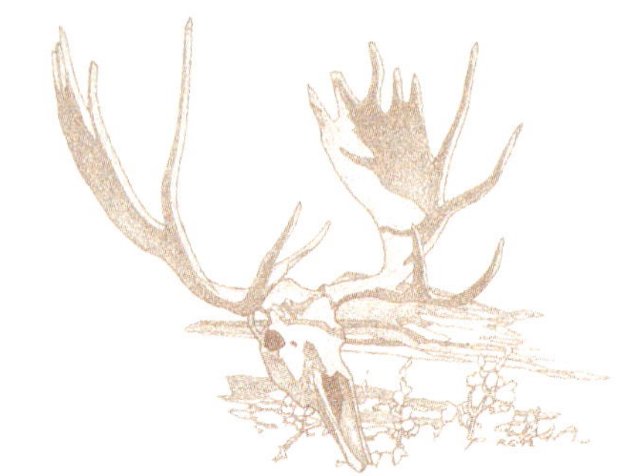

LIFE OF A MOOSE

The moose had quite an impact on the survival of the Indians and the early white travellers. It has been part of the fauna of North America for thousands of years, and has adapted to the climate and harsh conditions along the eastern slopes of the Rocky Mountains. The moose is a recognized symbol of unspoiled wilderness, and is established in native folklore.

The moose is the largest member of the deer family. While a cow moose can be formidable during the calving season, it is the bull that is considered the most dangerous. This is especially true in the late fall during the rut, or mating season, when a bull weighing anything up to a ton will attack and is capable of causing serious injury or death.

Bull moose at Nose Lake

TOP: Skull of a bull moose

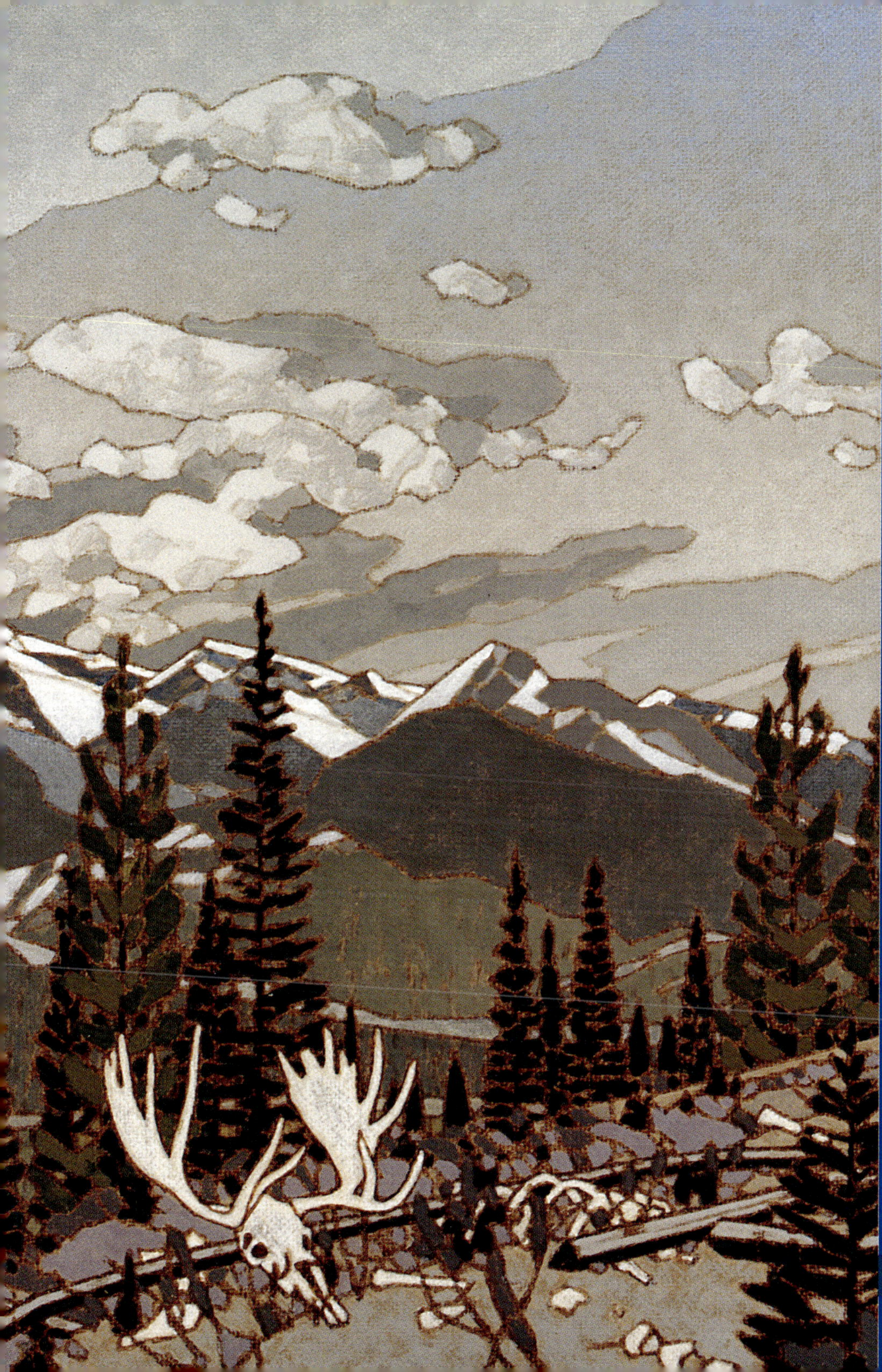

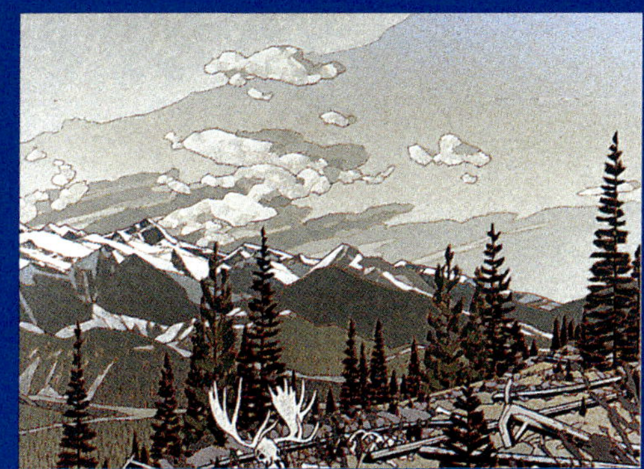

Beaverdam Creek along the Eastern Slopes

"While the horses were studying their lessons we were too. We could see in the near future unsweetened puddings, and sugarless cakes, and in time the tea and coffee so happily blended in flavour that only he who filled the pot knew which was in it."

Mary T. S. Schaffer, 1911

Copton Creek before Winter

To some extent, the section of Trail along Copton Creek was a winter route. This was low country where for miles it was necessary to cross and re-cross the stream, with horses and other animals, along gravel bars and through soggy meadows. Rainy weather brought flooding and pesky insects. Whenever travellers stopped for very long they needed to build a smudge. In winter, when the higher branches of the Trail became snowbound and exposed to biting winds, it was preferable to stay low, where there was firewood, shelter, drinking water, and grass under the snow for horses. The painting shows the first line of mountains to the southwest, upriver. The time of year is late October, waiting for that first fall of snow.

Packhorses at a smudge

TOP: Horseshoes for a rocky trail

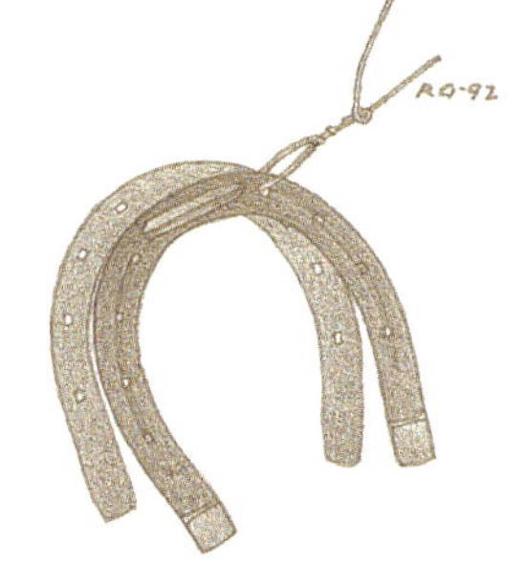

GUIDING FOR FUN AND PROFIT

Settlement in the south branched out, resulting in a variety of trades and local industries. One of the most influential was the guiding and outfitting business. From the early days, a number of exceptional people come to mind: Vincent Wanyandi, Adam Joachim, Donald Phillips, Jack Hargreaves and Albert Norris. Added to this list are the names of equally popular guides from a later period: Felix Plante, Louis Delorme, Art Allen, Tom Vinson, Deome Findlay, Carl Luger, and Edward and Frank Moberly. And there were others. The scenic beauty of the country coupled with the reputations of these people brought visitors and big-game hunters from all over the world. One of the most famous was Bing Crosby, the singer, in 1944.

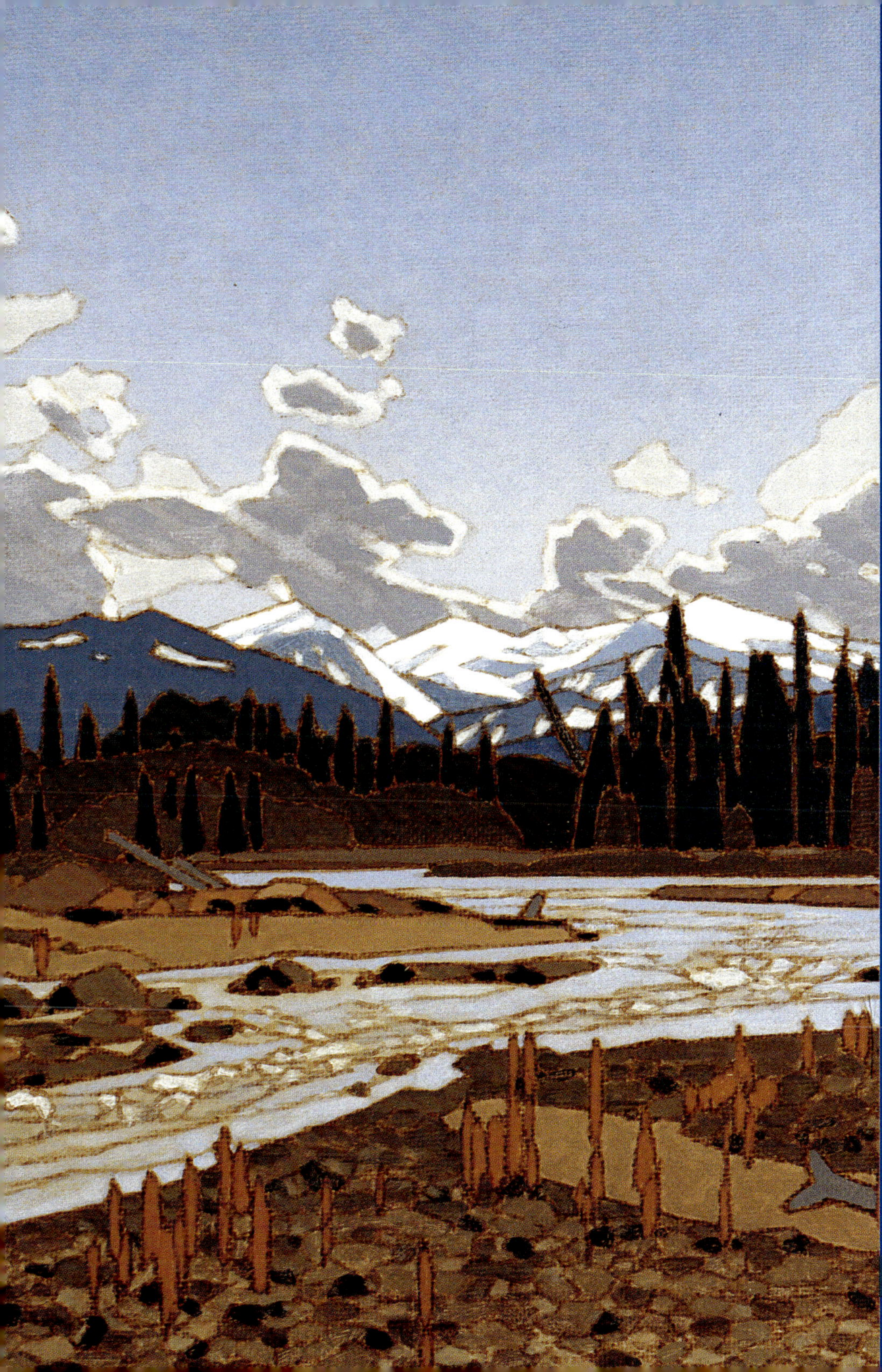

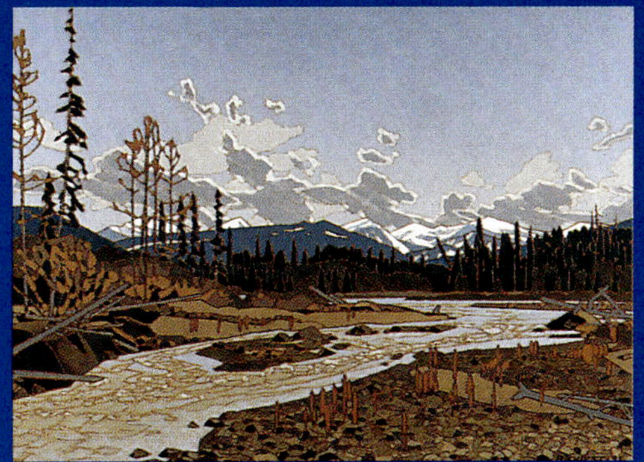

Copton Creek before Winter

"THE HORSES *certainly enjoyed the smoke and crowded in as close as possible. The building of smudges is something that the Indians very seldom do, so after a while a bunch of their horses came charging in to smoke their pipe of peace. They were met with a very cool reception. A short, spirited battle took place in which no punches, or in this case kicks, were pulled."*

John Glenn, c.1920

Trail Crossing on Prairie Creek

A few miles east of Copton Ridge was a divide in the main Trail. One part went uphill, kept to the height of land, and was preferred during summer. Usually it was much drier and had fewer mosquitoes and flies. The other branch of the Trail, along Copton Creek, was best for winter. Prairie Creek was on the higher trail, flowing to the northeast through a long, shallow basin rather swampy in places. Travellers crossed the creek in different places. Among other species of big game, the bushland caribou preferred this habitat and can be seen in the area to this day, although there are fewer now. The Prairie Creek part of the Trail eventually reached the banks of the Smoky River further to the southeast. The painting was taken from a trip in late spring, when a few patches of snow were still unmelted.

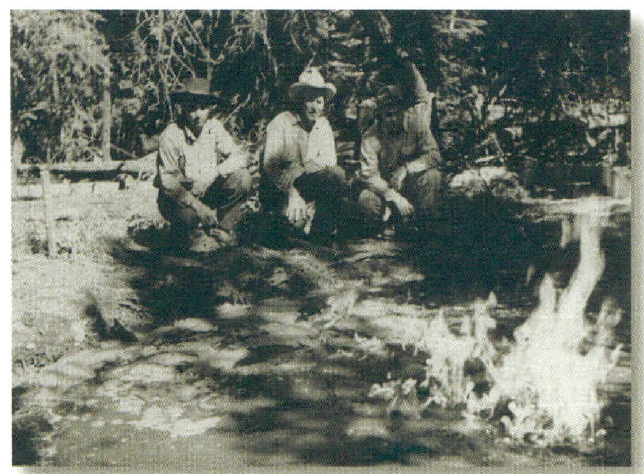

THE HAND OF MAN

It was about 1946 when the outfitting business began to change. Roads and technology were advancing, and the hinterland wasn't valued so much for its surface qualities as for its hidden wealth. Almost overnight, geologists employed in the search for gas and oil needed assistance to reach the remote country along the mountains and headwaters of the rivers. People like Bert Dalgleish were hired to get technical people into those areas to find minerals and petroleum-bearing strata. With a yen for adventure, Bert was a logical candidate, and was soon well known from camp to camp. His groups of packhorses scattered throughout the eastern slopes were, at one time, under contract to eight oil and gas companies. At the high point in his career, 186 horses were under Dalgleish saddles.

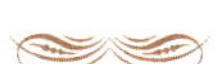

PHOTO: Bert Dalgleish and Frank Letendre demonstrate the presence of natural gas to an oil official, c.1950.

DRAWINGS: Bert Dalgleish's coal-oil can; moonshine jugs abandoned along the trail

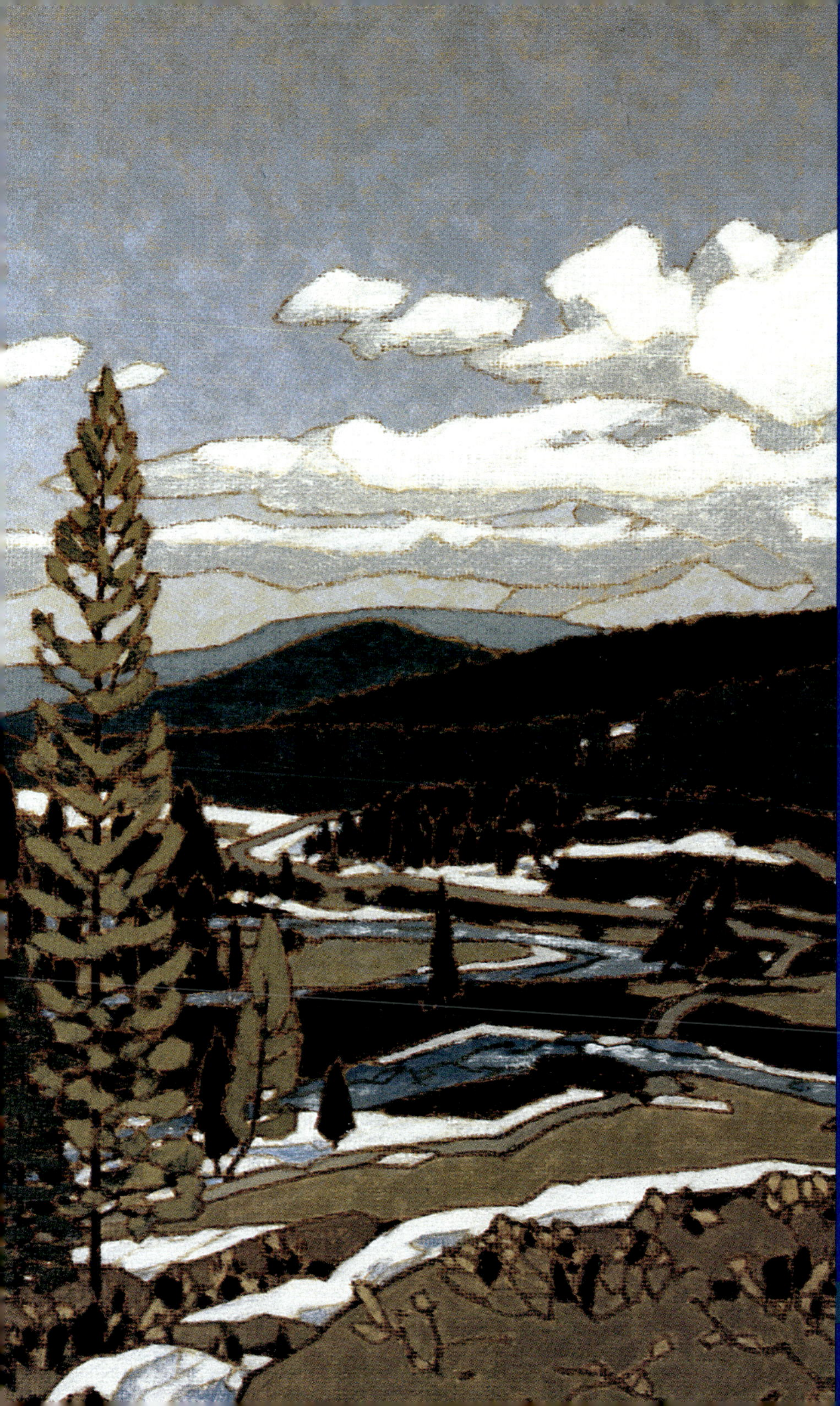

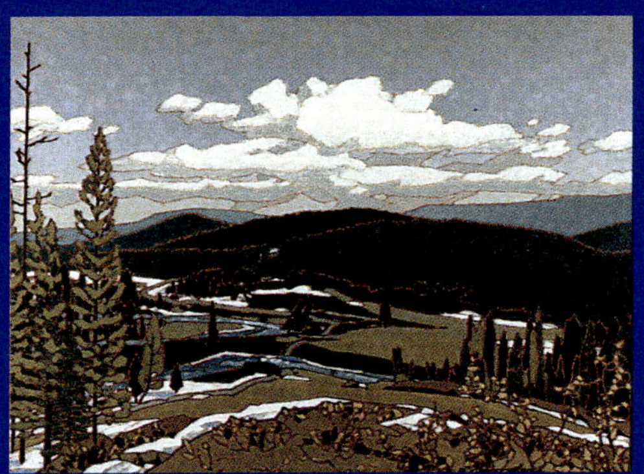

Trail Crossing on Prairie Creek

"PRIORITIES *for an overnight camp are: (1) Horsefeed, (2) water, (3) fuel and (4) a convenient campsite. In strange country without a guide, grazing opportunities cannot be anticipated, so the best use of daylight, so essential for following an unknown trail, cannot always be made. Good feed may occur too early in the day for an overnight stop, and no more may be found before darkness obscures all. The horses must then be tied up hungry and travel resumed next morning at first light, until feed is encountered. There a two or three hour rest stop for the animals to fill up must be made at the price of wasting precious daylight."*

Gerry S. Andrews

Trail over Morley Hill, Facing North

The Copton Ridge branch of the Trail went uphill, making a long swath through the trees in a southeasterly direction. It was quite steep in places for packhorses carrying heavy loads. But once on top, the Trail levelled off along a kind of plateau that continued almost as far as Prairie Creek to the south. This was the western edge of Morley Hill. It was the summer detour, a better way to go than following the lower valleys with the willows and long, swampy areas. Out in the open, the view was spectacular and panoramic, with mountains along the western horizon as far as the eye could see. This was one of the highlights of the Trail. The painting is based on a visit to the area by helicopter in May.

◆

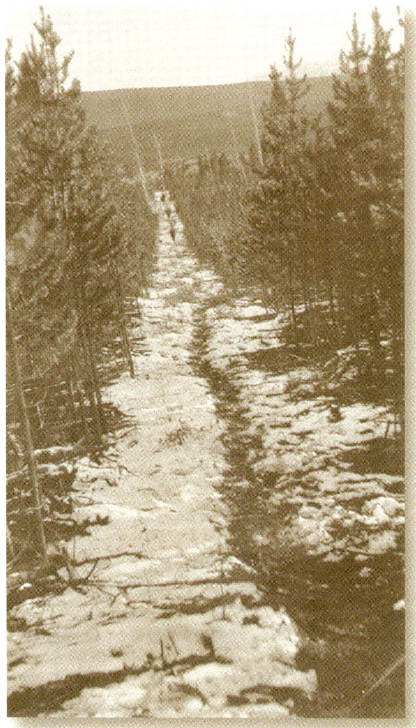

A typical section of the Lower Trail, c.1920

THE TAMING OF THE TRAIL

As a rule, settlement followed the trails. The demand to reach settlements resulted in the widening and clearing of parts of the Hinton Trail. Some people walked in over the Trail to speculate on land available for farming or ranching. These settlers would bring their families, livestock, and equipment in at a later date. Long sections of the Trail needed widening to accommodate teams of horses and wagons. Little by little the widened road would improve with use, and supplies could be hauled in on a regular basis, on wagons in summer and sleighs in winter. The old Trail was upgraded in places to the status of a dirt road, or ploughed under altogether. Examples of improved trails would be the Moberly Trail between Grande Cache and the Athabasca River, and in the north, the one cleared by axe, from the Redwillow River to "Wapiti" Brown's log house on the north banks of the Wapiti River.

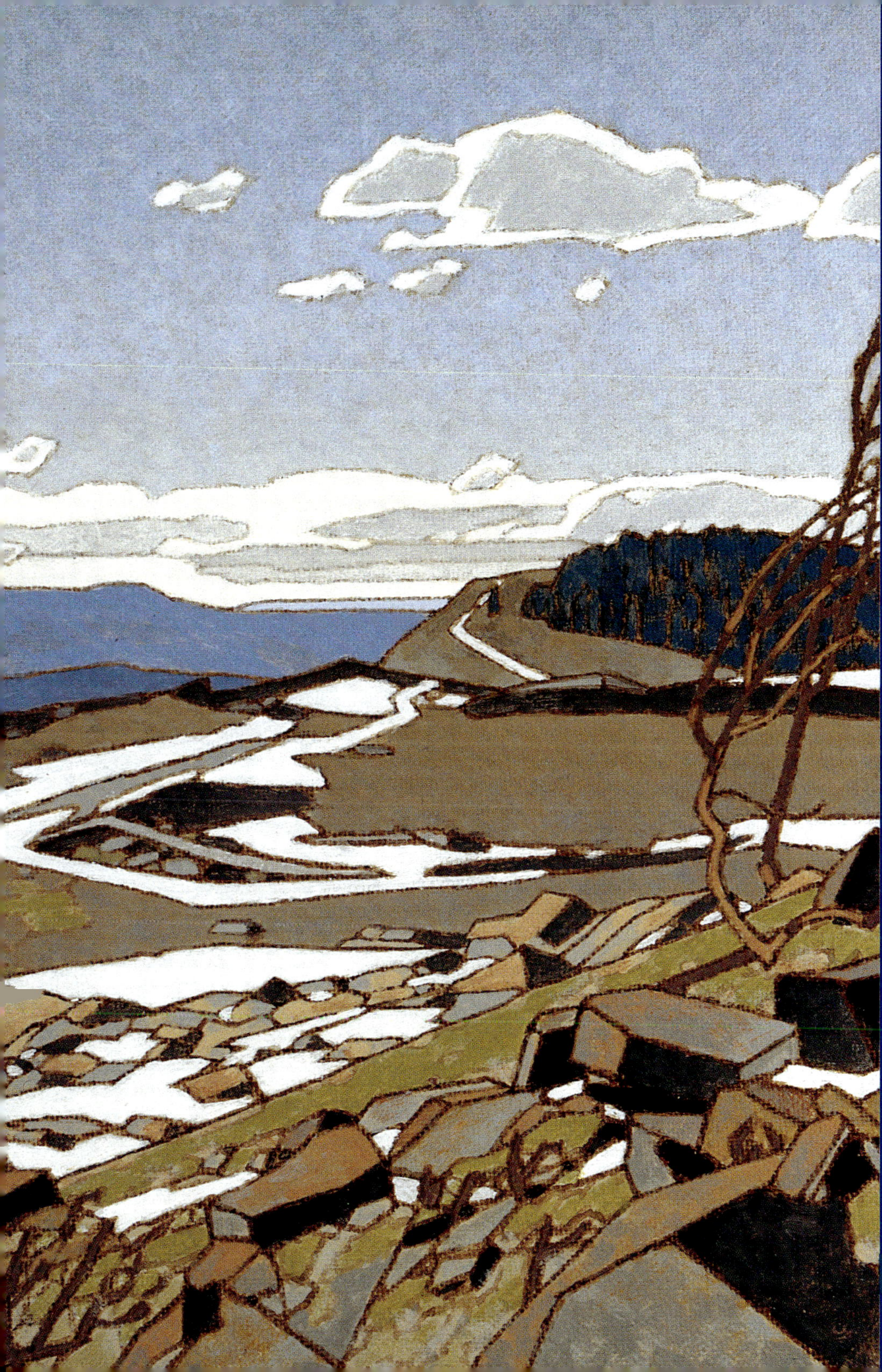

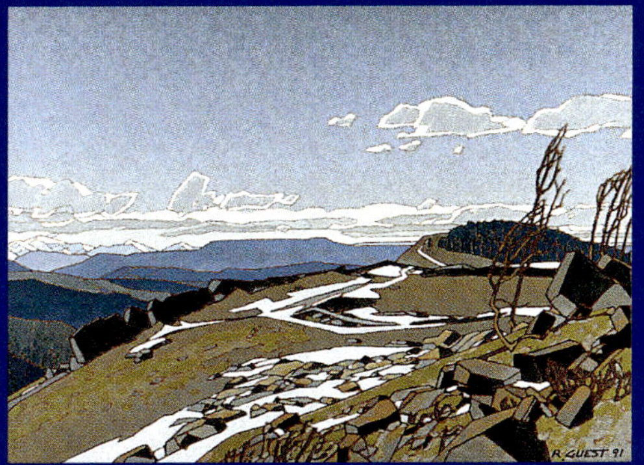

Trail over Morley Hill, Facing North

GERRY compared the Pine Pass trip (1924) with his trip a year later down the Nose Mountain Trail to Entrance. He said he found the flies in the Pine Pass area to be more of a problem than on the southern trail.

From Gerry S. Andrews

Flats along the Kakwa from the Air

The Kakwa River was a halfway point between the settlement in the north on the Wapiti River, and the trading post at Grande Cache in the south. Quite often, by the time travellers had reached the Kakwa, they were glad to take a little time off to fish, rest their horses, and meet some of the natives living in the valley. It was a haven for many species of wildlife, including elusive herds of horses that were considered wild, but were often tame ones who had escaped from their home pastures. It was a day in late fall, and the view from a helicopter showed the flats along the river with their variety of meadows, groves of trees, willows, and other shrubs. The aircraft, a type of Beaver, was used by the Forestry Service to help spot forest fires during the early 1960s.

WHERE GRAVESITES ARE FOUND

Included in the painting, but not obvious, are some log cabins that once belonged to Henry Joachim, and the grave of a girl who drowned trying to cross the river some years back. It is an old-style grave, made of carved wood, and is a silvery-white colour. There are Indian graves at various locations throughout the foothills, with a number of them close to the Hinton Trail. From his research, Dave Schenk identified the following locations: Shuttler Flats, Sherman Meadows, Gunderson Creek, Porcupine Cabin, Copton Creek, Nose Lake, and along the Kakwa and Cutbank rivers. Most of these are now overgrown and have disintegrated through the years. From my own observations, no graveyard has been found in the mountains, although the odd single grave has been identified. It seems that the mountain valleys and lower passes were not used for burial, and, with few exceptions, the dead were transported to the traditional graveyards east of the slopes.

Lone girl's grave, Kakwa River

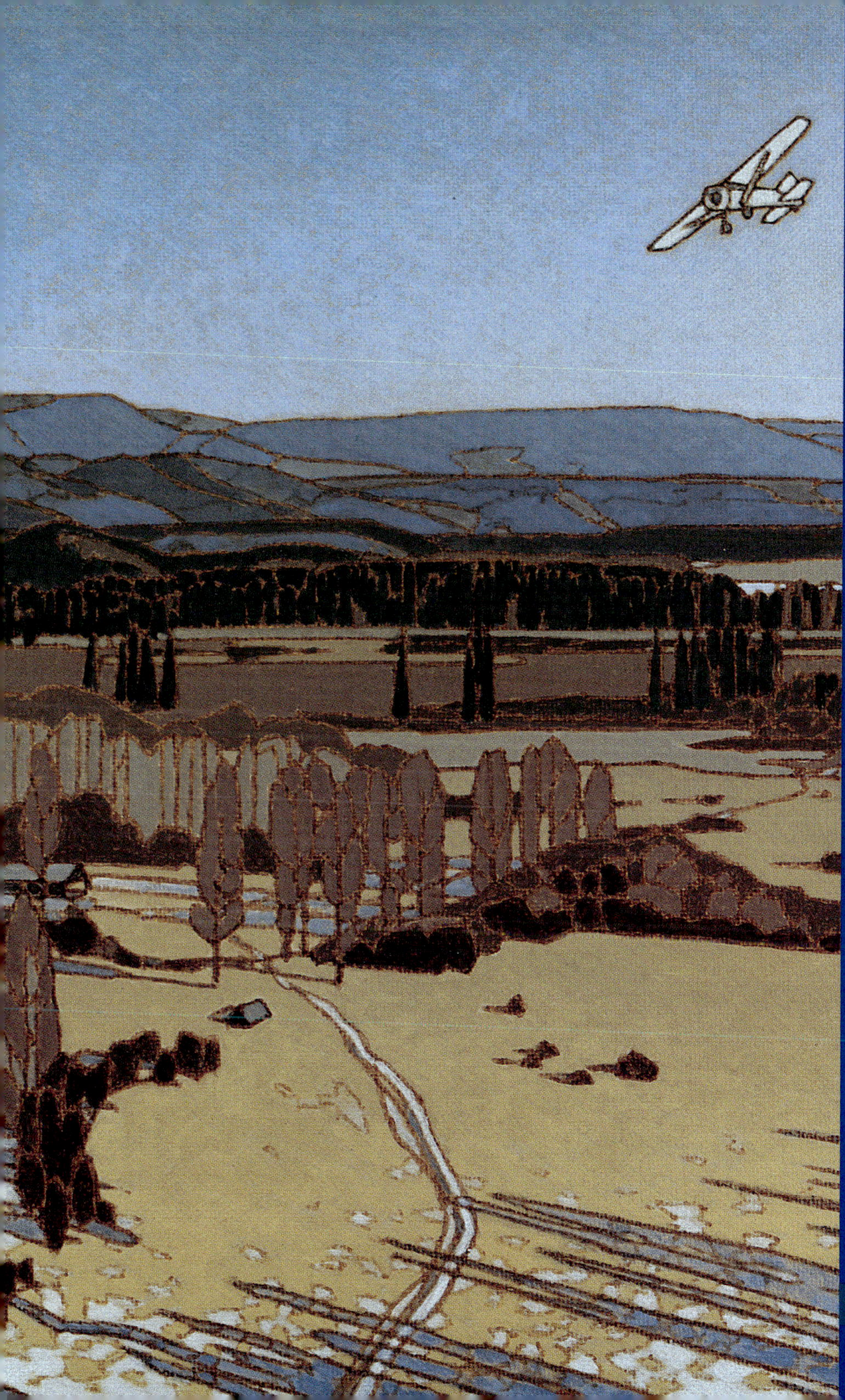

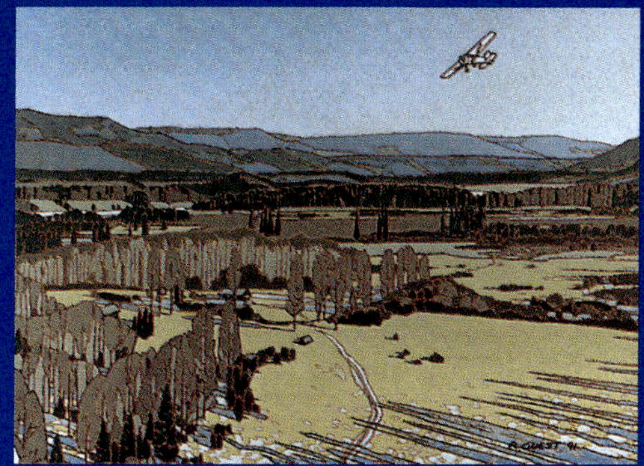
Flats along the Kakwa from the Air

"ON SEPTEMBER 1, 1967 I was working in the Nose Mountain area and chose to overnight at the Porcupine cabin on Kakwa River. While cooking supper, I heard the sound of laughter and voices and stepped out to investigate. A group of approximately ten native men, women and children were approaching on horseback followed by a small string of packhorses. Homeward bound, with their journey almost over, the horses were moving at a very brisk pace. Sitting astride the lead horse was a very proud looking man holding a sleeping child in his arms. Against the backdrop of foothills and forest this was a memorable sight."

Mort Timanson

Mad Wolf's Hill, East of Copton

A flat-topped hill stands alone about three miles east of Copton Ridge. It isn't as high as the ridge, but its sharp outline against the sky makes it look higher. The hill overlooks the west bank of Copton Creek, where the packtrail wound its way along the valley floor, gaining elevation as it headed southwest to the Rockies. The hill is ancient, a prominent landmark in the area, covered with windswept shrubs, and the rock has been worn smooth over eons of time. It's a legendary spot, sometimes called Mad Wolf's Hill. When a fiery-red setting sun strikes the high country, the colouring seems to reinforce the strange legend. I made the painting from an earlier one, painted on the spot at Copton Lookout in 1965.

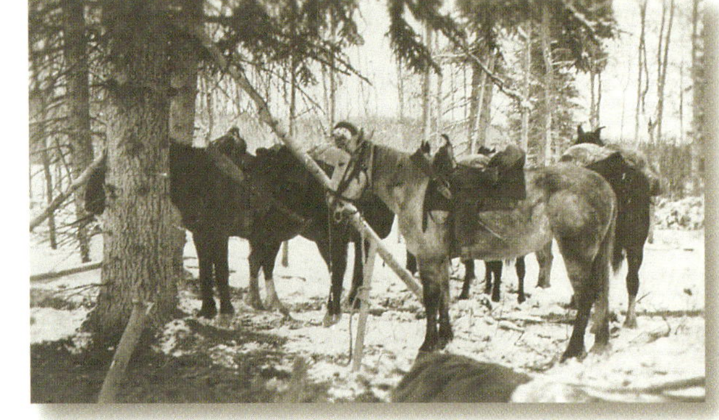

THE MAD WOLF

The story behind Mad Wolf's Hill is about a legendary timber wolf. Years ago, it was said, a large grey timber wolf became rabid, lost its fear of man, and harassed dogteams passing through the area, sometimes killing valuable sled dogs and pack animals. This would happen out on the Trail, or during the night when drivers and their dogs made camp. Eventually the wolf disappeared but his legend lives on in the minds of a few oldtimers.

Early snow, saddle horses at Nose Creek, c.1938

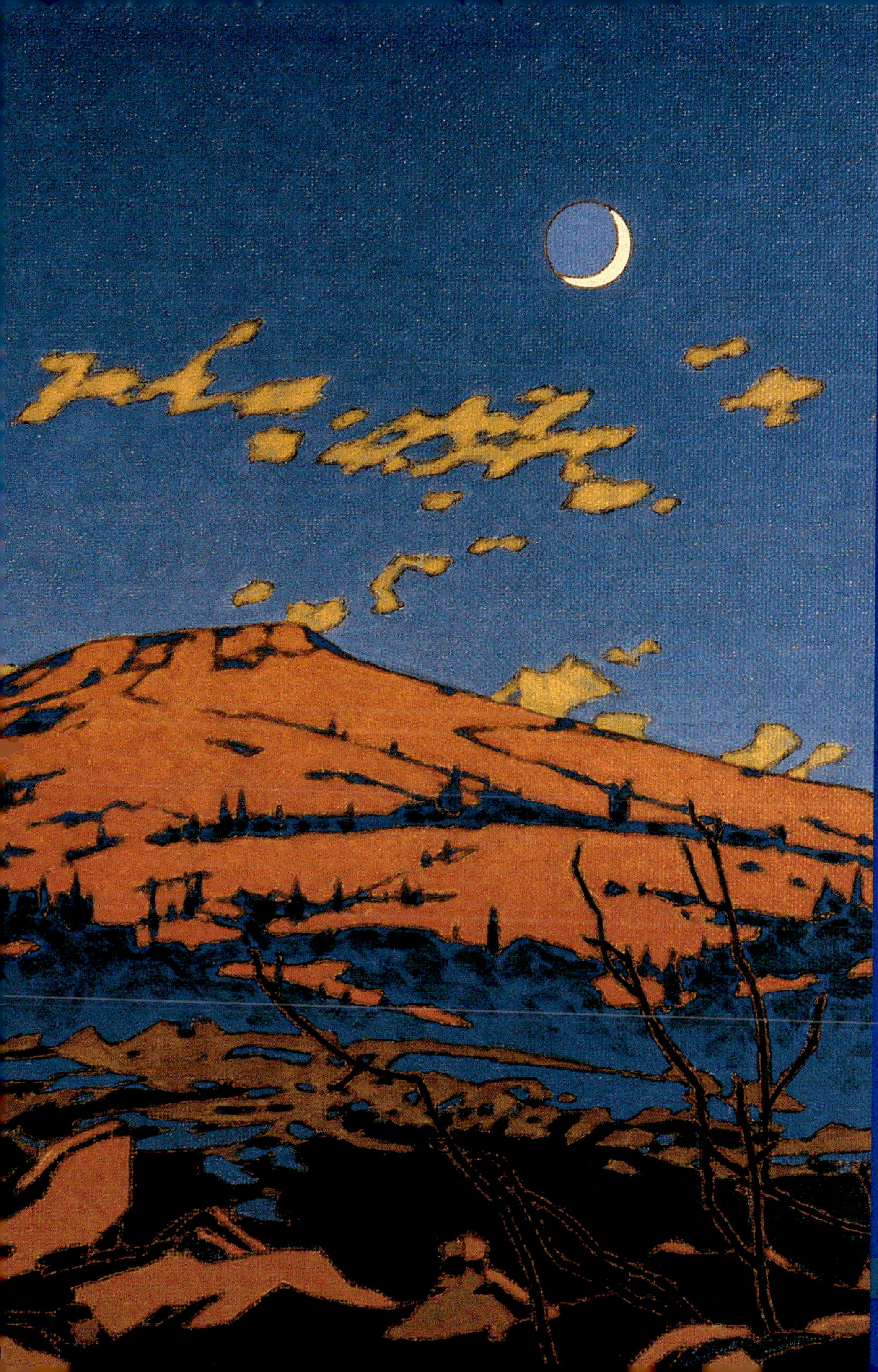

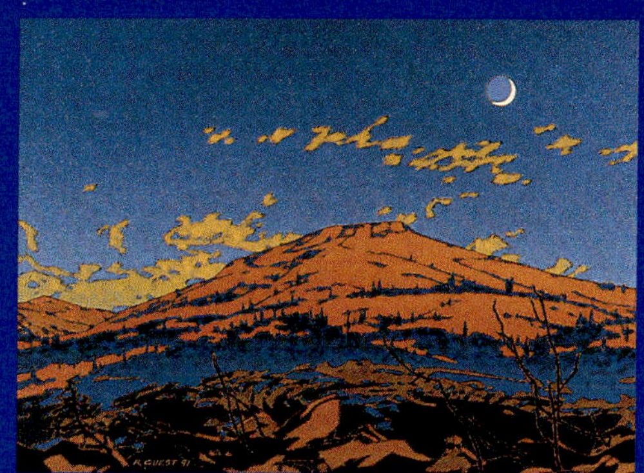

Mad Wolf's Hill, East of Copton

"When I had almost dropped off to sleep a timber wolf howled quite close to the cabin. I almost hit the roof and from then on sleep became impossible."

John Glenn, c.1920

La Force Creek Fire from Copton Lookout

The lookout cabin at Copton gives a panoramic view of the country through which the Hinton Trail passed. If visibility is good, even the faint blue edge of Nose Mountain can be detected in the far north. Using binoculars, it is possible to trace the Trail route as it went across country on the east side. The Trail crossed the Kakwa River about seven miles away, the closest it came to Copton Ridge. It followed Copton Creek to the Beaverdam, and finally dropped out of sight in the large valley of the distant Smoky River. It was a hot, dry, early-June day in 1961 when lightning started a forest fire close to La Force Creek. The towering column of smoke was visible for miles. Because of its hillside location and limited accessibility, it was difficult to extinguish the fire, and the surrounding country took on a bluish haze. I made the painting partly from memory.

◆

TRAIL UNDER SIEGE

Resource exploration and development probably claimed as much of the original Trail as anything. The branch of the Trail coming down from La Force Creek to Sheep Creek was defaced out of existence by the open-pit or surface coal mining established over a wide area along that part of the Smoky River. The logging industry was even more noticeable, especially where large areas were clear-cut to sustain one pulp mill at Hinton and another at Grande Prairie. In some places, their scarifying and harvesting techniques have erased all traces of the Trail. The petroleum industry has left its mark too, permanently scarring much of the foothills. In addition to the many well sites, the oil companies needed a vast network of access roads. Some were redundant and wasteful, to say the least. Now, these roads and seismic lines provide a means for destructive all-terrain vehicles to enter the wilderness, following the last few traces of the packtrail.

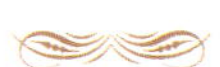

Heavy pail from Big Grave Flats

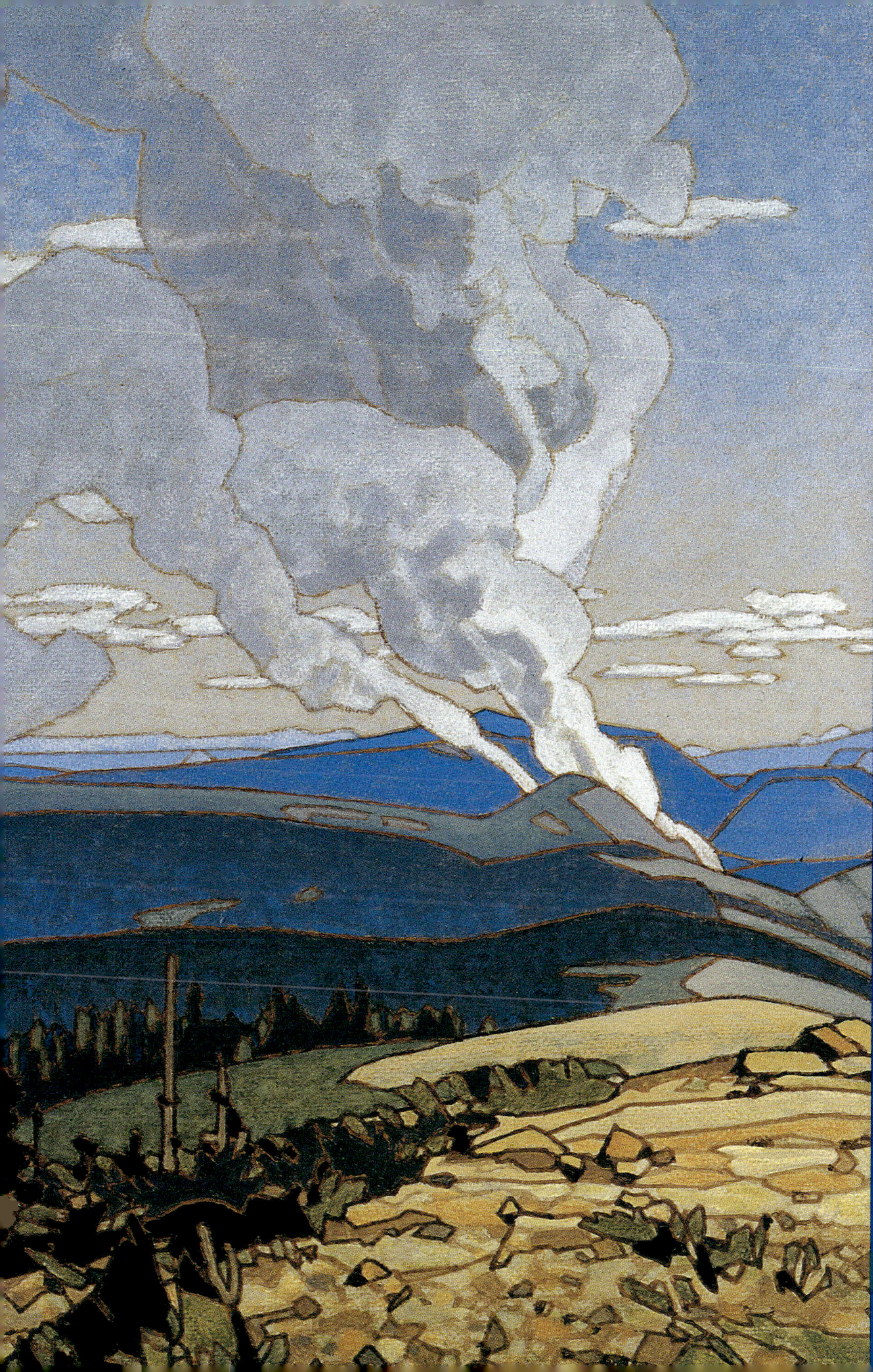

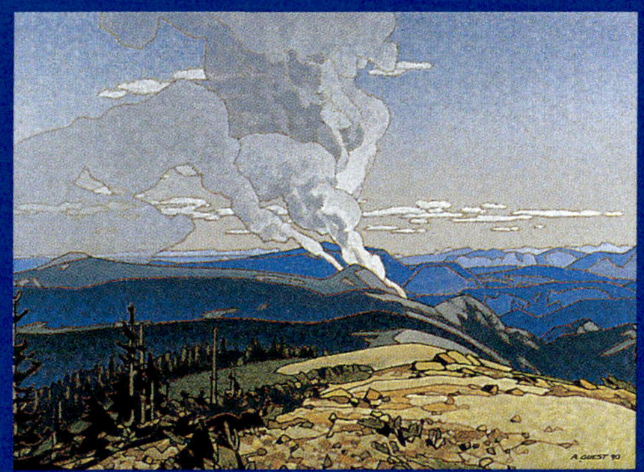

La Force Creek Fire from Copton Lookout

"AS WE HAD no chance to stop the fire from burning up the side of a mountain we tried to prevent it from coming down.... Rocks were the worst offenders as there was generally moss and needles sticking to them. I have seen some of them travel a quarter of a mile before stopping, leaving a trail of fire all the way."

John Glenn, c.1920

Chicken Creek Area from Copton Ridge

Copton Ridge was about halfway along the Trail to Grande Cache. The long, low mountain is parallel to the front range of the Rockies. The summit on Copton Ridge gives a commanding view in all directions. This is why the spot was selected as a lookout point in 1956. The packtrail had to go many miles through what was considered some of the most inaccessible country along the eastern slopes. It hasn't changed very much over the years. To the north, on the far side of the Kakwa Valley, one can pick out the Chicken Creek area. This was a favourite trapping and hunting spot, particularly for the Indians, and, closer to the Kakwa, some of the earlier cabins are still visible. The painting shows the area in late summer.

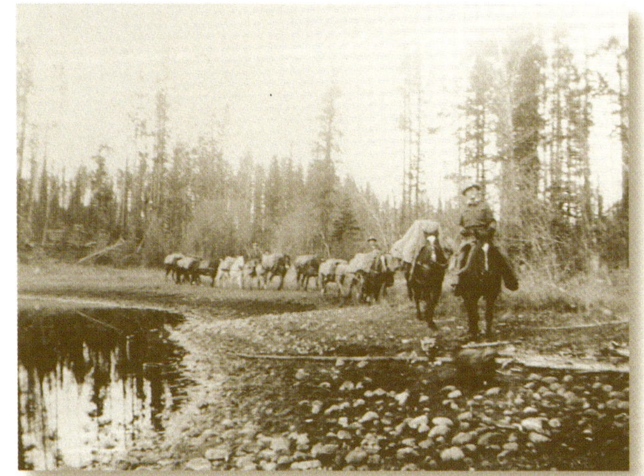

Packtrain coming down from the North Country, c.1946

MAKE YOURSELF AT HOME

During the settlement years the main Trail took on a new importance. Until about 1916, the packtrails were used primarily by the Indians, many of whom lived along its route, concentrated to a certain extent in the river valleys. Other than a few traders, and some big-game hunters and trappers, not many white people had reason to take the long Trail south to Hinton. If Indians had not made their paths over much of this territory, some roads would not exist where they do today. Their paths helped scouts, prospectors, and land surveyors get into remote areas during the early years of the century. The reports they brought back glowed with optimism. This was a time when newcomers, mostly white settlers, came to Alberta looking for good, cheap farmland. This population increase soon resulted in the claiming and clearing of new land for farming, market gardening, ranching, and other livelihoods.

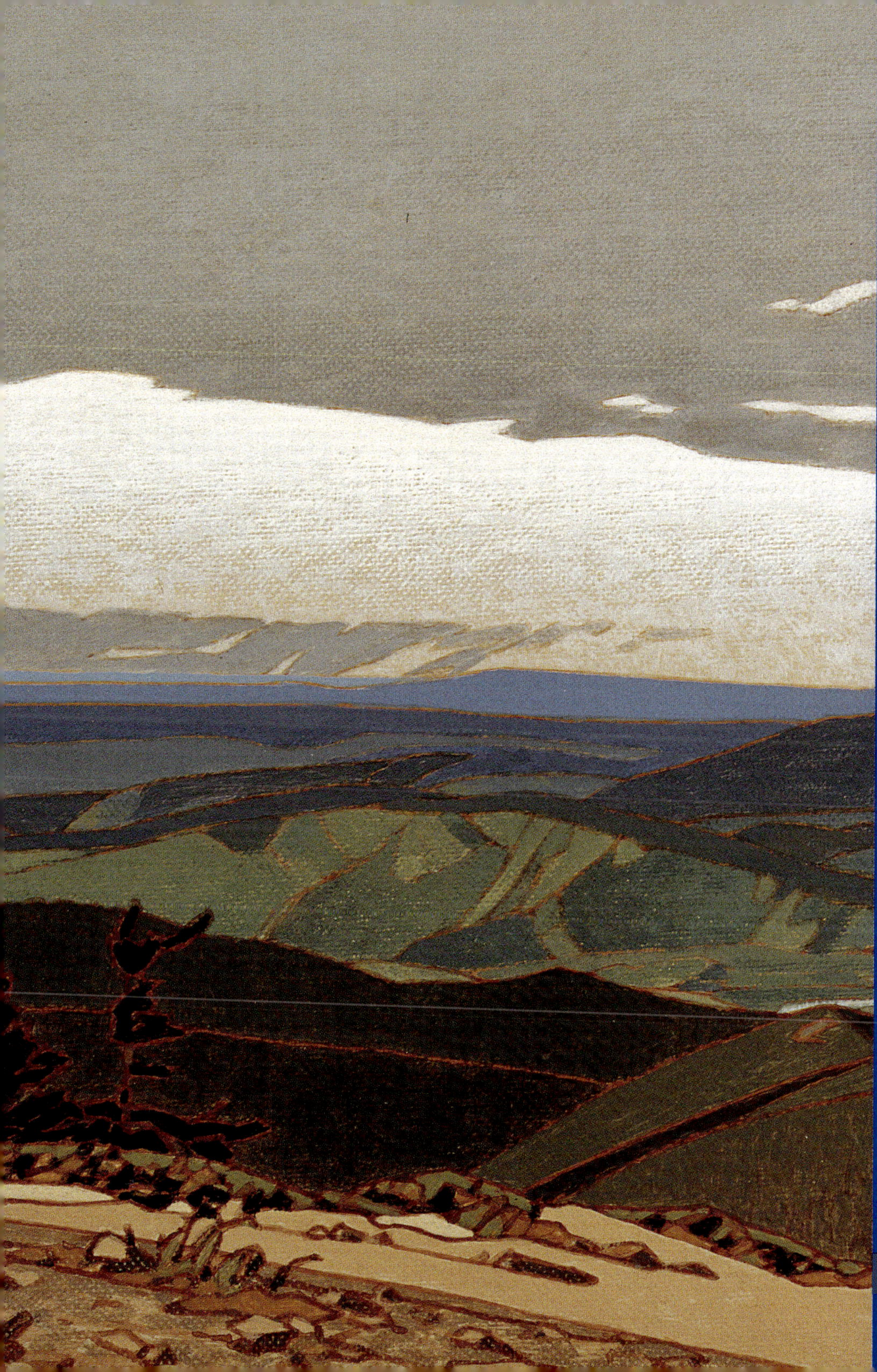

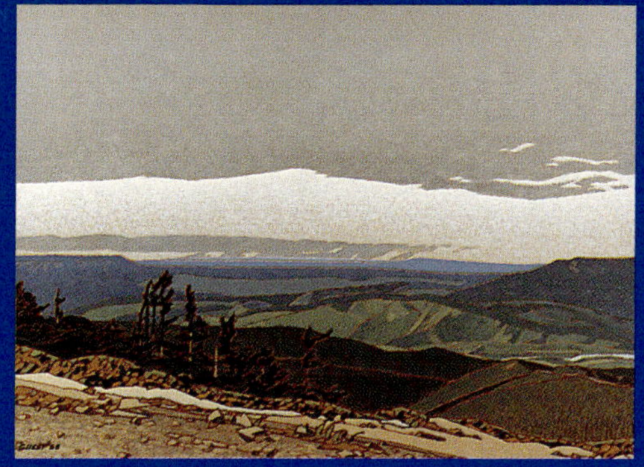

Chicken Creek Area from Copton Ridge

ANOTHER *difficult trip, according to Sam, was made from Nose Lake, where they had camped a day too long, heading towards Chicken Creek. The deep snow was up to the panniers which dragged as the horses tried to move along. There was a twelve-mile stretch of this before conditions began to improve when they reached Kakwa valley. As well as exhausting, it was almost impossible for the horses to paw away the snow to find grass.*

From Sam and Betty Unruh

Wickiup on Chicken Creek

In the old days, one could sometimes find a wickiup under a canopy of spruce and pine trees. A wickiup was like a tipi, but it was made from materials found on the spot, such as logs, moss, tree branches, and bark. It was normally a forest dwelling. Some people have said it was as comfortable as a cabin and almost as sturdy. A wickiup was built for winter use, and fairly heavy logs were used in its construction so it could withstand a heavy snowfall without buckling. In the north there were at least two designs: the long or horizontal type in the shape of a standard tent, and the conical variety similar to the Plains tipi. After a year or two, the forest dwelling was camouflaged by the moss that began to grow over and between the logs. The wickiup in the painting was still being used by Ernie Karakonti, a local trapper; I saw it just before winter.

◆

GRANNY

Her name is Alice Joachim, but her friends call her Granny. She is the wife of the late Henry Joachim and, although she has no children of her own, it is said this kindly lady took in more than 30 needy youngsters over the years. Alice was born at the Horse Lake Reserve near Hythe around 1905. Like many native people in the early days, she travelled the various packtrails through the north country, and south as far as the Athabasca River. Alice cannot speak much English, but she is very adept at using sign language. Alice is one of the better-known full-blooded native women, elegant in manner, lively, and someone who enjoys a good laugh. Even at her age she still does some trapping, and her moccasins and beadwork continue to delight the young and old. When trapping, Alice mostly goes after weasels and martens, but she told me trapping was not as good as it used to be.

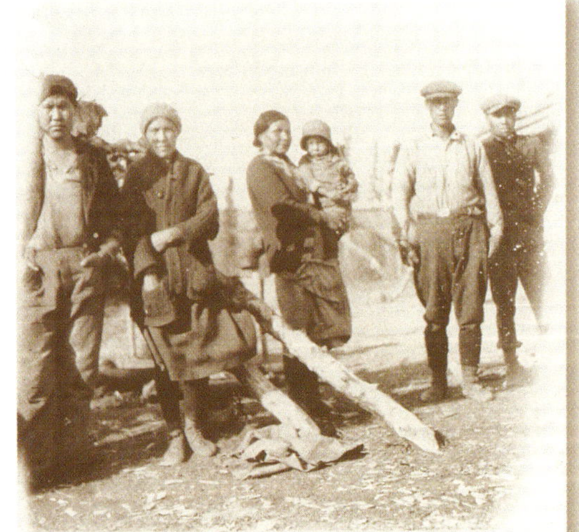

Few natives of the Smoky River are better known than the resourceful Alice Joachim (shown beside Mrs. Shettler and Little Joe, c.1920).

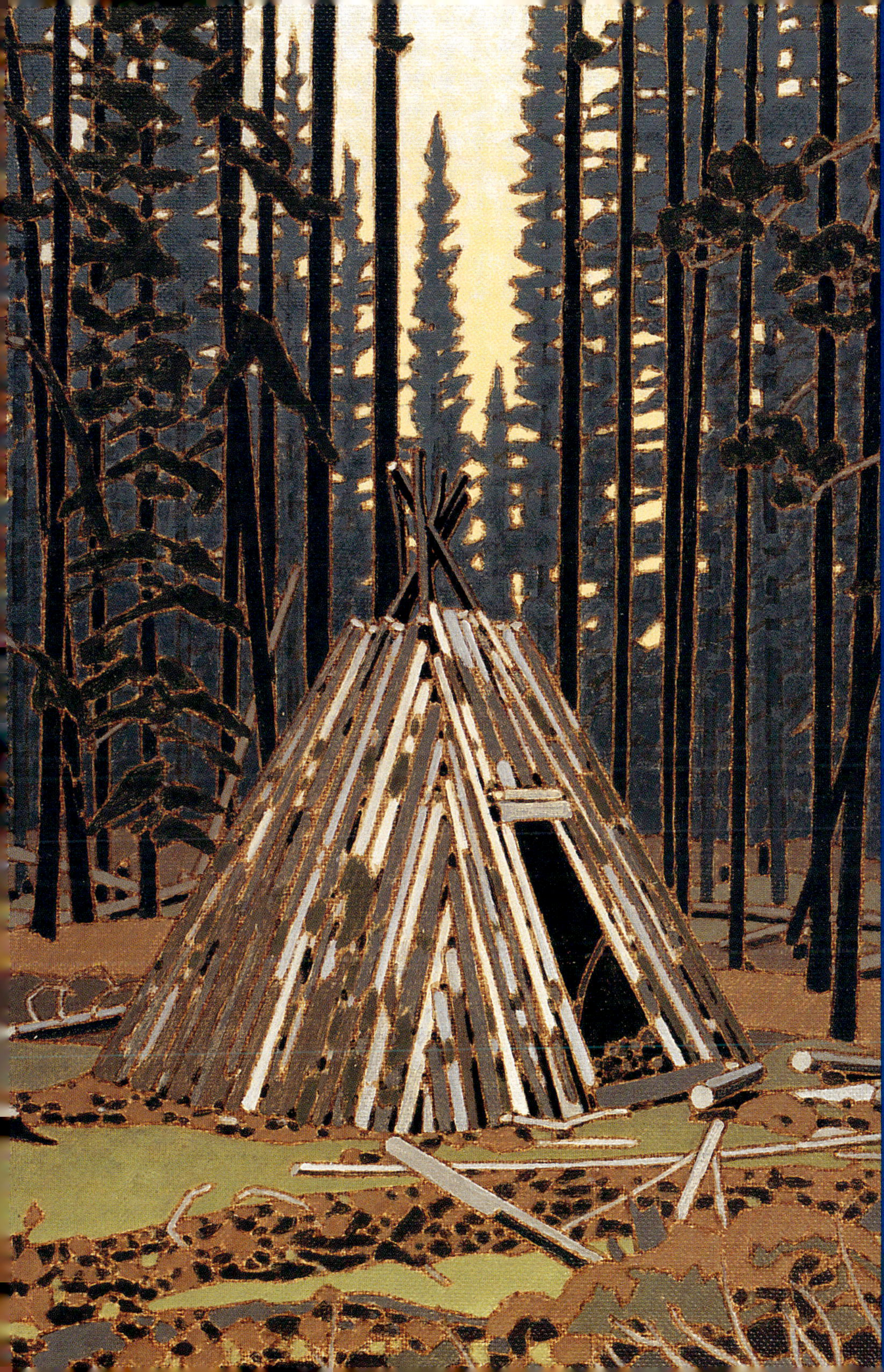

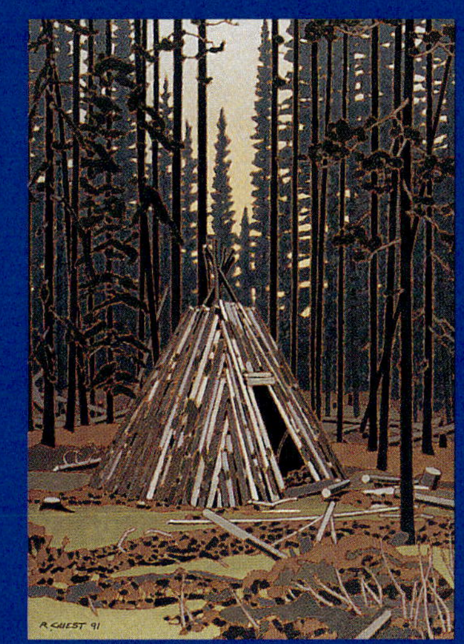

Wickiup on Chicken Creek

"He [Curly Phillips] showed them how to be comfortable without a tent by building a 'wickiup' from small trees and boughs."

W. C. Taylor, 1984

Kakwa River under Full Moon

There was something special about being on the Kakwa River at night. The place was alive with moving shadows and wildlife. In the light of a late-summer moon, the tales and images of the past seemed to return and haunt the riverbends, meadows, and dark spruce groves on both sides of the valley. It was bear and wolf country, still a wilderness after the last resident natives left the valley in the late 1960s to move to Shuttler Flats. The view selected for the painting included the same general area as where the old packtrail crossed the river downstream. Somewhere in the mountains there had been a forest fire, and the resulting smoke haze gave the full moon an orange cast, reflected on the moving surface of the rapids. It was a night in late August.

◆

FATAL AIRPLANE CRASH AT KAKWA LAKE

In October 1945, Carl Brooks made his last trip to Kakwa Lake. He lived in the Pipestone Creek area, and was one of the best-known outfitters to travel that part of the Hinton Trail. A special plane was hired to fly to Kakwa Lake to bring back hunters who were anxious to leave before the weather changed. Some say the visibility was poor, with a low cloud ceiling over the lake. The plane made a crash landing in a meadow. Carl was the only passenger killed. Word of his death reached his family about three days later when the pilot, Mr. Cormack, and the Indian guide, Ed Stoney, arrived on saddle horses. The rare twin-motored Barkley-Grow was one of two in Alberta at the time. I could still see the registration letters CF-BTX on the sides of the fuselage when I made sketches of the plane in 1981.

Kakwa Lake aircrash, 1945

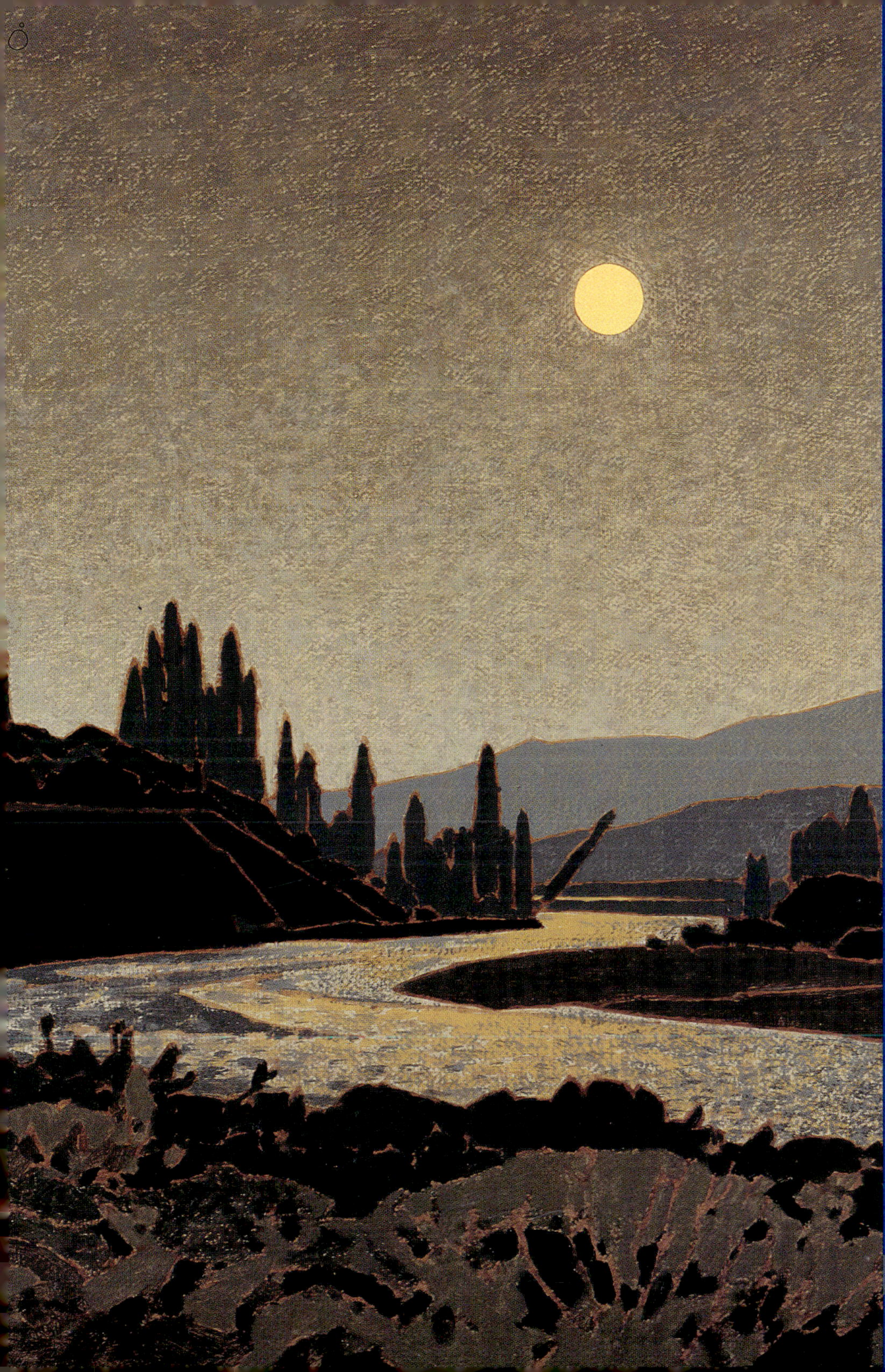

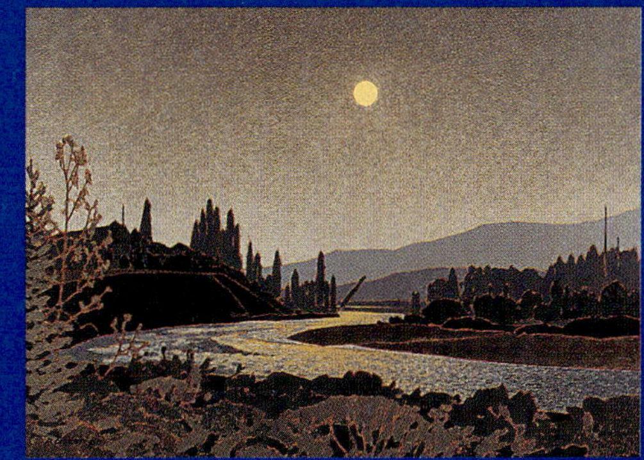

Kakwa River under Full Moon

*W*HEN I *walked down to the Kakwa River one evening from Copton, I saw a small group of wild horses. One stood out in particular. It was a beautiful white animal with a very long tail and flowing mane. They were down on the gravel bar on the north shore, and didn't seem to notice me on the old Forestry road across the river.*

Robert Guest, 1963

Indian Graves at Night on the Kakwa

Most of the many graves along the Kakwa are now overgrown and lost, but, in a few places, some of the old spirit houses can still be seen, in their weathered condition, with fences to protect them from grazing animals. It was one thing to see the graves in daylight, but quite something else to stay through the night, studying the effects of moonlight on the scene. The setting was remote, and peaceful with the harmony of the natural world. Everything seemed transformed and mysterious, with the full moon half-hidden by dark poplar trees. The moon was orange, and on the surface of the river was a moving, golden shimmer. The painting is based on a night in August when shadows seemed to come alive—if only in the imagination.

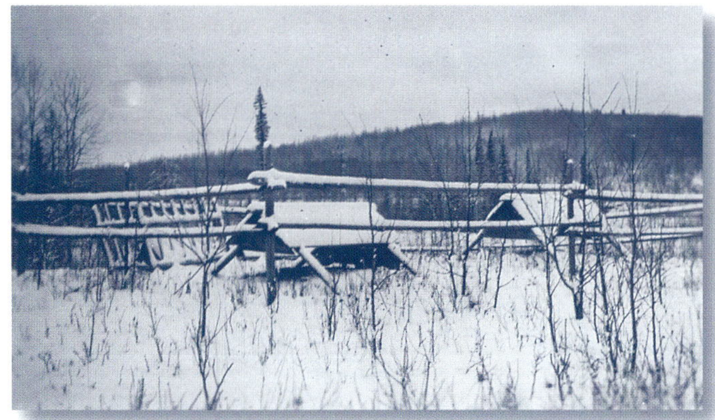

In a quiet, timeless setting, snow covers a graveyard in Shuttler Flats.

MAKING THE SPIRIT HOUSE A HOME

Especially eye-catching is the iconography or decoration of some of the graves. Some are quite simple, others have symbols of playing cards, or gothic motifs linked with the Christian church. It is believed that the choice of designs was personal, according to what happened to be most convenient or attractive at the time. Some spirit houses were complete with floors, walls, roofs, and even windows (but no doors), and it was believed the spirits within enjoyed the opportunity to look out on the world.

As in other cultures, important individuals were given more elaborate markers. The more important shelters were beautifully carved, especially the cross, the ridge-line of the roof, and the containing fence, if there was one. The individual size of a grave usually indicated whether it was a child's or an adult's, but there were some exceptions, probably depending on the status or influence of the family.

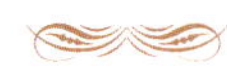

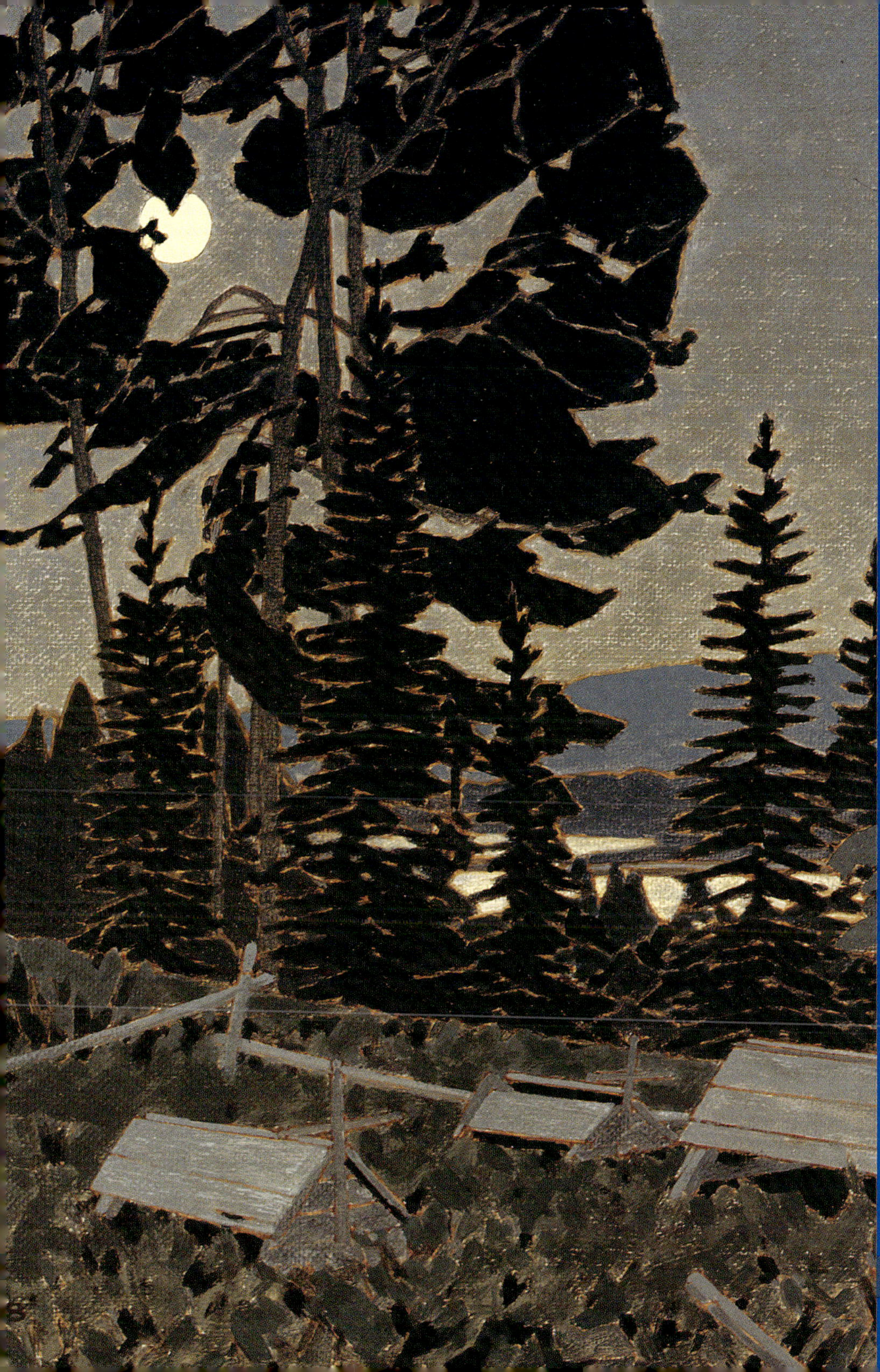

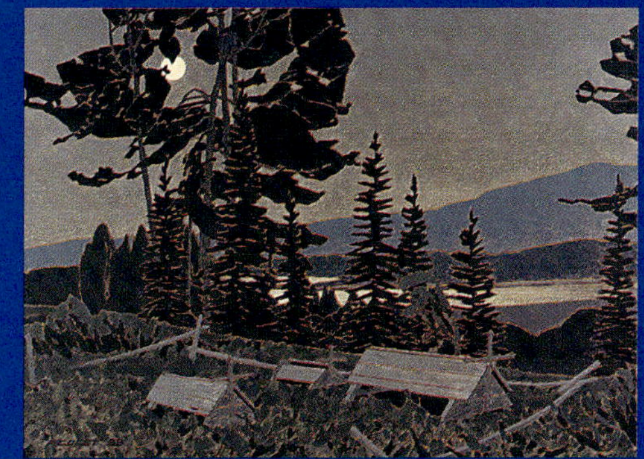

Indian Graves at Night on the Kakwa

"The adoption of the spirit house burial appears to date from the mid-1800s in the interior of British Columbia. If my speculation regarding the spread of this trait is correct, I would expect the appearance of spirit houses in the Kakwa area to date somewhat later in time, say around the late 1800s or turn of the century."

Milt Wright, 1991

Metis Cabins on the Kakwa

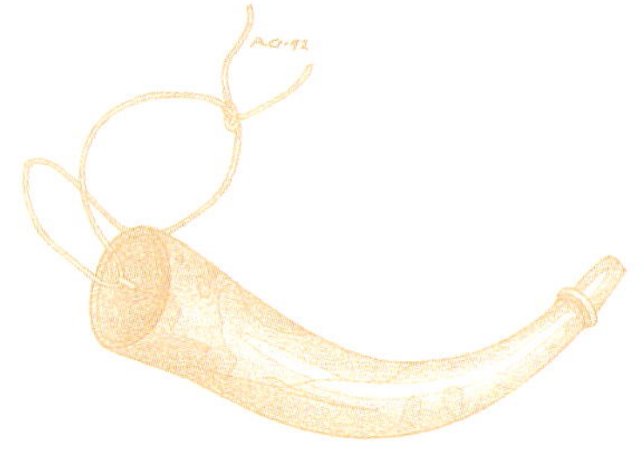

For years, the Kakwa valley has been a choice area for hunting and trapping. From the river's origin at Kakwa Lake in British Columbia, along the miles of flats and oxbows to where it joins the Smoky, it was home to the Indians. Some lived there year-round, while others migrated back and forth with the seasons. Packtrails were their highways. One can still find log cabins dating back to the 1920s, but in most cases they have fallen in and are camouflaged by the forest. Other, more recent cabins, such as the group below Copton on the north side of the river, still stand with their rail fences. Most of them belonged to the Karakonti family, who moved away in 1969. It was a wonderful place, unspoiled and remote, where the natives lived in peace and raised their families on an abundance of wildlife and fish. But things have changed in recent years. The painting shows some of the cabins in the early fall.

THE TRAIL IN 1875

An early reference to the Trail was made in 1875 when surveyor Edward W. Jarvis gave an account of travelling through the upper drainage of the Kakwa River. Jarvis had instructions from Sandford-Fleming to explore the Smoky River Pass through the Rocky Mountains. His party left Fort George on January 14, 1875, and ascended the Fraser and McGregor rivers. They headed across country from the Kakwa valley in about the same place the old packtrail headed for new Entrance on the Athabasca River.

After a long, rough trip through deep snow, they reached the Athabasca and the trading post of Jasper House. Nearly starving, they were greatly disappointed to discover the post had been abandoned. Fortunately, a small band of Indians revived them with rabbit stew and shared some provisions so the group could continue on to Lac Ste. Anne, about 200 miles further on.

Roof garden on one of the Karakonti cabins

TOP: Joe Dupuis's powder horn c.1870

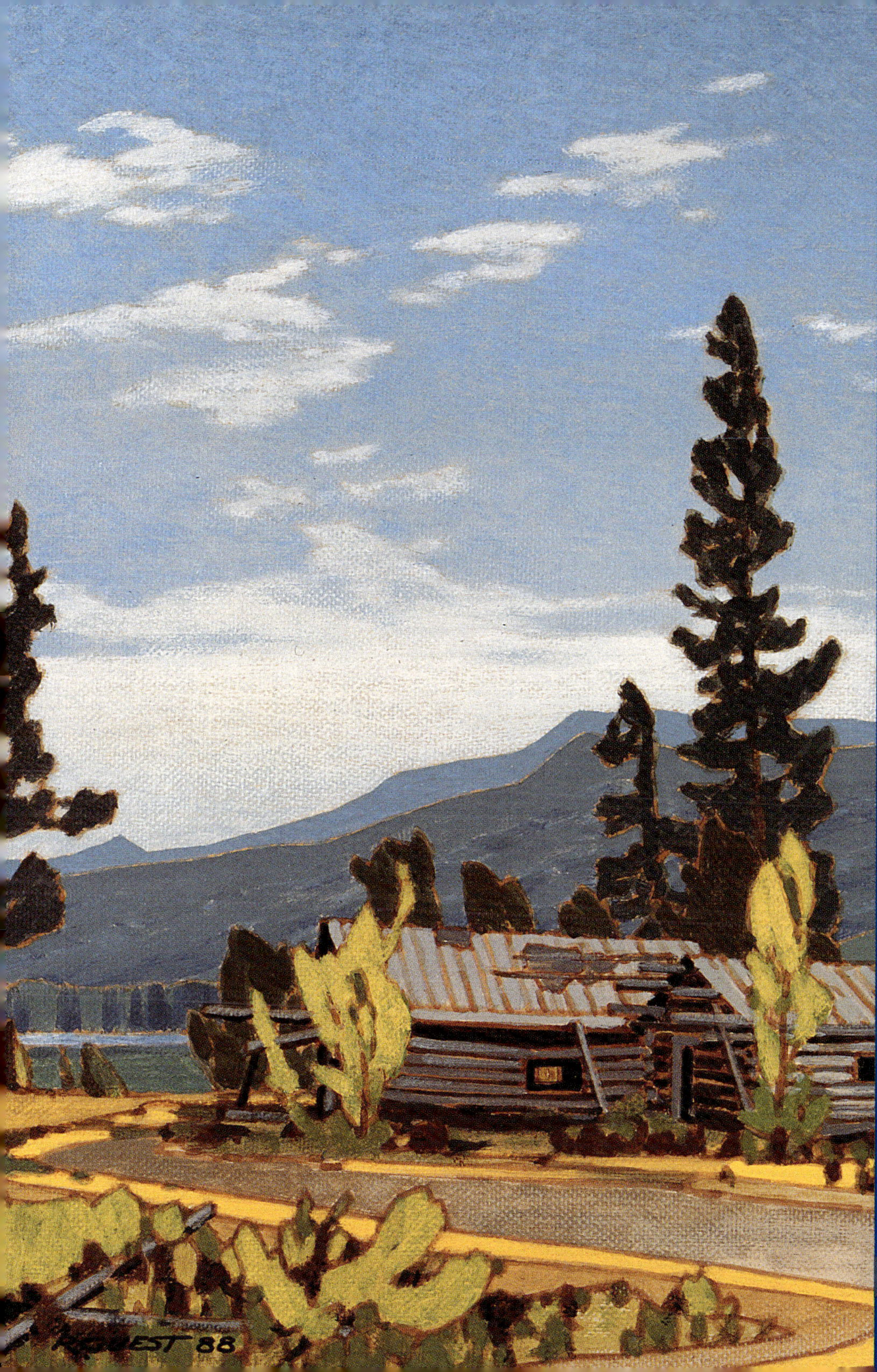

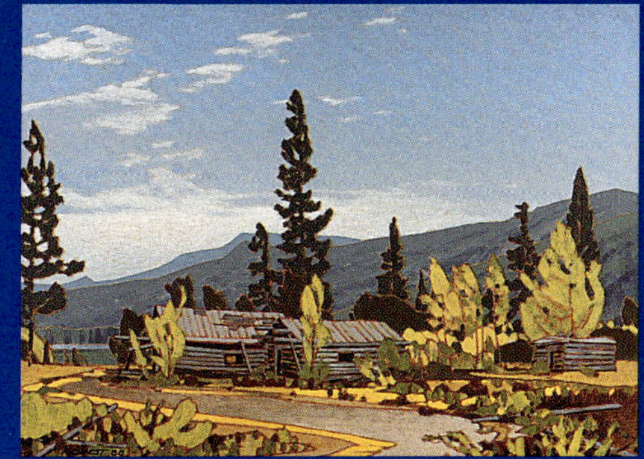

Metis Cabins on the Kakwa

IN 1963 A *helicopter pilot gave me a lift and we flew fairly low over the Karakonti cabins. There were children out in the yard with faces turned skyward. I noticed that one of the cabins, a large one, seemed to have a garden up on the roof, with vegetables, flowers, etc. This was out of the reach of horses.*

Robert Guest, 1991

Fort Porcupine on the Kakwa

Some of the trading posts along the Trail operated early in the century, while others, like Fort Porcupine, were built in the mid-1930s. These posts were set up for trade with the local trappers who were mainly Indians. A few of the posts were connected, indirectly, to large fur buyers such as the Hudson's Bay Company, but most were run by freetraders. Alan Watts was one of these adventurous people. He built the post on the south side of the Kakwa River (*kakwa* is a Cree word meaning porcupine), hauling in supplies and trade goods by packhorse. The Fort Porcupine post was likely the last in the area to be built specifically for the fur trade. Remnants of the cabin can still be found, although its location is largely inaccessible. The painting is a reconstruction, based on an old photograph and a visit to the location in 1991.

◆

ABOUT THE FORT

Of the different posts on the Hinton Trail, Fort Porcupine was the only one with a distinctive name. The post was established about 1936, and it wasn't very long before it had a lot of customers in the area. Unlike other posts, this one became a sort of centre from which Watts and his assistants would fan out on horseback, dealing directly with the Indian and other trappers on their own doorsteps. The log building was connected to the main packtrail by an eastern branch that came along Red Rock Creek, crossing the Wapiti River at Pipestone Creek.

The following are some of the more practical items taken over the Trail for trading at posts like Fort Porcupine:

tea	dried apples	flour
coffee	rice	cans of butter
lard (3 lb. pails)	bacon	raisins
syrup	tobacco	sardines
jam	snuff	Klim (powdered milk)
cheddar cheese	matches	sugar
bologna/wieners	prunes	baking powder
beans	yard goods	ammunition

basic medicines, and a few items of hardware.

Tom Wanyandi's pack saddle

TOP: Outdoor items of the trail era

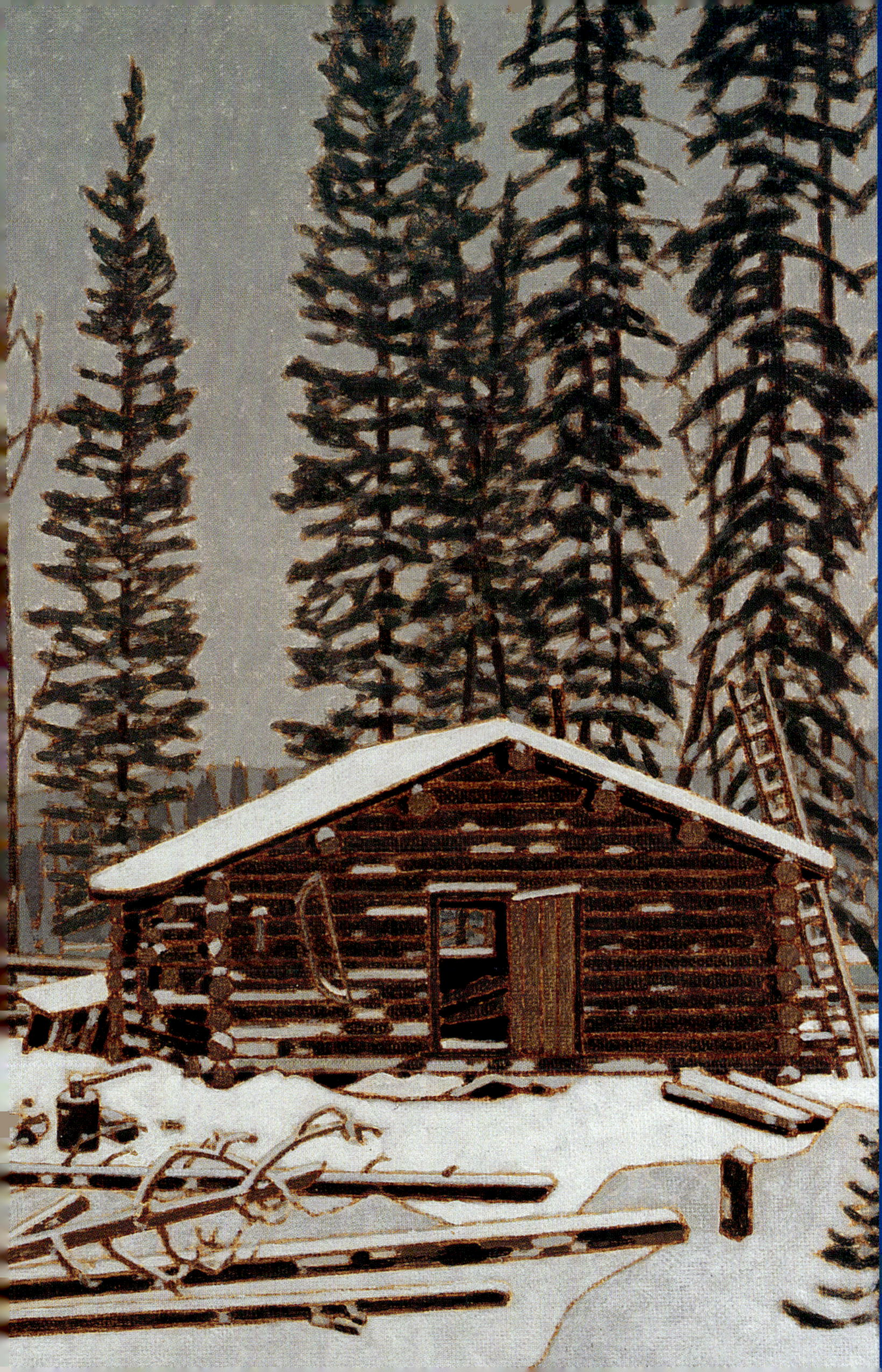

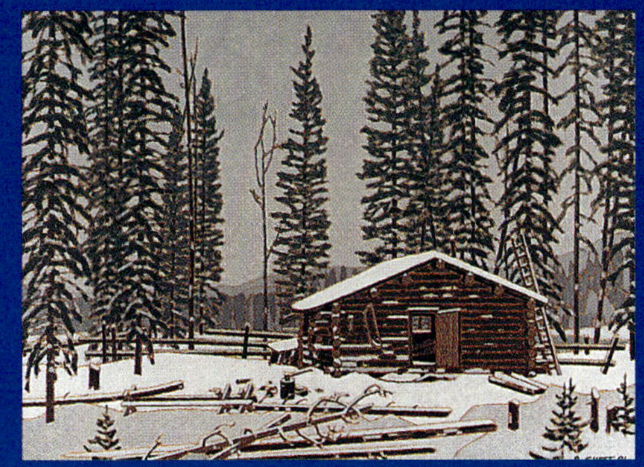

Fort Porcupine on the Kakwa

"I was shown how to throw the diamond hitch, quite a complicated business if you didn't know how. On one side of the pack saddle was the tent rolled up; on the other, blankets and a waterproof sheet; in the middle, a sack containing bread, potatoes, salt, etc. Stuck on the top we had a frying pan and an axe."

J. B. Bickersteth, 1911

Lower Red Rock Creek

In the north, in the Nose Mountain area, was a branch of the Trail sometimes called the Lower Mountain Trail. There was an Upper Mountain Trail that went further to the west and over the top. The lower one followed the creeks and low valleys, connecting Pipestone Creek on the Wapiti with Red Rock Creek. The area was thought to be valuable to the Indians in the past, partly for the quantity of exposed, red-coloured rock along the creekbed and in the cliffs. The rock may have been used for special purposes such as carved pipes and other ceremonial items. The bright red hue, akin to a brick colour, is believed to have resulted from underground fire that burned many years ago. The stream itself had some fish in it, and the territory it flowed through was a popular area for trapping.

BERT AND THE DODGERS

Bert Dalgleish and his wife, Jean, started a guiding business that drew clients from all over North America. The war interrupted the growth of the business when Bert joined the army in 1941. Just before he left for overseas he received an unusual request from three would-be trappers. They wanted to be taken to a spot and left there. It was in the foothills north of the Kakwa River, not far off the eastern branch of the old packtrail. The men built a log cabin and survived there for four years. Bert never thought much about them again until the war was over and he returned home. Then, in 1946, as one of his first commissions, he was asked by the Royal Canadian Mounted Police to fetch the three men. Apparently they were conscientious objectors, but in the end all charges were dropped.

Trap set, along La Force Creek

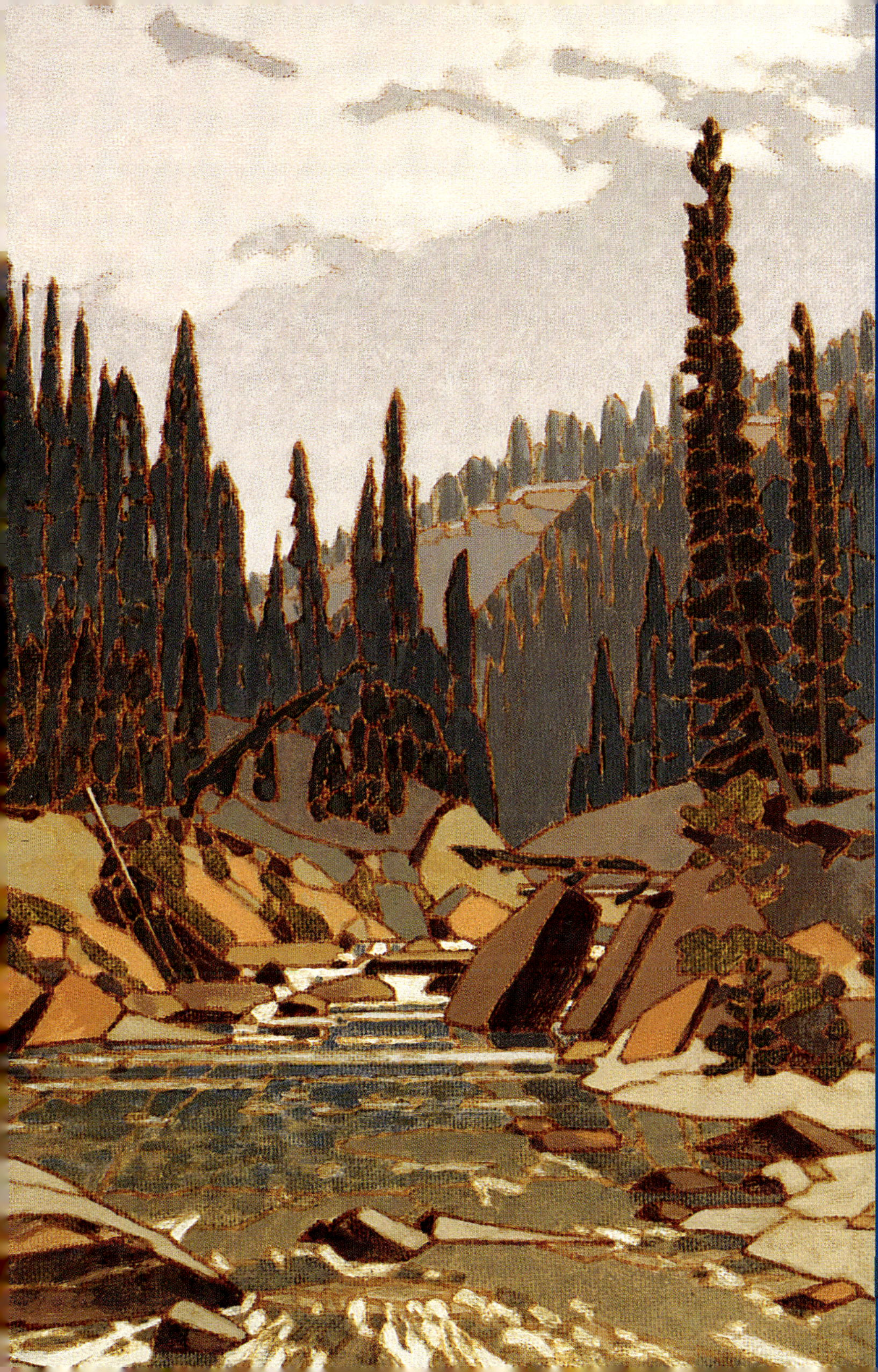

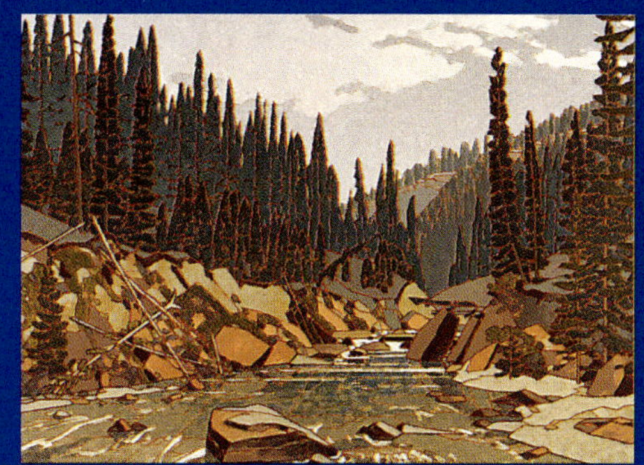

Lower Red Rock Creek

*T*HEY WERE *trapping one winter along Red Rock Creek. There was an enormous grizzly around, and it had a den large enough to walk into. Sam also saw the eyes of timber wolves when sitting around the campfire at night. He lost his horse Silver, and thought it could have been the wolves.*

From Sam and Betty Unruh

Old Cabin at Gunderson and Nose Creek Junction

The wild, scenic country along the upper Nose Creek was difficult to reach except on horseback in summer, or by dogteam in winter when it became safe to travel on the ice. This was the mode of travel the trappers used long before the age of snowmobiles. The territory is the main drainage of Gunderson Creek with its source at Two Lakes, and of the wide valley southwest of Nose Mountain where Nose Creek winds its way northward for many miles. At one time a branch of the original packtrail followed the valley, and made a connection with the main branch along the tip of Nose Mountain. Near the junction of the two creeks was a small old Indian settlement. The painting was based on a trip to the area in late September.

◆

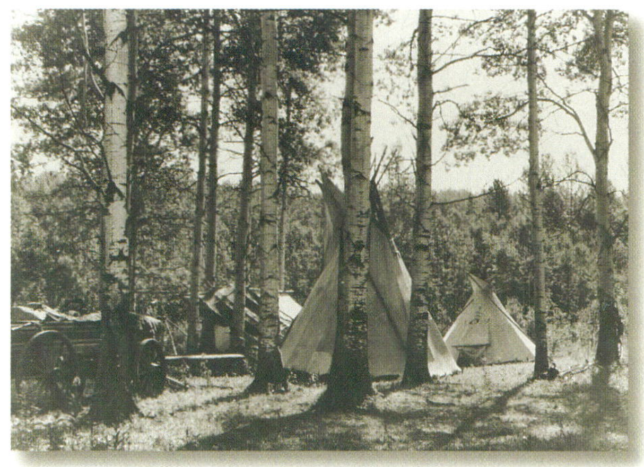

Alex Moberly's tipis, Nose Creek, 1970

THE EPIDEMIC HITS THE TRAIL

Dotted along the banks of upper Nose Creek, cabins made of logs from the surrounding forest became a landmark on the old trail system. Likely, the small community had its start in the late 1800s, and the cabins date back to about 1915. It was an isolated settlement of a dozen or so cabins, connected with the outside world through a network of packtrails. The residents were resourceful native people who made a living in their broad valley much as their ancestors had done for centuries. Their settlement was peaceful and predictable until the flu epidemic reached them about 1919. Within a few weeks these resilient people were decimated. The few and disheartened survivors moved away for good, heading north to the Peace River country and leaving their cabins, log corrals, and a graveyard behind. Today only a few rotted logs show where the cabins once stood and, except for the odd cutline, the place is almost inaccessible.

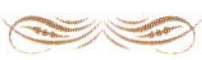

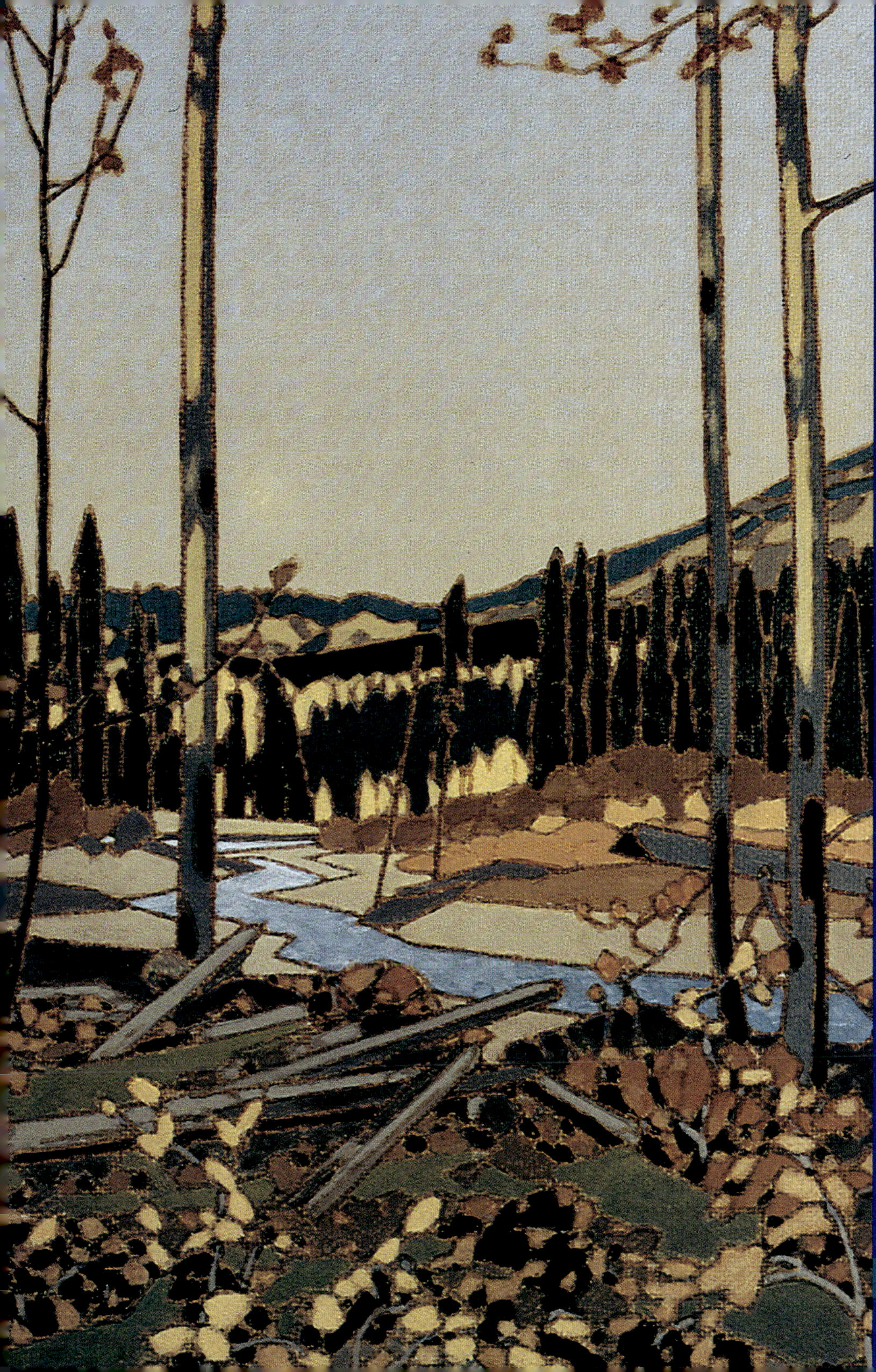

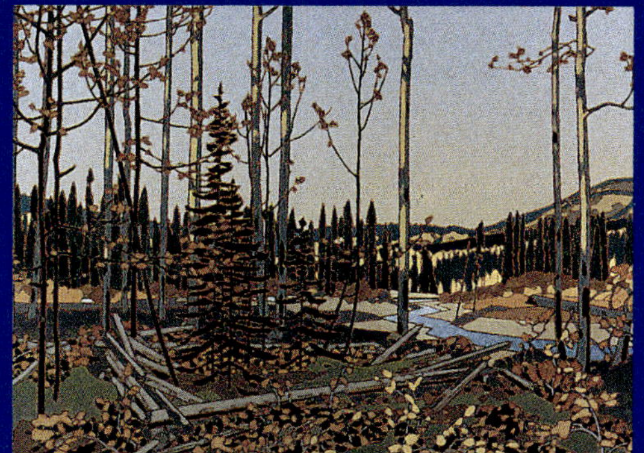

Old Cabin at Gunderson and Nose Creek Junction

"ALMOST AT your very feet there lies brooding a nomadic race whose life is a great tragedy. There is nothing to show for the trails that run from the post like silver threads into the unbroken wilderness of the North. They live and die. A little weather-bleached cross of wood marks their grave, and a friendly Indian hangs upon it a rosary and a few leaves from the balm of Gilead."

Cortlandt Shoonover, 1974

Old Campsite at Nose Lake

Few places along the Hinton Trail can compare with the old campsite at Nose Lake. Nearly everyone who made the long journey down the Trail stayed there at least once. It's an ideal spot. Men, women, and children have likely camped here since nearly as far back in time as the last Ice Age. The location was choice for a number of reasons: it was close to the old Trail route, there was a good supply of water for man and beast, there was excellent pasture for grazing animals, wild and domestic, and, tucked between forested hilltops, the lake had shelter and firewood on its shores. The lake itself is surprisingly deep, and contains fish believed to have followed the Cutbank River to its source. It was a bright fall day when I visited the area to sketch.

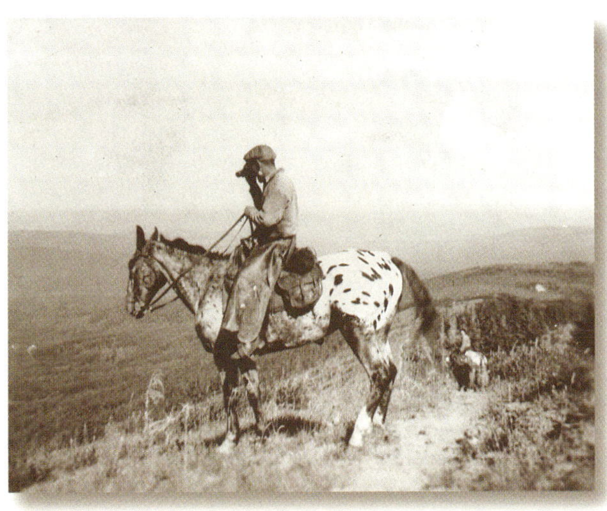

Bert Dalgleish on Patches around 1940, a pair synonymous with the foothills, with Jean Dalgleish in distance.

TRAPPING ON NOSE MOUNTAIN

Partly for the novelty of it, and partly for the money they would make, Bert and Jean Dalgleish decided to try their hand at trapping. Taking the old Trail horseback in late fall, they brought a tent and other supplies into the small lake at the top of Nose Mountain. Later, when the snow got too deep, the horses were brought back and exchanged for a dog team and sleigh. Near the traditional camping spot, on the west side of the lake, Bert and Jean set up a base camp and trapped until early March. They returned down the west side of Nose Mountain with a load of fur so heavy they had to find a way to slow their sleigh down. They tied a spruce tree behind the sleigh, and it acted as a brake when its branches caught in the snow. This was the winter of 1939–1940 when there was a demand for fur-lined jackets for RCAF pilots.

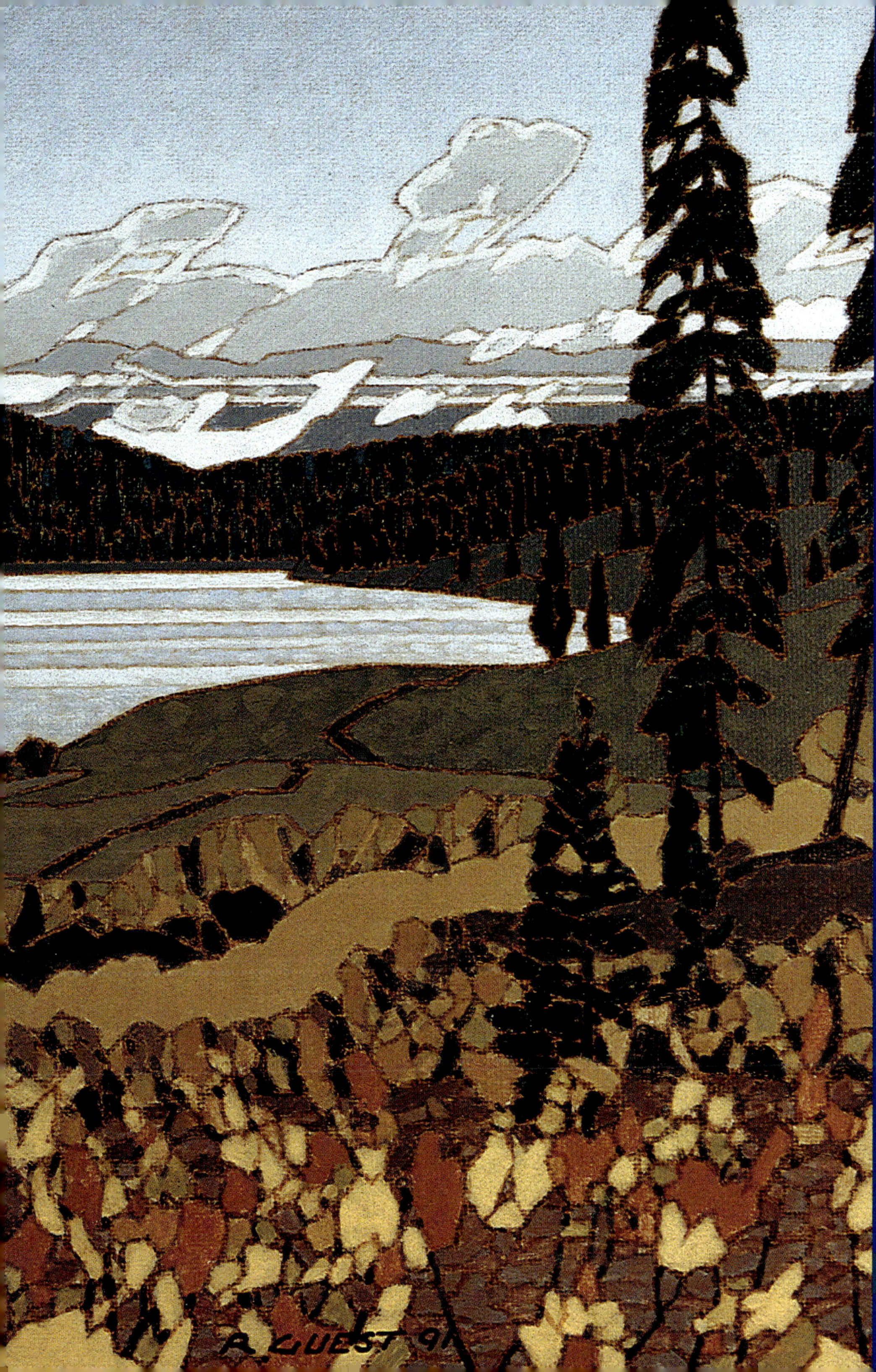

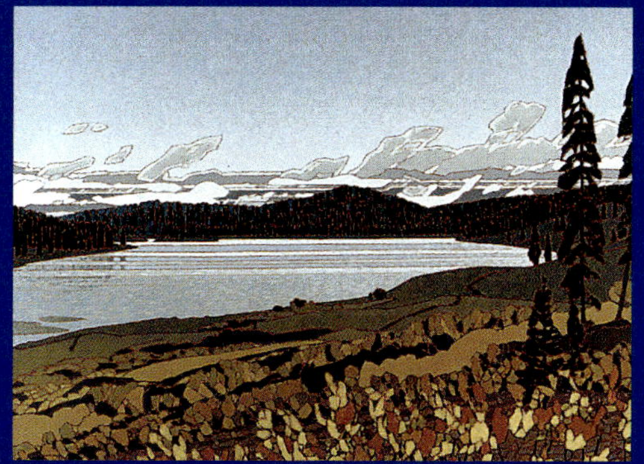

Old Campsite at Nose Lake

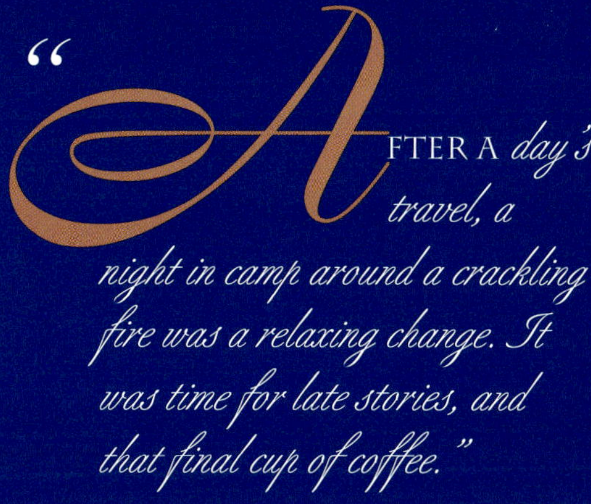

*"A*FTER A *day's travel, a night in camp around a crackling fire was a relaxing change. It was time for late stories, and that final cup of coffee."*

Euphemia McNaught

First Nose Mountain Fire Tower

One of the last fire lookouts built on the Trail was the metal tower built on Nose Mountain in 1951. About 80 feet high, it was situated east of Nose Lake, about three miles from the mountain's point. At that time, roads were few and not fit for much traffic, so the tower was rather isolated. A branch of the packtrail went almost through the yard where one of the first towermen, Sam Fomuk, was taken to by packtrain each year. In those days, it was the responsibility of towermen to take care of their own needs for firewood, drinking water, and other supplies. They also had to cope with nuisance bears. Although it was a lonely life for some, others thought it was an adventure. The painting is a reconstruction to a certain extent.

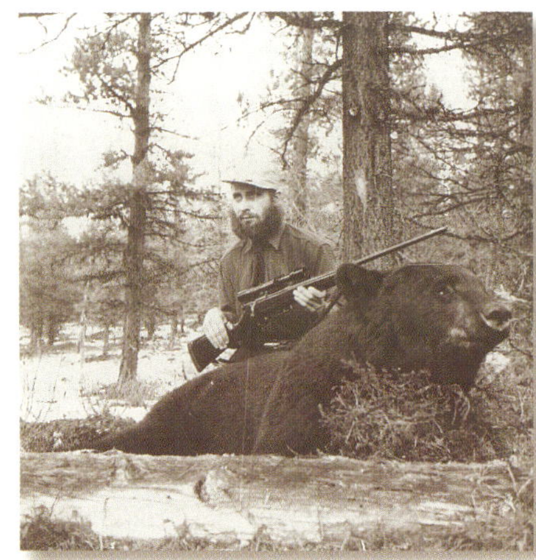

SAM FOMUK AND THE DECLINE OF THE TRAIL

By the early 1950s the original Trail was used less and less, and, in spots, had almost disappeared. The seismic activity advancing into the wilderness was first noticeable along the fringe of the settlement, where existing roads were improved for motorized vehicles. It seems the bulk of exploration was in the northwest part of the Peace country, but gradually it spread out in all directions, leaving scars across the landscape.

One person who witnessed this was the lookout man stationed in the original Nose Mountain fire tower. His name is Sam Fomuk, and his first season at the tower was in 1951. To this day, he is still working as a towerman, and likely holds the record for the longest service. In recognition of his long-standing service in Forestry, a creek in the Nose Mountain area was named after him.

DRAWING: Winter on Nose Mountain, view northeast

PHOTO: Sam, an excellent marksman, with his largest black bear, c.1956.

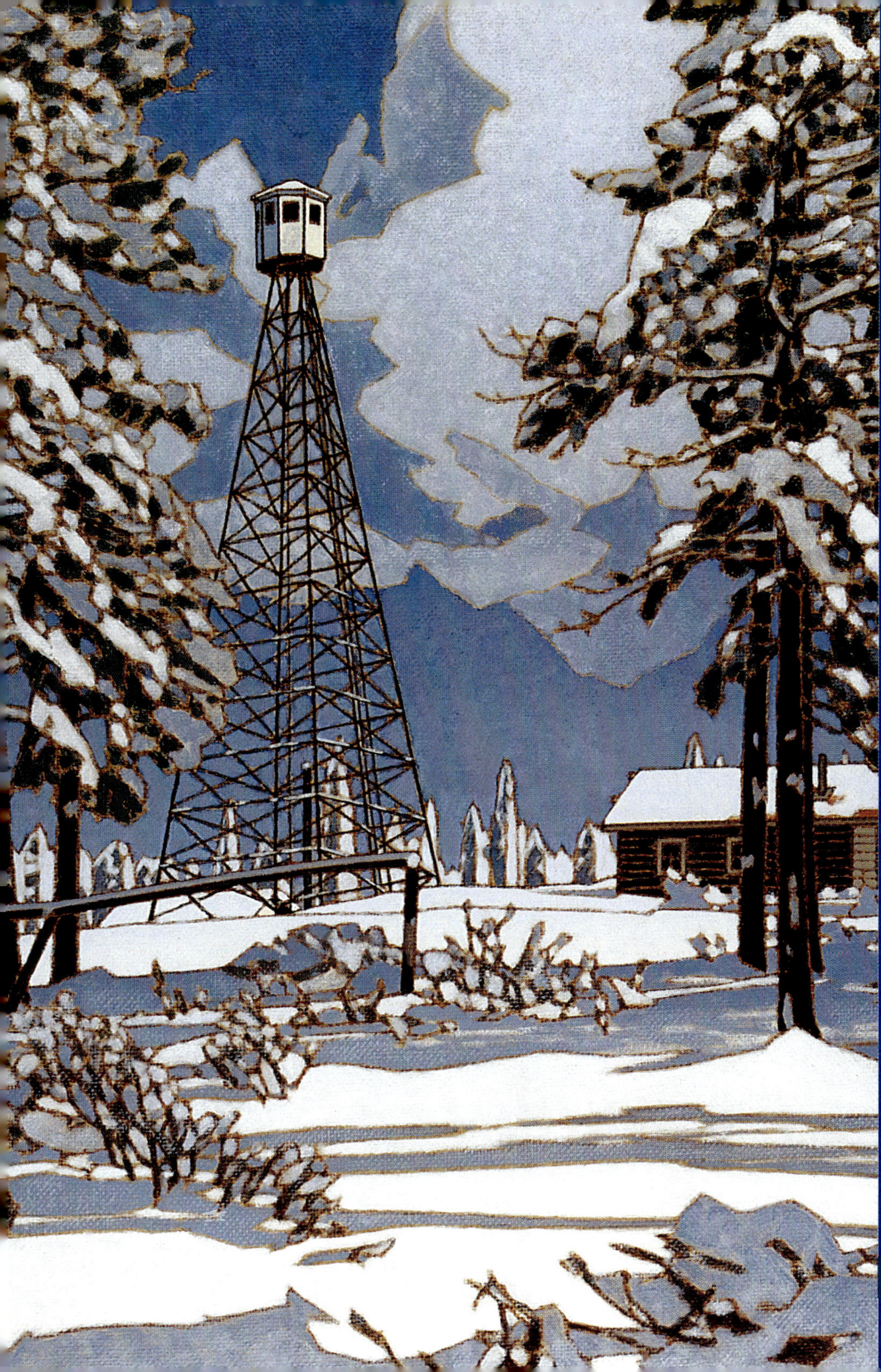

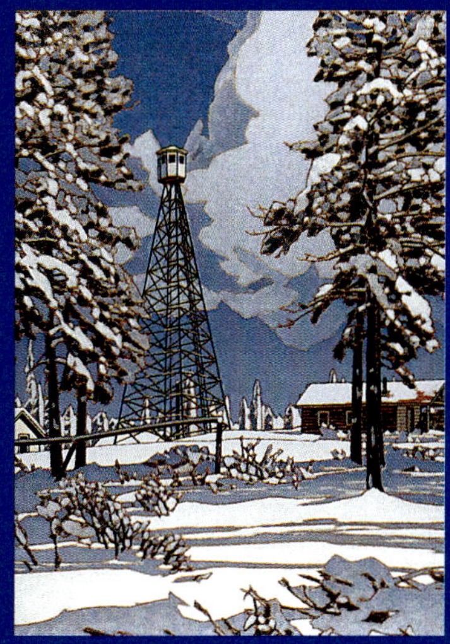

First Nose Mountain Fire Tower

From his station at Nose Mountain tower, Sam would go for long walks. These were made when the hazard was low, and in the early years when towermen were given a lot more freedom. Or as he put it, "Long before you became a prisoner of the loudspeaker."

From Sam Fomuk

Trail over Nose Mountain, Facing South

More than any other section of the historic Trail, the part along Nose Mountain remains the most distinct. It can be followed for at least twelve miles as it winds southeast along the mountain's edge. Its path has been worn down about two feet in places, from years of heavy use. It is still quite visible in spite of severe weather erosion. Spots of it are overgrown by alder bushes and trees, and sometimes the old Trail becomes braided, dividing into many lesser trails where it went around wet spots or outcrops of rock. In places, charred remains of old campfires can be found. The view for the painting was close to the point of Nose Mountain, facing south. It was midsummer, just after a rain shower.

Two campers with a lean-to

THE RECREATIONAL TRAIL

Outdoor recreation drew a lot of interest. At first, the national parks were the main sites for trail rides, fishing trips, and mountain hiking, but gradually this changed, and the well-established trails provided a summer playground for more and more people. The Trail was the preferred part of the province, especially where the packtrails kept to open ridges with views of the mountains.

During the 1930s, groups on horseback went south from the Peace River country, following the Hinton Trail. Some went as far as Nose Mountain while others reached the Kakwa River before turning back. Usually, trail riding was organized during the summer when people could get away on their vacations. A few enjoyed the trips so much they made it an annual event; in a way trail riding was almost fashionable.

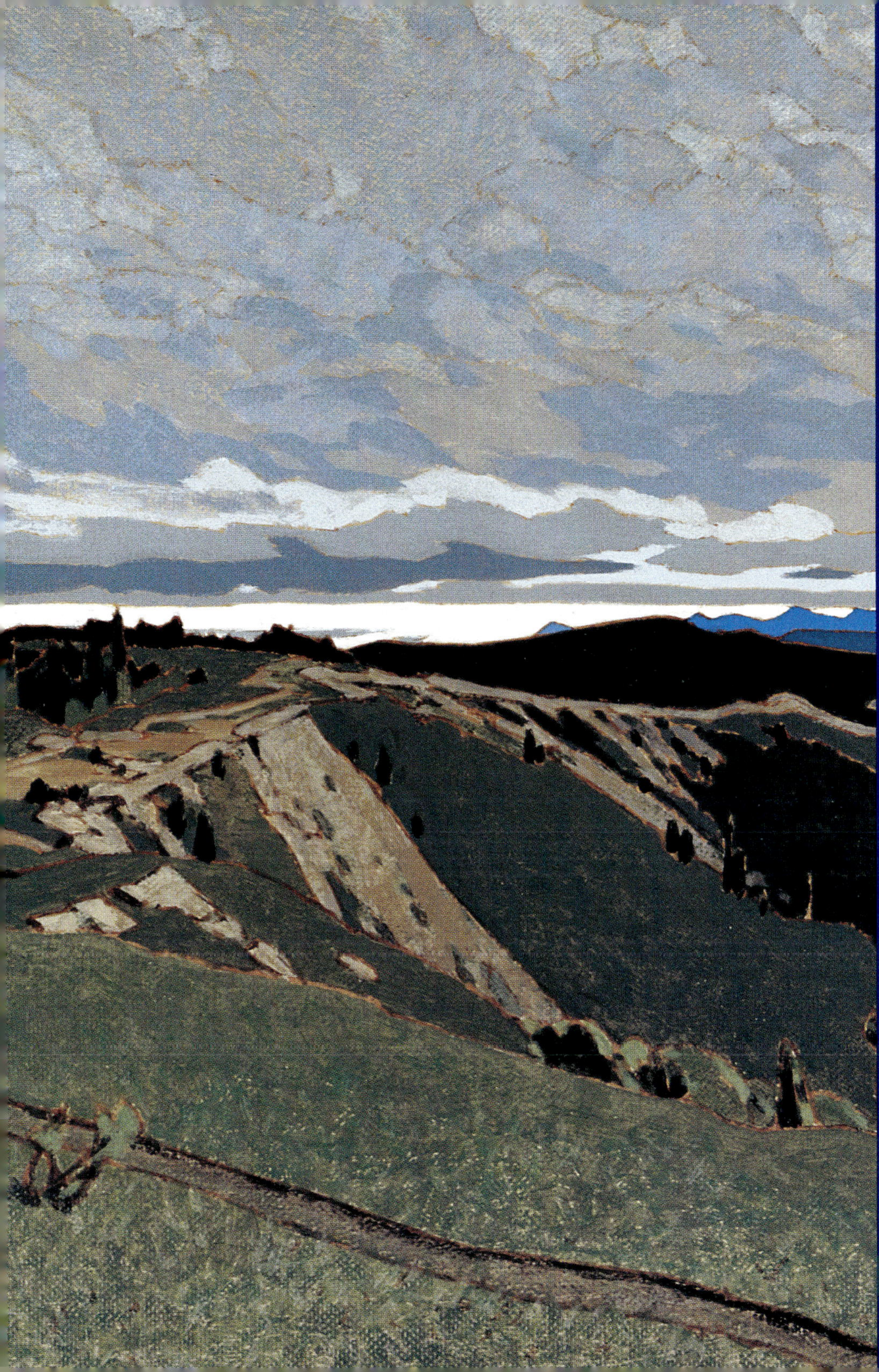

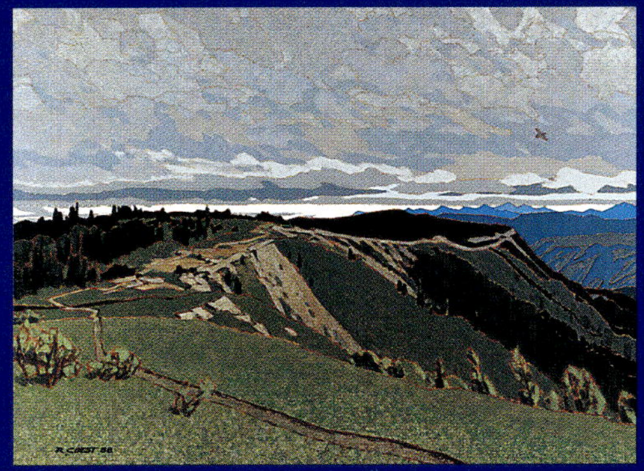

Trail over Nose Mountain, Facing South

"South from the Nose Mountain Tower, adjacent to the packtrail, there was a place where the natives ringed the bark of a number of large green trees. These pines would eventually die, providing excellent firewood for future trips."

Sam Fomuk

Trail over Nose Mountain, Facing North

The point of Nose Mountain has been a landmark for years, especially when seen from the Peace River country in the north. For people on the packtrail it was a favourite lookout point, in spite of the prevailing southwest wind. Usually when travellers camped in the area they picked a spot where the forest provided shelter and there was grass for the horses. Many camped on the shores of Nose Lake. But out on the point, the view was spectacular, and those who stopped there could see for miles in almost every direction. Part of the packtrail can still be detected, although it has been worn away by the wind and weather, particularly along the west side. The outline of Chinook Ridge is visible, and in the far north the faint blue shape of Saskatoon Mountain can be seen. The day was windy, as usual, when I made sketches for a painting in midsummer.

THE MISADVENTURES OF DORCAS

Looking back, the trip that Dorcas Dalgleish made in 1936 could be seen as typical of those made by many travellers. For her, and seven others in the group, it was a first trail ride. Various miscalculations were made, and a food crisis developed while they were out on the trail. Their idea had been to try to live off the land like the Indians did. But mishaps along the way,such as losing the pail of beans at the first river crossing, and the can of jam exploding when the pack-horse carrying it stumbled on a bees' nest, made things a little tight. Their food ran out sooner than expected, and the game they were counting on was extremely scarce. It was the same old story that has plagued many travellers—placing too much faith in the unknown.

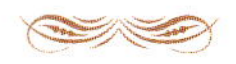

DRAWING: Bee's nest on the Trail

PHOTO: Dorcas Dalgleish on her 1930 trail rides. In later years she was my schoolteacher.

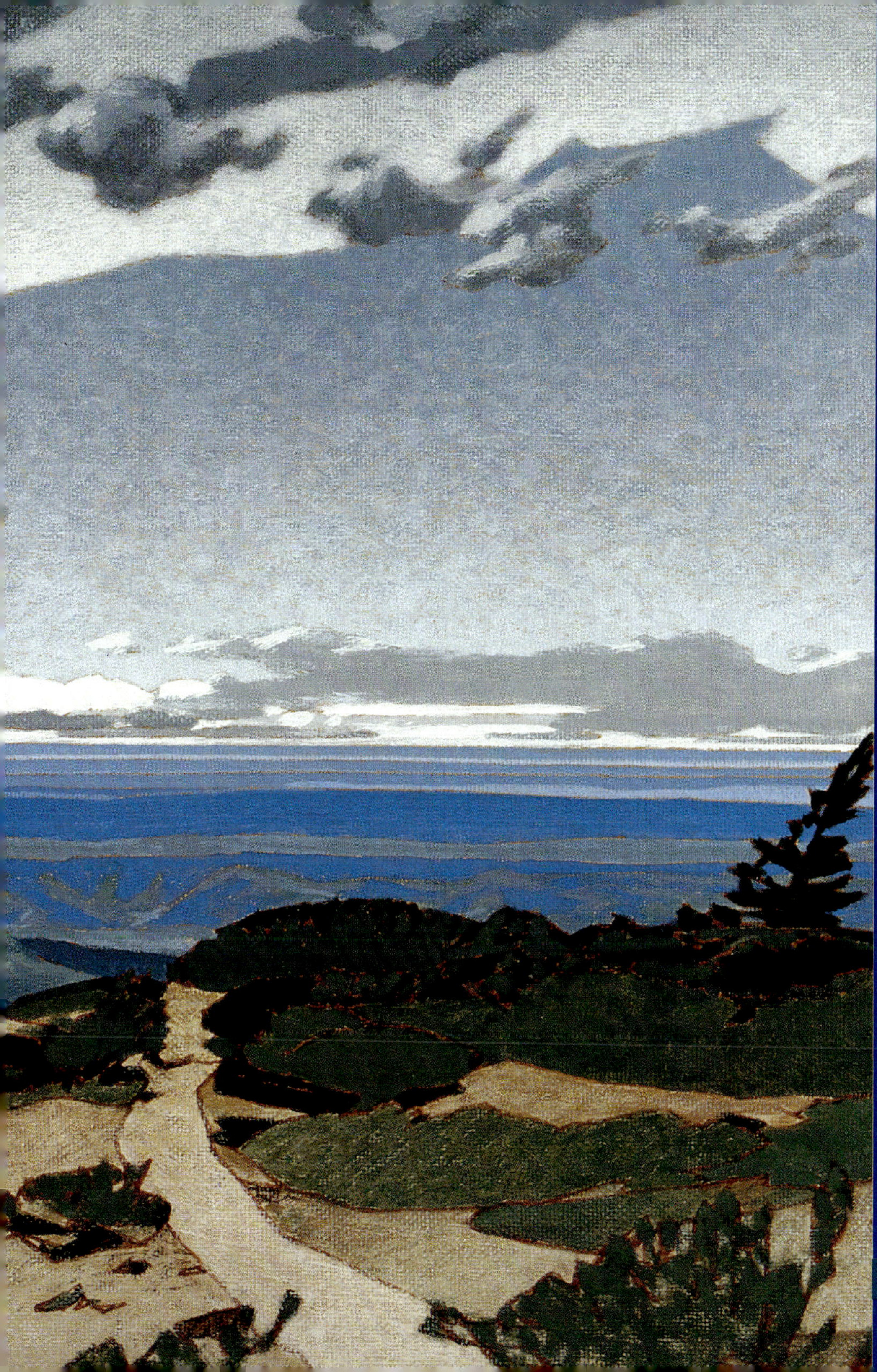

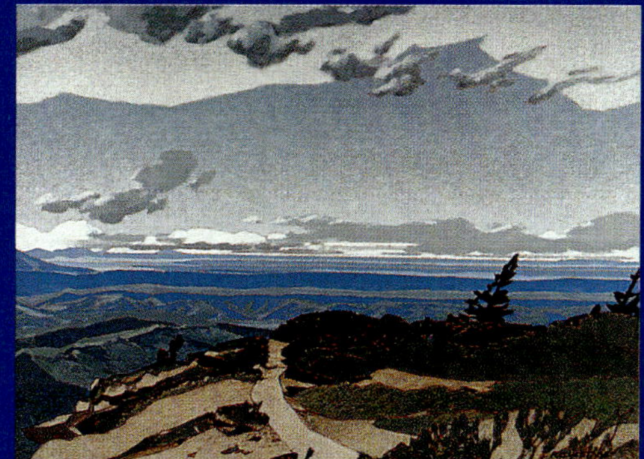

Trail over Nose Mountain, Facing North

BILL SPOKE of a clear, balmy night one late fall when he and Bert were camped on the top of Nose Mountain. They could see distant lights in the area of Halcourt-the lights of cars parked at a dance. How they wished they could be there. But, the next morning the view was lost in a howling gale, with several inches of new snow.

From Bill Smith

The Rocks, North Face of Nose Mountain

Not only was the trail over Nose Mountain the most spectacular part of the journey, to many it was the most challenging. This was especially true of the climb up the long, steep slope of the north face. There were two approaches. The trail from Hammer Creek was safe enough, but the older one from Grayling Creek, further to the west, could be quite tricky. It was impossible to avoid, and, in bad weather or winter conditions, it was downright treacherous. It was close to the top, in a spot exposed to the howling wind. There was a steep slope on either side, and sometimes drifted snow covered up holes and jagged edges. Travellers who experienced "the Rocks" took extreme care with their animals, and even people with dogteams had problems. The painting shows the location in late fall, with a few snow drifts already beginning.

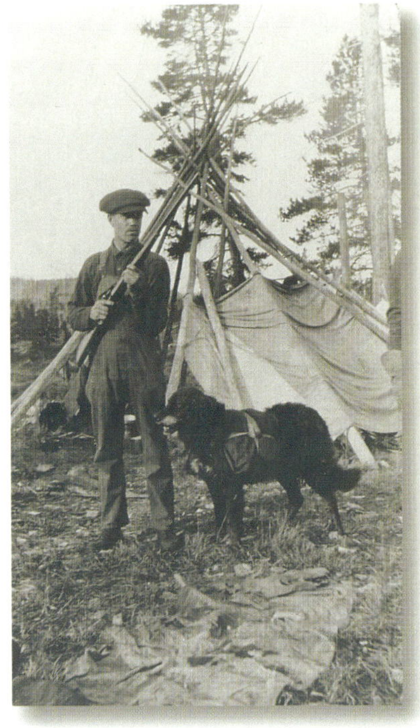

Bert Osborne with packing dog

BARKING AT THE MOON

From prehistoric times dogs had been the main travelling companions. Before domestication, at least in North America, most of them had wolf origins. Gradually they were tamed and put to work, and they often served as an emergency food supply when other sources became scarce. They also provided security for early travellers against wild animals and unpredictable humans. Even after the introduction of horses, dogs were often used by women to transport personal cargo from camp to camp, a mile or two at a time. The dog would pull a sleigh or travois, or carry a pack on its back. Sometimes these short trips resulted in a dog taking off after a rabbit or a deer, scattering some poor woman's belongings over the countryside. Dogs could survive well in deep snow and very cold weather. They were more flexible when it came to finding food, and they almost never drank water, preferring to snatch mouthfuls of snow.

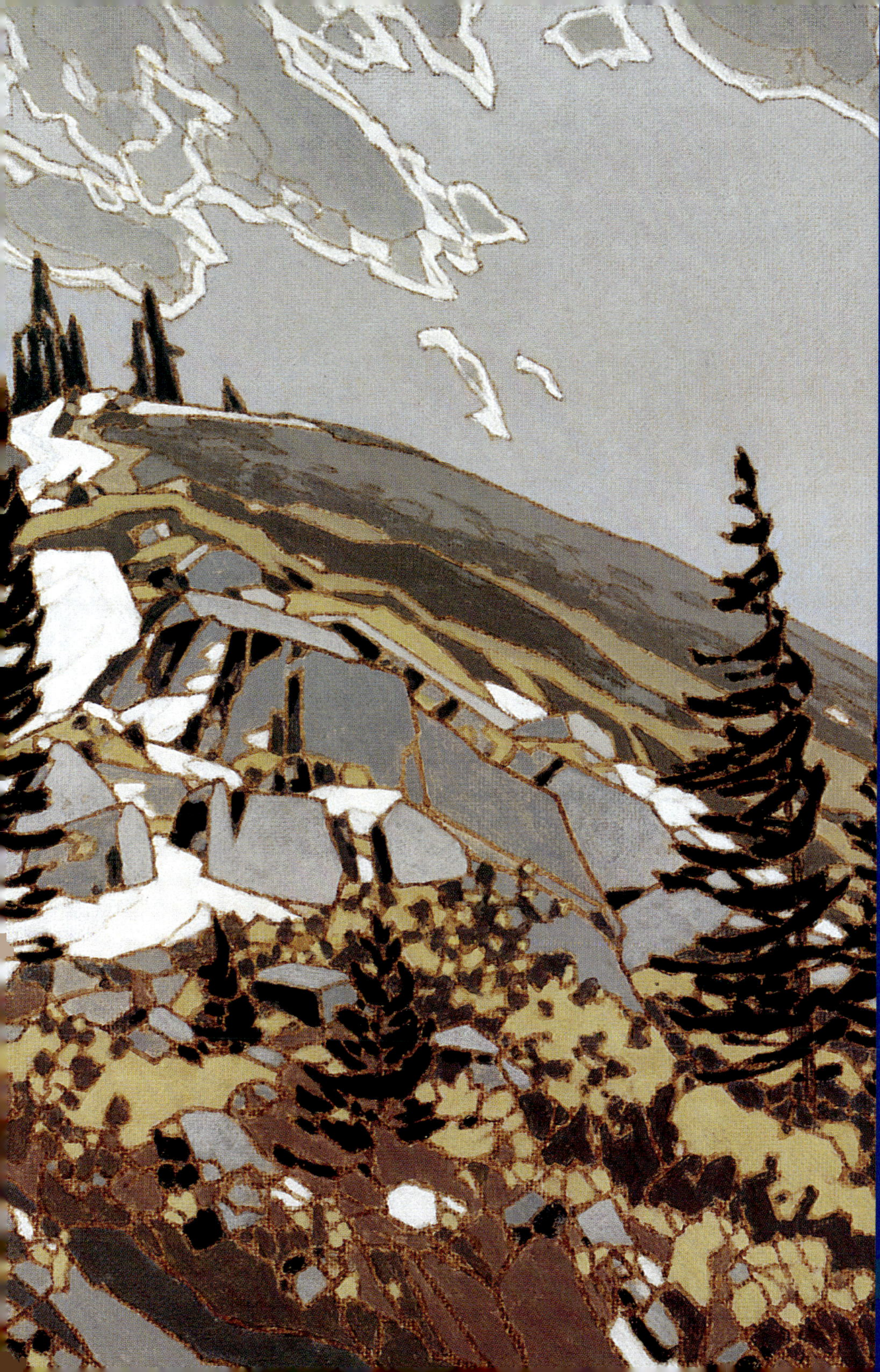

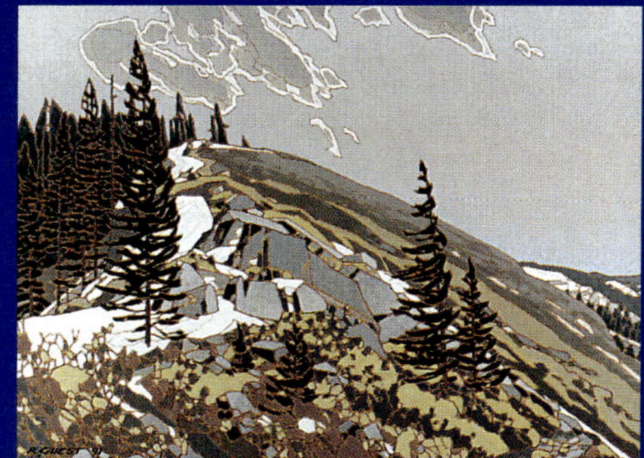

The Rocks, North Face of Nose Mountain

"SO LONG as the blue sky is above the green grass you will be the friend of the prairie children. Then, when at last we cross the great river, and see behind the Divide, we hope we shall find awaiting us our old friend, the Dog, that we may take up our friendship again, and continue on and on in the good country where no white man or smallpox ever comes."

Ernest Thompson Seton, 1911

Pierre Lake, Low Clouds and Wind

Even from the air, Pierre Lake looks isolated. It is in a hollow about halfway through the bush between Shettler (now spelled Shuttler) Flats and Nose Mountain, and has been identified as a large kettle lake. It was on the main packtrail route, and over the years its east side provided an overnight camping spot among the large trees still around the shores of the lake. In a few places, some very old axe blazes and carved initials have been etched in the bark of larger trees. Trappers, and others, have developed a respect for the lake, with its deep mysterious water and stories of the supernatural. To observe the spot on a stormy day in the late fall when there are low clouds and wind sweeps the surface of the lake, is to understand how some of the stories could get started. The painting shows the location in the last days of October.

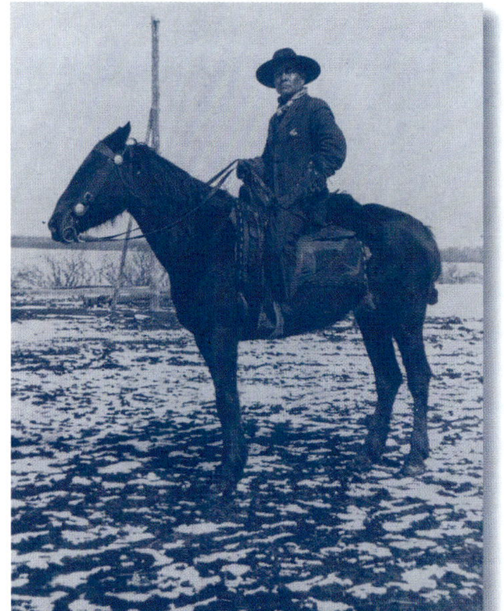

A proud and popular leader, Chief Shettler knew the Trail well.

STRONG LEADER

Pierre Shettler was widely known in the Peace River country and along the northern half of the Hinton Trail. He was a much-respected chief of the Beaver Indians, from the Horse Lake area. He was one of the few natives in those years to learn the English language and could communicate with settlers coming into the country from eastern Canada and the United States. Today, Pierre is remembered by landmarks along the Hinton Trail that bear his name, such as Pierre Lake and Shuttler Flats.

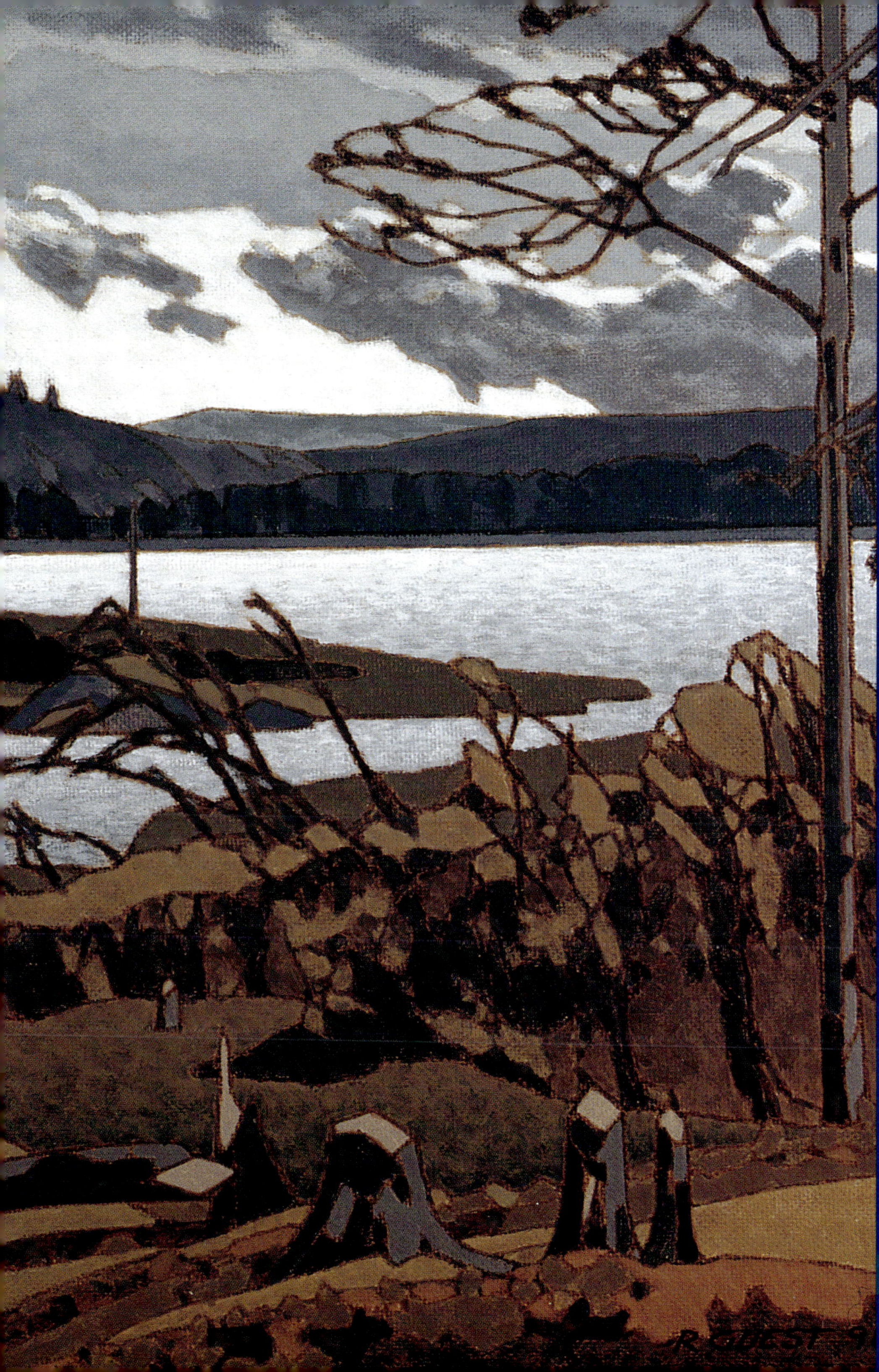

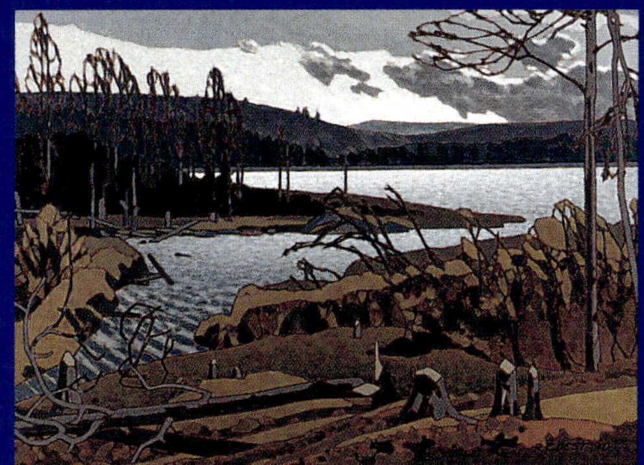

Pierre Lake, Low Clouds and Wind

"IT IS A *classic example of a kettle lake. These lakes are found in many areas of Alberta and were formed during the decline of the last glacial ice sheets. The lake basin is thought to occur as a result of single blocks of ice being detached from the glacial ice sheet, and then being rapidly buried by sediment flowing from the glacial front. This rounded basin profile is typical of kettle lakes, which as shown, form when the buried ice mass melts and the thin mantle of covering sediment collapses into the water-filled basin."*

Milt Wright, 1990

Shuttler Flats on Nose Creek

The old trails met at Shuttler Flats, a crossroads where the Pipestone Trail came in from the east to join the main route. The main route crossed the Wapiti at a spot referred to as the Jasper Crossing, at Hans Hoglund's. The Indian settlement of Shuttler Flats had been established for many years, and had its own school. Some of its residents had moved from their previous location along the Kakwa River in the late 1960s. At one time, the packtrail passed over the flats on the west side of Nose Creek, then recrossed to strike out in the general direction of Nose Mountain, visible on the southern horizon. It was late fall when I collected information for a painting that included a great grey owl, a species common to that part of the country.

◆

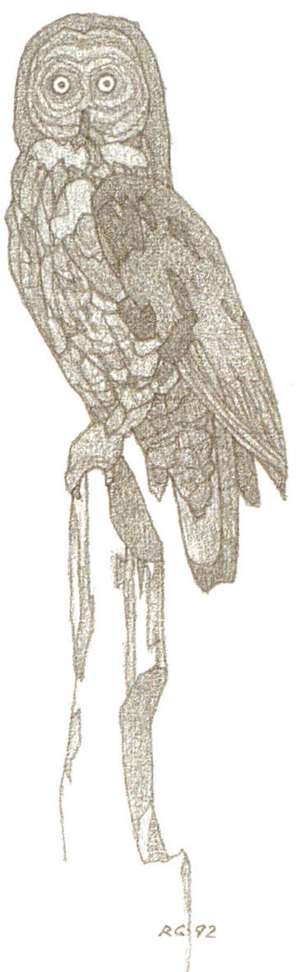

Great Grey Owl, Hinton Trail community

ON FOOT WITH STEVE SAWCHUCK

At 16, Steve Sawchuck must have been the youngest person to travel between the Wapiti River and Grande Cache alone. He made the trip on foot during the early summer, when most of the creeks and rivers were high from spring runoff.

Like Tony Roteliuk a few years earlier, Steve was expected to take a message to Fletcher Smith. The long trip caused some worry in the Sawchuck household, and before he left, Steve was given some advice about crossing rivers from his father, John. He was to find a large, dry log that he could hang on to and half ride and half walk across the river at an angle. With a backpack, Steve had no choice but to try the log technique.

He had no problem with bears, and walked through grizzly country, sleeping each night by a small campfire. After about a week Steve reached the first trading post at Sheep Creek Junction and delivered the important message.

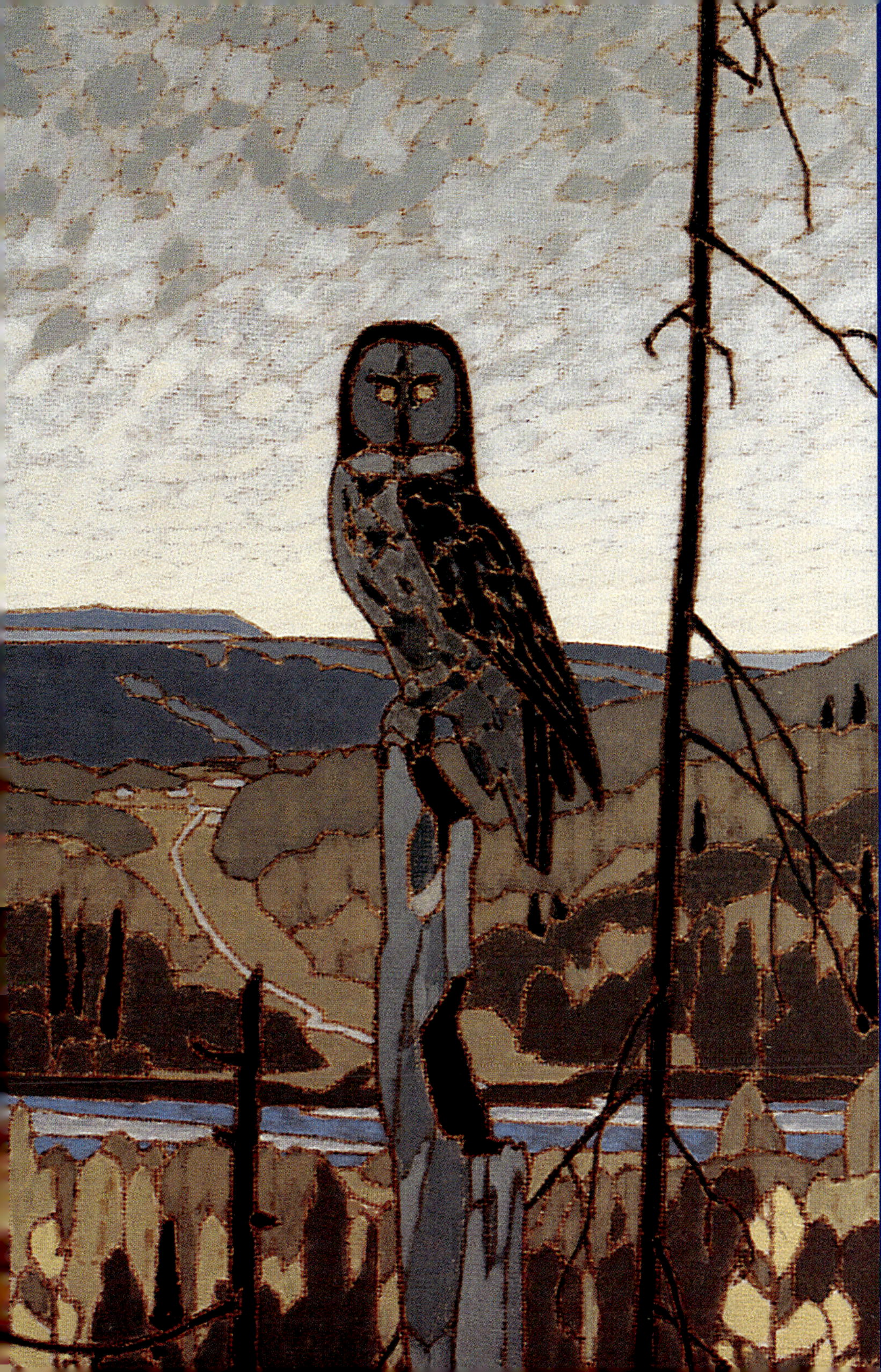

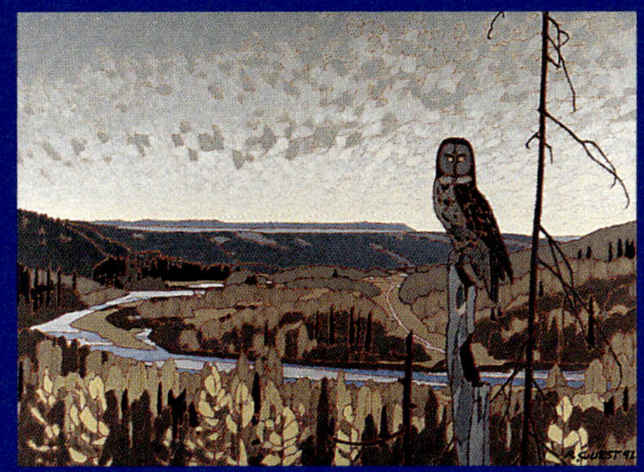

Shuttler Flats on Nose Creek

On his trip south, Tony stayed at an abandoned cabin at Shuttler Flats. Timber wolves howled quite a lot about a quarter of a mile away. It made him uneasy, and even in the cabin he felt chills running up and down his spine.

From Tony Roteliuk

Chatelaine Cabins on Pinto Creek

At one time, this native settlement on the upper Pinto Creek was a busy place. It was known as Stoney Meadows. There were a number of cabins and other buildings, complete with corrals, drying racks for meat, and, roughly 200 yards away, a graveyard on the bank above the creek. The east branch of the pack-trail went through the area, heading towards Pipestone Creek and crossing the Wapiti, and so the residents lived practically on the Trail. A wagon road went northwest along the top of the east bank of Pinto Creek close to Alex Connell's homestead, crossing the Wapiti at the old ford. Nowadays, all the cabins have been abandoned except one used during the winter by two local trappers. The painting records a clear, cold night with a moon.

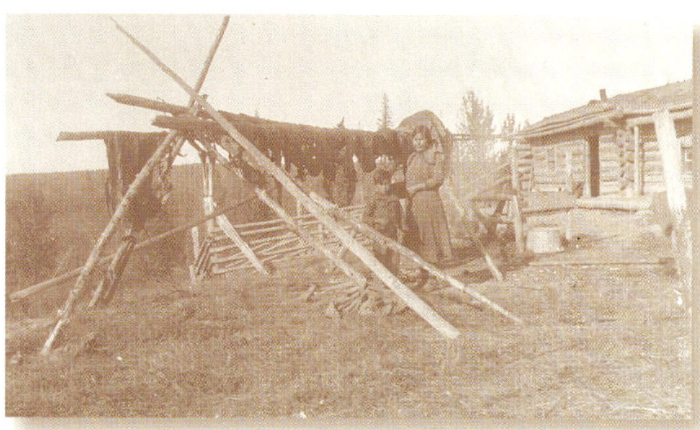

Mrs. Shettler and Little Joe, drying meat on the Upper Pinto, c.1941

A Story of Two Brothers

Henry and Pete McCullough came into the country in 1928 and settled along the Wapiti River close to the Pipestone Creek crossing. Henry was good with horses and was soon guiding big-game hunters who wanted trophies. He also had his own sawmill and, on the side, did some packing for the Alberta Forest Service. From his farm Henry travelled the foothills extensively, making no less than 12 long trips to Hinton, sometimes with up to 50 packhorses. He said that for every seven horses there was, on average, one rider. In 1958 he was given the honour of bringing the city charter to Grande Prairie from Edmonton on horseback.

Pete is Henry's younger brother, and he still lives on the farm. His late wife, Lena Wanyandi, was related to the Wanyandi family who left Jasper Park in 1910. Pete's most notable memory is the trip when, accompanied by Bert Vardy, a senior forest ranger, he went on a six-week trek through rough country, to check boundary markers along the Alberta-British Columbia border.

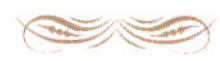

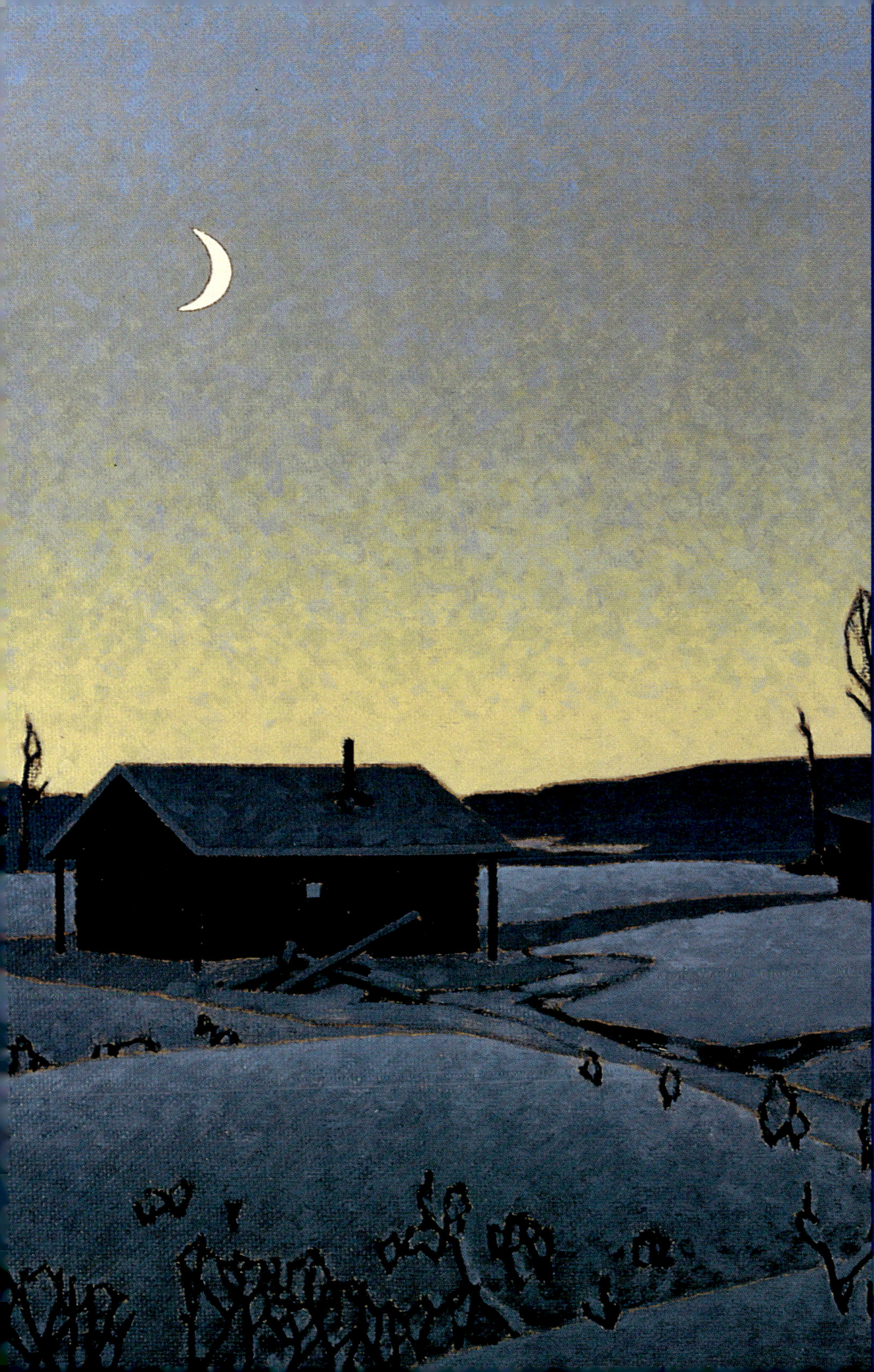

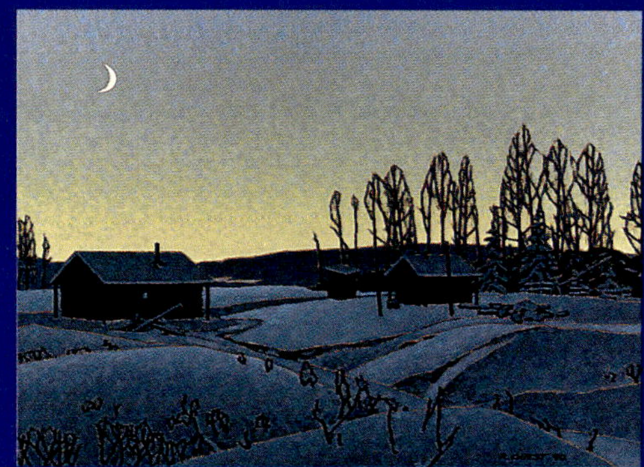

Chatelaine Cabins on Pinto Creek

FRED drew attention to the small, fenced enclosures on the north side of the cabins along the edge of the bush. Here, he thought, some of the Chatelaine children had been buried, although the main graveyard was about 200 yards further west, overlooking the Pinto Creek.

From Fred Comeau

Wapiti Crossing at Lingrell Flats

This spot was sometimes referred to as the "upper" crossing on the Wapiti. There are other fords upriver but they did not link up with the Hinton Trail. From the Lingrell crossing, most of the traffic went to the Rio Grande area and points beyond, including those on the British Columbia side of the border. For years the Indians travelling to Rio Grande stopped and made camp on top of the riverbank on the north side. It was a wonderful place to rest horses and pick blueberries under the large pines. After attending church at Rio Grande and taking part in the annual sports, they returned to their cabins along the Kakwa River. Whole families would make the journey in the summer when the water level had subsided after spring runoff. The view for the painting is from the junction of the Calahoo Creek and Wapiti, facing downstream. It was a cold winter evening in early January and the moon was just beginning to show.

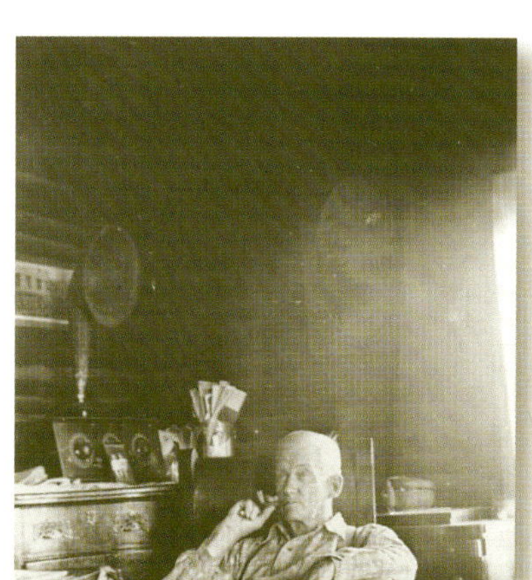

COME ON DOWN TO WAPITI BROWN

One of the earliest settlers along the upper Wapiti River was Frank Brown, better known as Wapiti Brown. He came into the Peace River country from Idaho in 1916, and filed for homestead in what would become the Haven School District, on the north side of the Wapiti. Frank was responsible for having the Trail widened so that wagons and other implements could get through to the banks of the Wapiti River. This took weeks to do and was the first improvement to the old Trail in the north. It was rough, but it was a start. About the same time he made quite a name for himself by attracting big-game hunters to the area. He was so successful that his outfitting services were covered in a feature article in Outdoor Life magazine in 1936. This brought Wapiti Brown into the international spotlight, and big-game hunting became associated with northwestern Alberta.

Frank Brown was a pioneer and one of the country's best promoters, shown listening to his radio in 1918.

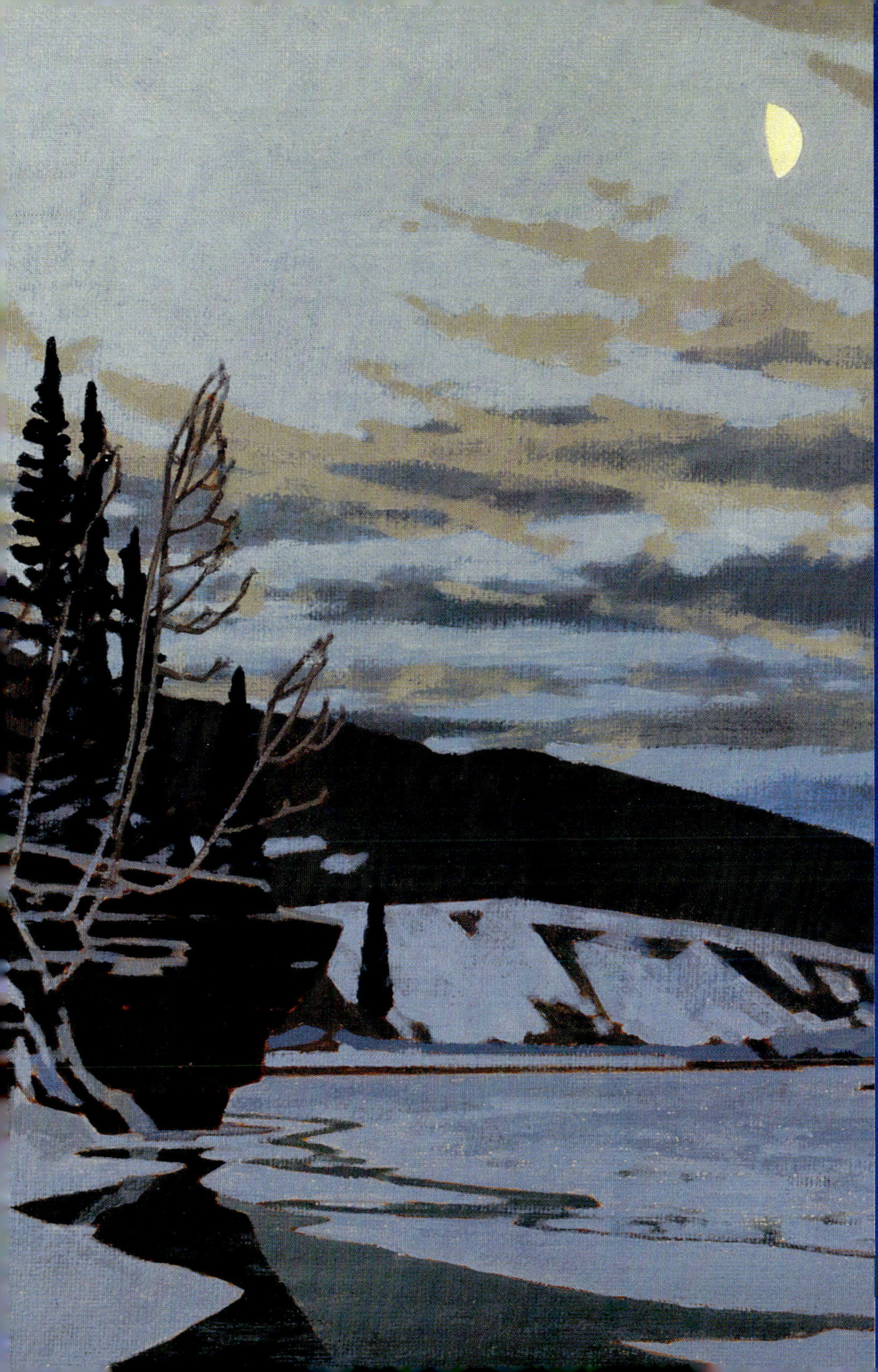

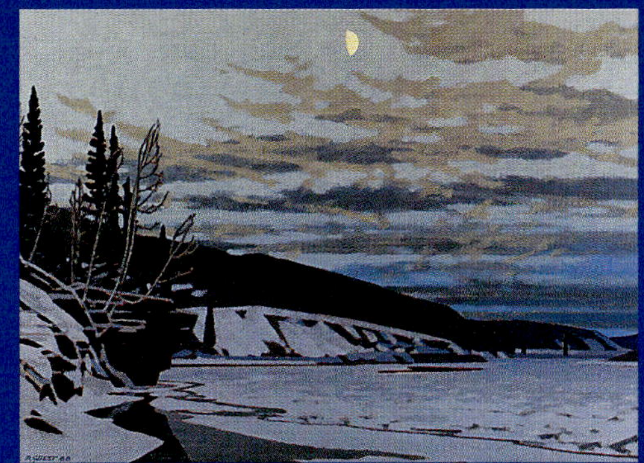

Wapiti Crossing at Lingrell Flats

"THE ICE *was bare and the horses were afraid of it. We had a battle at every crossing to drive them in and break the ice and their tails became solid chunks of ice. The saddles and packs were also covered in ice which made packing and unpacking a miserable job."*

John Glenn, c.1920

Forest Fire at Lingrell Flats

The upper crossing on the Wapiti was at Lingrell Flats, downstream from the mouth of Calahoo Creek, and once the location of cabins, fences, and structures related to an early sawmill. This was Nick Lingrell's place, and the packtrail practically went through the yard. Across the river, the packtrail joined the main branch and struck out for Shuttler Flats and Nose Mountain. A common hazard, especially in late spring before the new grass and leaves came out, was the outbreak of fire. Forest fires, once started, were impossible to control, and many settlers lost their entire holdings when a dry wind fanned a blaze caused by human carelessness or lightning. According to early residents, the fire of 1940 was the most devastating. The cabins were never rebuilt. The painting is a reconstruction based on the location.

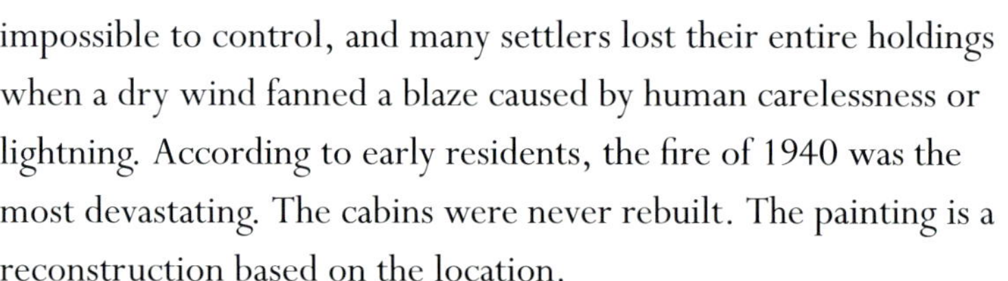

Party combing the foothills for forest fires, c.1935

THE PROSPEROUS FLETCHER BREDIN

At the north end of the Trail lived a successful trader by the name of Fletcher Bredin. His post was along the Redwillow River, not far from today's hamlet of Rio Grande. He operated the post in the 1920s, generating business with local trappers throughout the Rio Grande area to the mountains along the border. Considering the times, Fletcher Bredin was quite well-to-do, having had several successful business ventures in the Peace River country, and he was once a member of the legislative assembly. As the Hinton Trail became acknowledged as the only link between two major areas of settlement—the Yellowhead Pass in the south and the Peace River country in the north—more travellers took to the Trail with their packtrains and dogteams. With increased traffic, more trading posts were established along its 200 mile length.

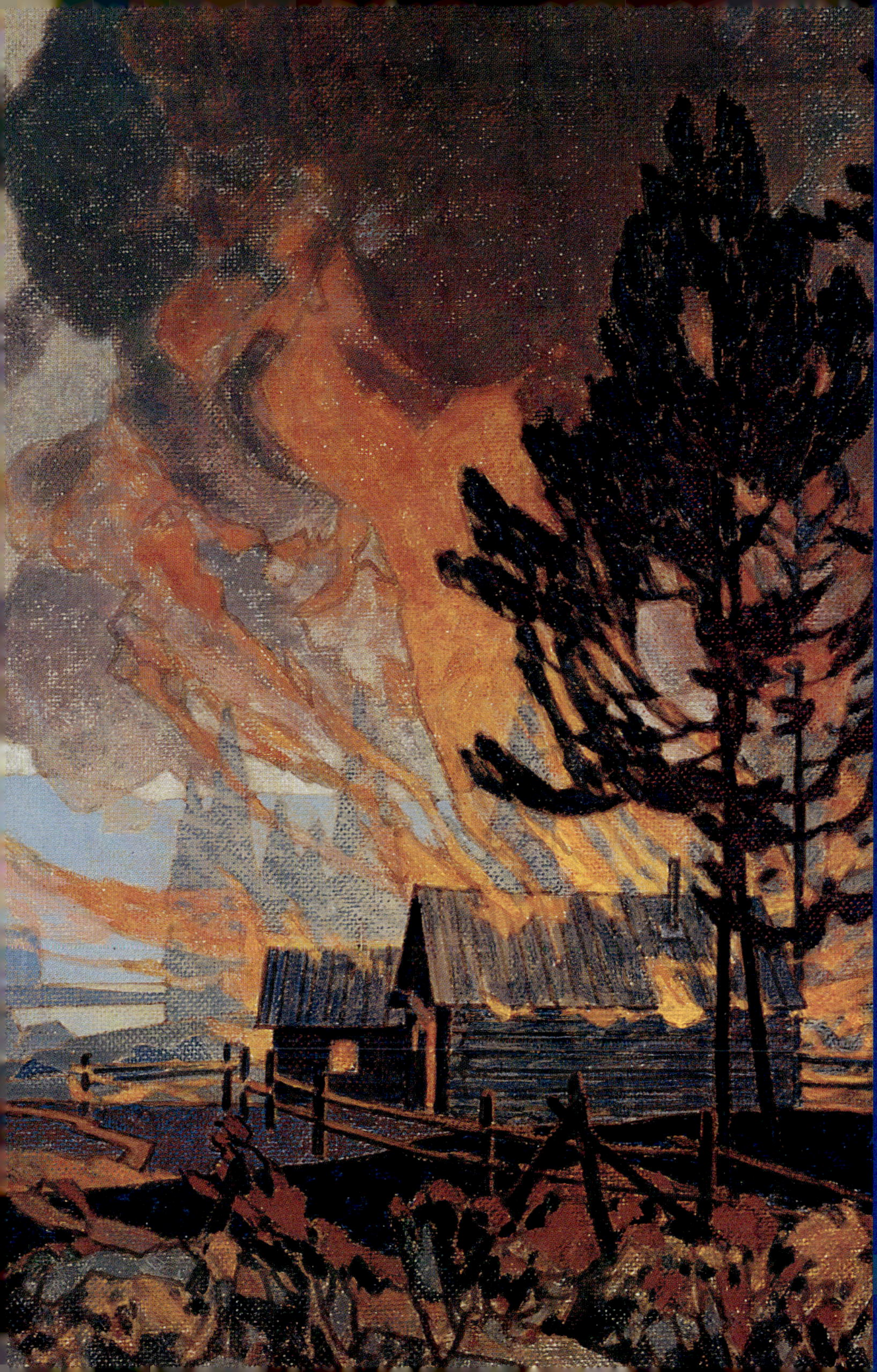

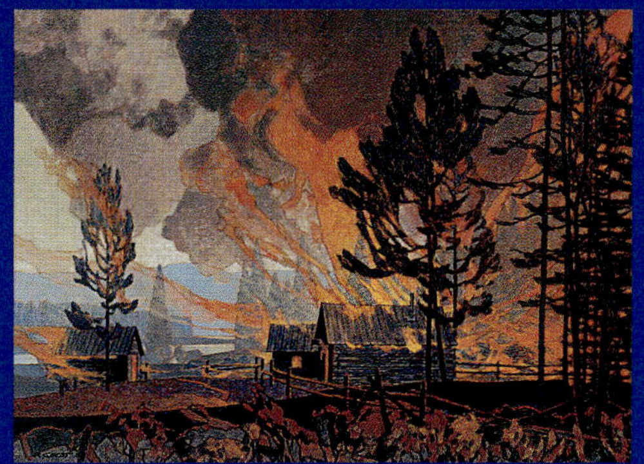

Forest Fire at Lingrell Flats

"Most of the time I had to have Indians to fight fire when I was in the mountains, as one could depend on them to get to the fire in a hurry as they travelled light and did not spare their horses. Generally they brought a tipi and, for food, a small sack of flour, tea, pemmican, or dried meat, lard and a fry pan to bake their bannocks on. They slept in their saddle blankets."

John Glenn, c.1920

Campbell Homestead at Elmworth

A western branch of the Trail crossed the Wapiti at Lingrell Flats, then angled towards the Alberta–British Columbia border and today's settlement of Kelly Lake. On the way, the old packtrail left a deep furrow through miles of bush, much of which later became farmland. One area was named Elmworth by the first settlers. Like their neighbours, Clyde and Merle Campbell applied for a homestead and within a few years had a small pioneer farm. They soon got to know some of the Indians who followed the Trail across part of their land. They also met the nomadic character, Frenchy Billedeau. After a few years fences went up and visitors could no longer follow the old trails. The painting came from several visits made to the old homestead to gather sketches and make small paintings on the spot. It was in the late spring and a little snow was still visible.

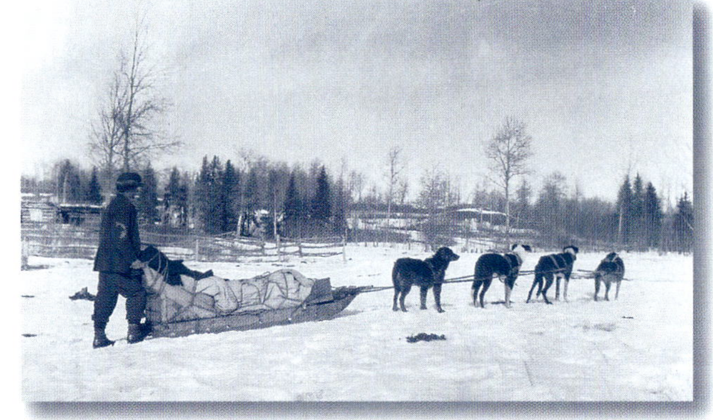

Frenchy loved his dogs and the winter season. He is shown here living the outdoor life around 1945.

THE UNCOMMON FRENCHY BILLEDEAU

Frenchy Billedeau arrived in the Elmworth district of the Peace River country before 1918. He was noted for his colourful clothing and used to sport an outfit reminiscent of a coureur de bois, with a toque and a wide woolen ceinture. He was a man of incredible stamina, and he covered the area along the Wapiti River from its head-waters, where he had his trapline, all the way down to the Smoky River and into Jasper Park, usually by dogteam. He was also a great walker, often having to break the snow along the winter trails so his dogs could follow pulling the sleigh. Frenchy travelled light, with little more than a tarp for shelter, and not much in the way of food or heavy winter clothing; he often spent a winter's night sleeping under the stars. His dogs were well cared for when, it was said, he didn't have food for himself. Frenchy was a solitary person, never able to settle down for very long, preferring the great outdoors to the civilized way of life.

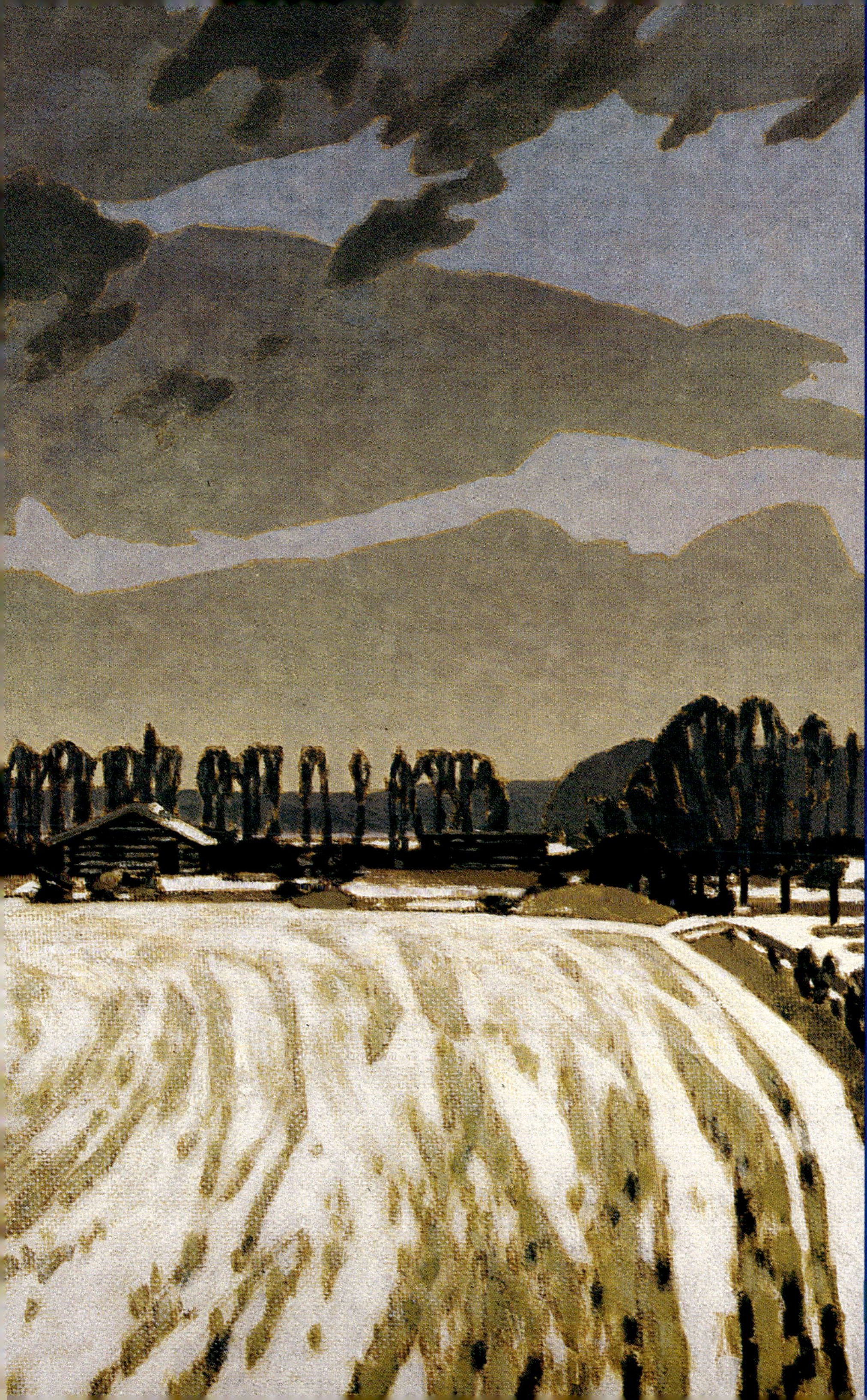

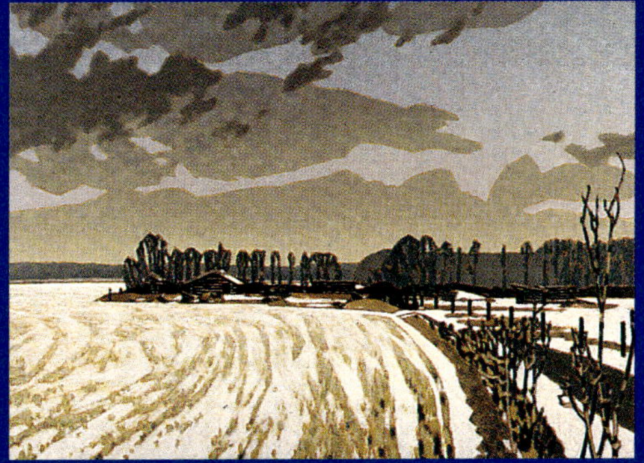

Campbell Homestead at Elmworth

"THE FAMOUS *Indian trail called the Wapiti Trail runs right across our land and we have made a trail from our cabin right into it.... The Indians always come up the trail from their hunting, loaded with moose and bear. The other night they went down the trail singing their Indian songs and it sounded so weird and beautiful. The Indians up here are surely good looking and their ponies' outfits are of the best–saddles and bridles spic and span, their clothes clean and moccasins all beaded. Even some of the saddle blankets are beaded."*

Clyde Campbell, c.1921

Rio Grande, Facing South

An important stop on the western branch of the Trail was at Rio Grande. It was a pioneer community, complete with a log church built in 1917. There was also a store, a hall, and eventually a one-room school. Like other stores near the Hinton Trail, Rio Grande was a supply centre and enjoyed a brisk fur trade with the Indians. Since the Catholic church at Rio Grande was the nearest one for native families living as far away as Kakwa River, they occasionally made the long journey north to attend mass, and for other special occasions. Over the years many people stopped at the store before heading down the long Trail to Grande Cache or Hinton. Sketches for the painting were done in late spring.

For rodeo practice at the Wanyandi's

THE LURE OF THE RODEO

It was part of the yearly cycle to have a large group take their string of horses from summer cabins along the Kakwa River to attend the July rodeos. In the north there was the Rio Grande Rodeo and in the south, the Muskeg Rodeo, both of which drew large crowds. The period of the 1930s and 1940s marked the peak in terms of participation and attendance. Certain events, or contests, were favourites year after year, like the half-mile free-for-all, quarter-mile pony race, relay race, saddle bucking contest, wild cow milking, democrat race, bare-back riding, and the Indian horse races. The rodeos were special, not only because of the sports, but as an occasion to renew acquaintance with old friends, attend the Catholic church, and have children christened.

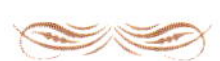

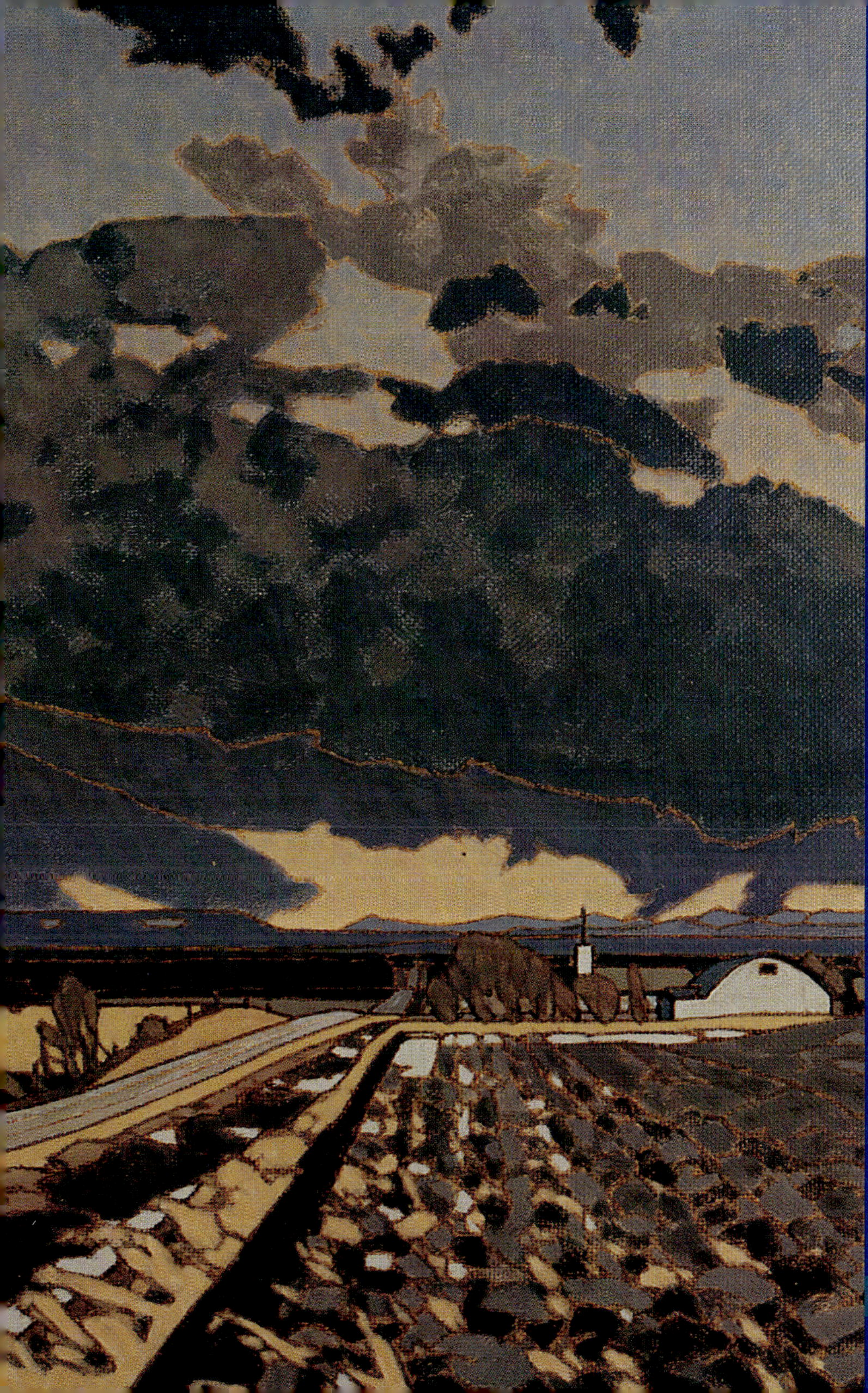

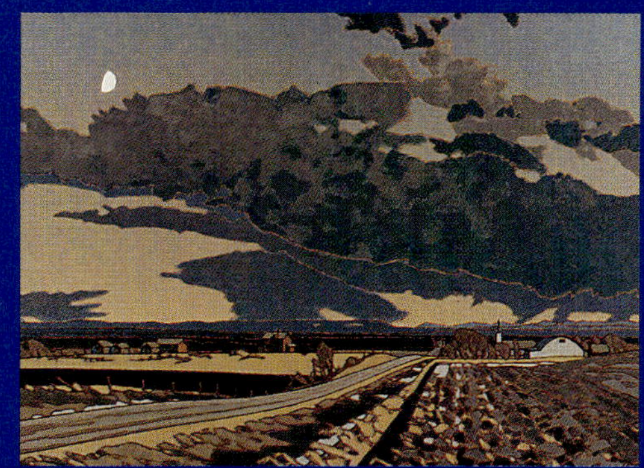

Rio Grande, Facing South

ISABEL TOLD *of one late evening long ago when she made a trip on horseback to Rio Grande. She took the ford on the Redwillow River known as the Kenny Crossing. As she got closer to the river, she saw an Indian tipi. She could hear the beating of drums, and from inside a wild, thrilling voice of a man singing. Campfires were burning, and no one was aware of her presence. But the wonderful mood was soon broken when some dogs caught sight of her and started to bark.*

From Isabel M. Campbell

First Kelly Lake Store and School

Before the turn of the century the packtrail passed Kelly Lake and linked with a trail going to the Yukon goldfields. The Metis settlement scattered around Kelly Lake dates back to the early 1900s, when trappers came to the area in search of better hunting. The first ones came from Flyingshot Lake, and eventually the population grew to a small community. In the 1920s, a store was opened. A freetrader by the name of Jim Young was the owner and he brought in the first teacher, Gerry Andrews, who set up a classroom in 1923. The same log building accommodated the store and school, in different rooms. Gerry's efforts were rewarded, and at the end of the second term he left, but not before sparking the enthusiasm that led to a modern Metis school. This composition is a reconstruction based on the advice of Gerry Andrews and an early photograph. A sketch was made at the location, and the final painting combines the cabins in a winter setting with the phenomenon of a blizzard sun.

BIRTH OF KELLY LAKE

The small community of Kelly Lake was started around 1910 when a few Metis trappers ventured west in search of new hunting territory. Originally, their families had come into the country from Lac Ste. Anne by way of the Snipe Lake Trail, settled at Flyingshot Lake near Grande Prairie, and then decided to move on. These people reached the semi-wilderness shores of Kelly Lake just inside the boundaries of British Columbia. This was during the years when most people were dependent on the great outdoors to sustain their way of life.

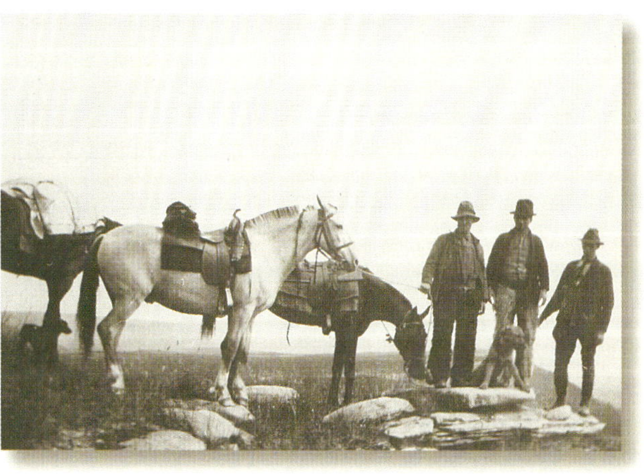

Gerry Andrews took this picture of his party atop Nose Mountain in 1925.

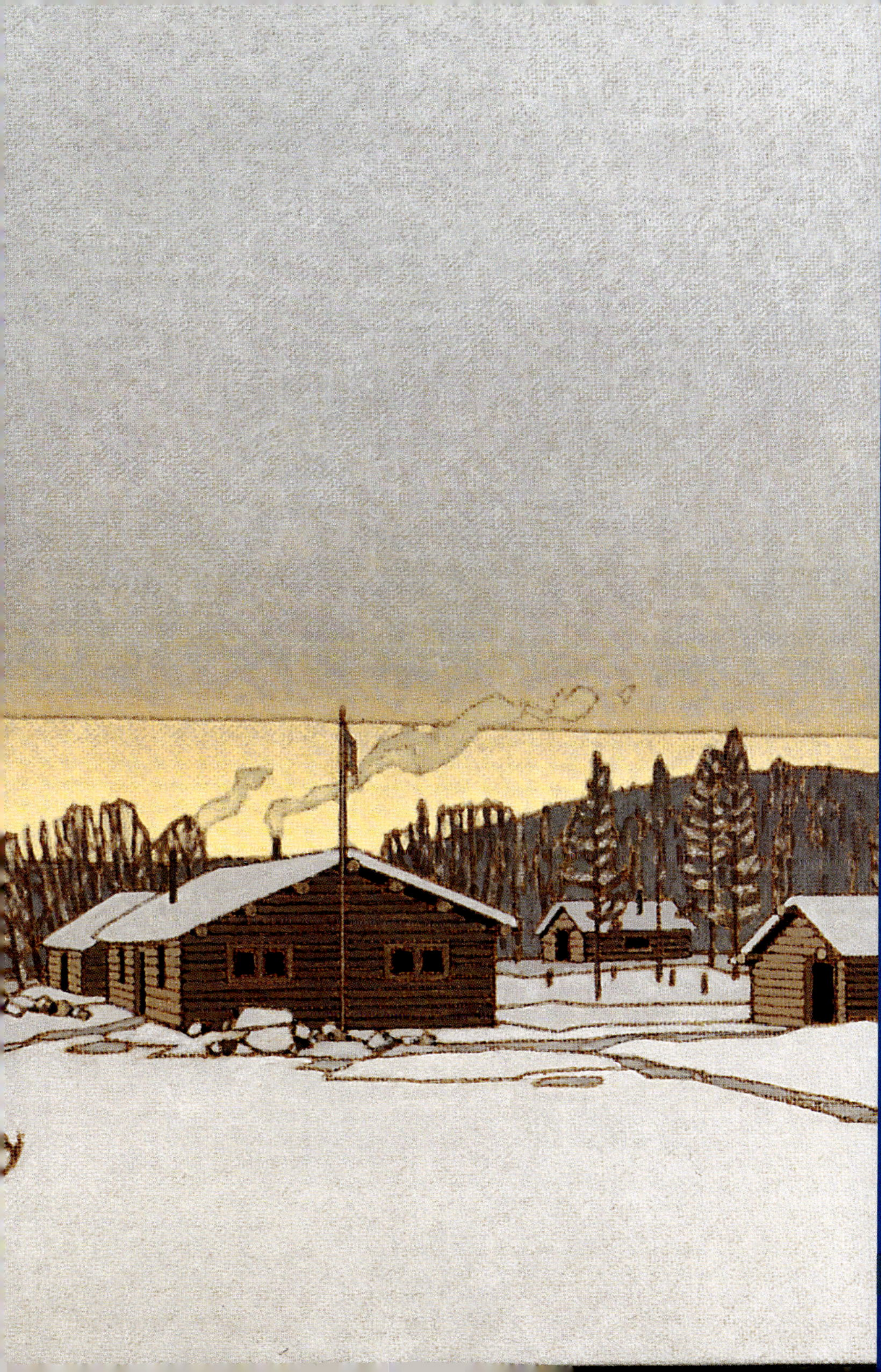

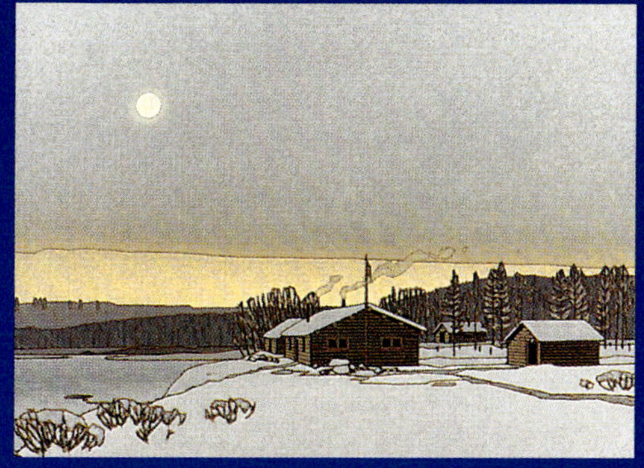

First Kelly Lake Store and School

"The tiny Metis 'Shangri-la' at Kelly Lake has thus endured for over 70 years and more than two generations with some inevitable changes in lifestyle. There is now better access and electric power. Moose and other game continue to supply food, raiment and pelts for trade. Lakes still yield fish and fowl. Berry-picking safaris are one-day jaunts by pickup truck instead of week long treks with horses. The Metis still enjoy their fun and sociability."

Gerry Andrews

Winter Camp on Denning Creek

Compared to some packtrails, the long Trail to Hinton was difficult. It was a summer and winter route used by working people, and, depending on conditions and the time of year, their packhorses and dogteams. During the winter the main group to use the Trail were the trappers. In all kinds of weather they hiked to remote traplines scattered throughout the foothills. Some went alone, some took dogs, many of them walked or rode horses. For the painting I chose a site south of the Wapiti. Based partly on a real situation and on observation of a nighttime campfire, I put a composition together. Sketching at night became more difficult as the temperature dropped.

◆

THE EARLY TRAPPERS

In the early 1800s the average trapper faced a long winter hunting for furs to sustain himself and his family. When at last spring arrived, he took his family to the trading post of his choice, which was quite a holiday for all concerned. Frequently this meant travelling a fair distance on horseback. Once at the trading post, the trapper's first obligation was to see that he had enough fur to cover his bill from the past season. If he was lucky, he came out ahead, with a little extra for himself, his wife, and his children. This was sure to be the case if he was fortunate enough to catch a silver fox or two along with the other animals. At that time such a fur could bring one thousand dollars at the big fur market.

RG-92

Gavin Craig's trap and stretcher boards

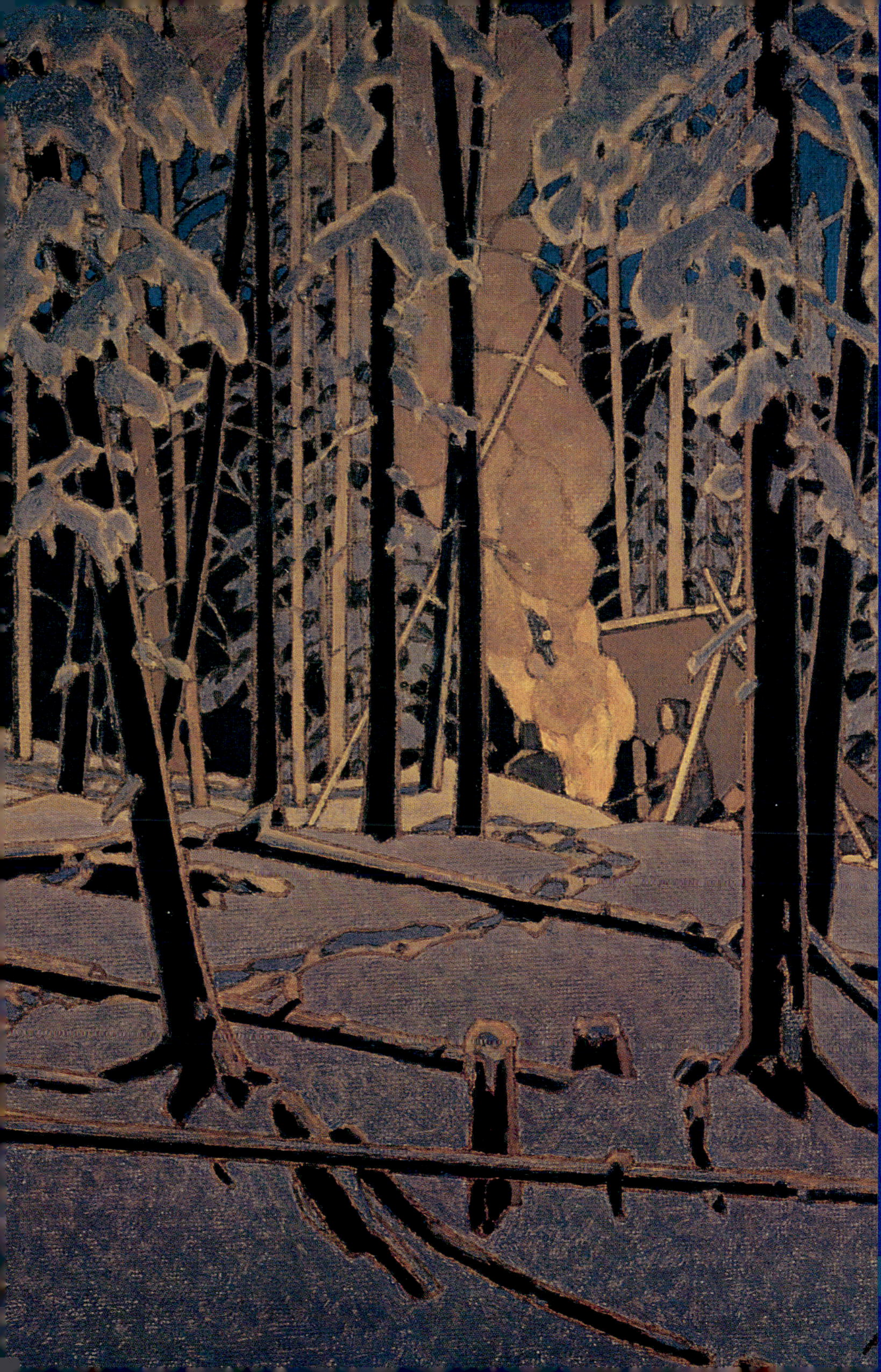

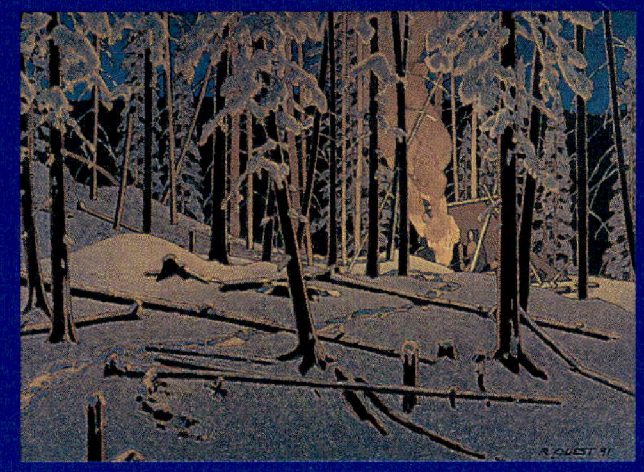

Winter Camp on Denning Creek

"It took a terrible lot of courage to emerge from the warm blankets, from which position we could note six inches of snow over everything, and every few moments the howling wind would send a fresh supply down over us."

Mary T. S. Schaffer, 1911

Moonlit Trail through the Poplars

As the long Trail from the Athabasca Valley reached the Peace country, the forest gradually changed. By the time it had crossed the Wapiti River it was winding its way through endless stands of aspen poplar. During the dark days of winter with cold weather and deep snow, travellers felt isolated and were glad to reach their destinations. Some people wore snowshoes, which were not always practical. Travel was often tedious, especially during days that were overcast and grey. But when the moon came up and flooded the winter landscape with pale blue light, spirits began to lift. Nowadays it's interesting to hear oldtimers talk—almost as though they were lucky to have been there—about the deathly cold, frostbite, howling wolves, roaming bears, and desperately trying to get a campfire going under the cold light of a winter moon. The painting was based on trail located close to my cabin.

◆

Big game hunter's tent, first fall snow

TOP: Dave Schenk's snowshoes

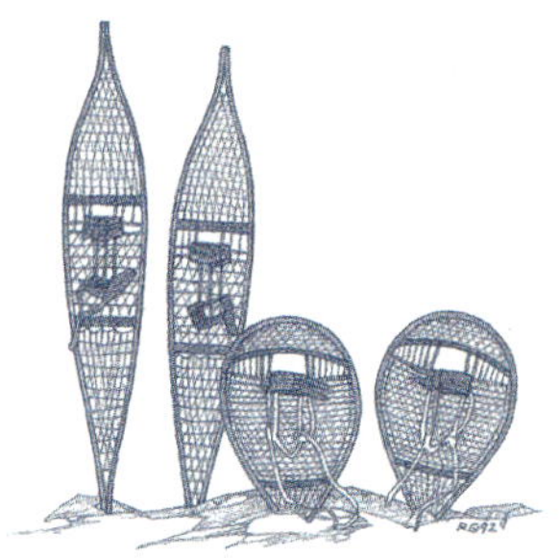

NOT IF I SEE YOU FIRST

In the south Peace Country Ike and Peggy Doerkson have had their share of bear adventures. They farmed in the Goodwin area prior to a long tenure with the Forestry Service. Their encounters with troublesome bears were mostly in the 1960s and Ike's most memorable experience was with a large silver-tipped grizzly that roamed a section of bush in the vicinity of the Economy fire tower. He stumbled on a 'burial ground' consisting of bones and rotting carcasses of game animals that the bear had cached. It was partly covered with leaves and debris, and when Ike approached the area, quite by accident, he couldn't help thinking that he could be added to the strange collection. When he spotted the large bear just before it spotted him, he kept his cool and managed to back off without getting into trouble.

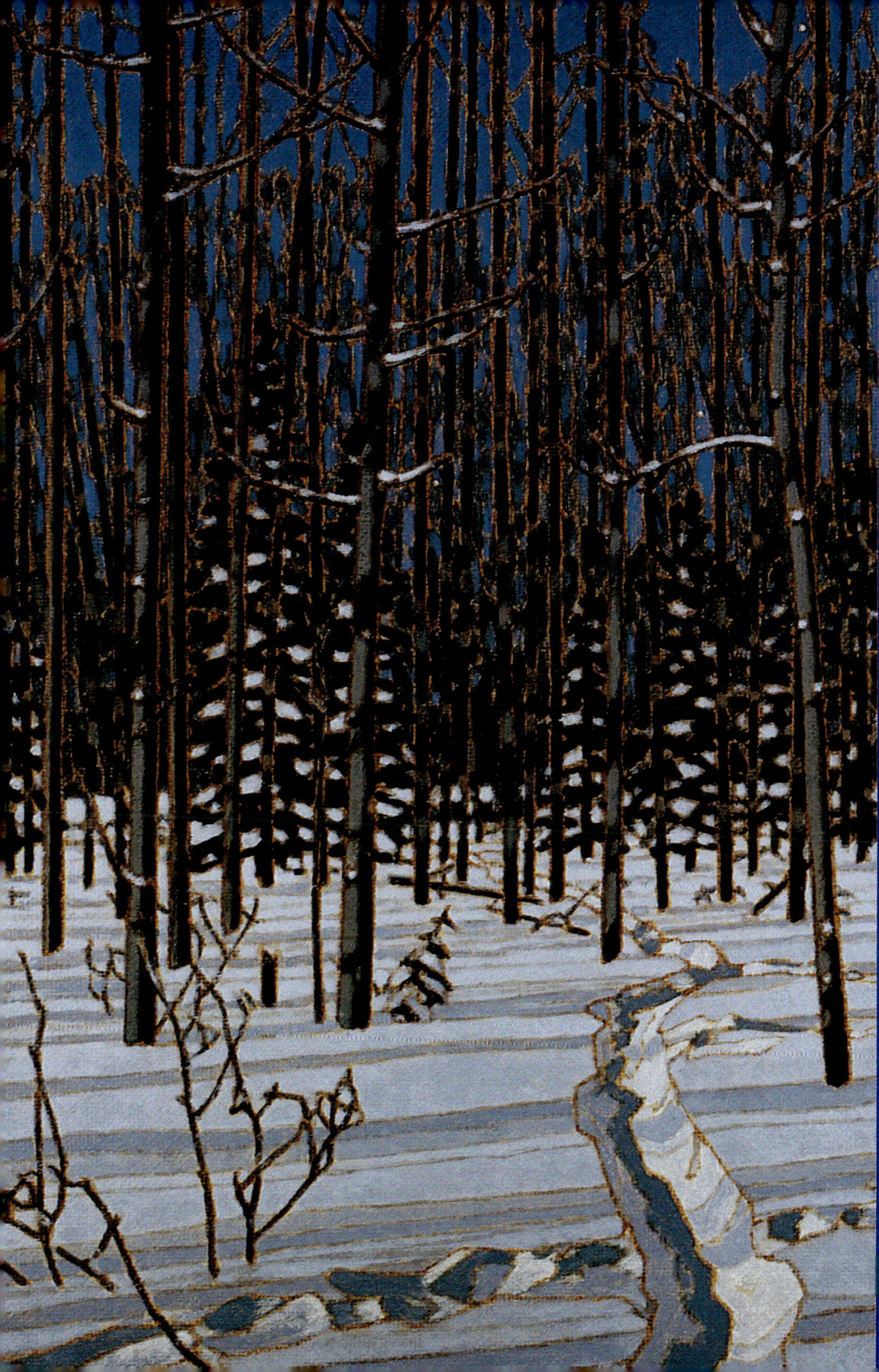

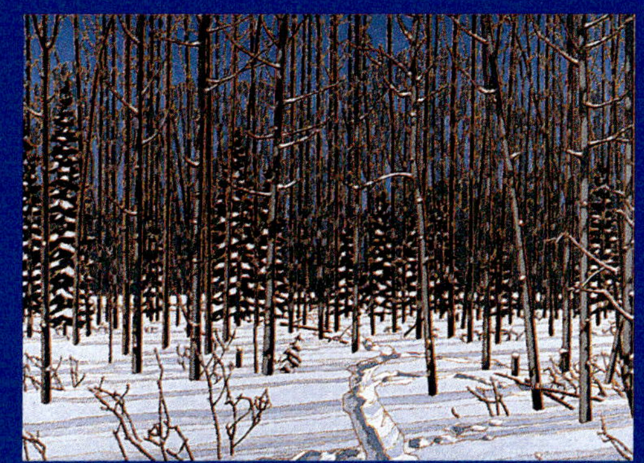

Moonlit Trail through the Poplars

"IT WAS *a land girt about with hardships, a land whose highway was a difficult trail or no trail at all.*"

Mary T. S. Schaffer, 1911

Jasper Crossing on the Wapiti, Full Moon

Of the three fords on the Wapiti River, this is believed to be the oldest, based partly on early survey maps. It is known as the Jasper Crossing, reflecting the fact that the Hinton Trail went on to Jasper Park. From the Grande Cache area one branch continued through the mountains to Jasper, while the other branch went east to Hinton. Travellers of the 1930s remember following the Trail and camping out on clear, moonlit nights when they could hear trees cracking in the frost and timber wolves howling. Although horses were often used, people were sometimes better off on foot. They didn't have to look after animals and find feed for them, and it was easier to keep warm walking. The view in the painting was from the top of the north bank, facing upriver to the southwest. On the far horizon, a faint line of snow-covered peaks shows the nearest range of the Rocky Mountains. The moon was full and it was very cold.

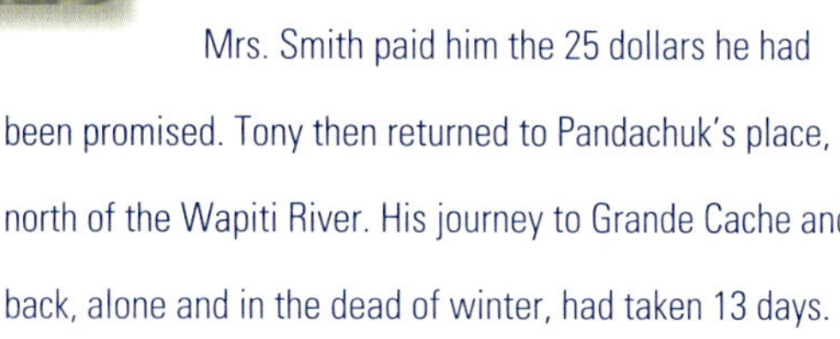

OUT FOR A WALK

Not many people walked the Hinton Trail alone, but Anton (Tony) Roteliuk covered about half of it on foot in the winter of 1935. In January, Ione Smith needed someone to take an urgent message to her husband, Fletcher Smith, at his trading post in Grande Cache. Tony was the only person who would go. He travelled from Fletcher's Hinton Trail store to the trading post. Today, by road, this distance is close to 100 miles. Tony had not been over the Hinton Trail before, and he lost his bearings at times. Once, after a day or so of resting, Tony had to head back up the Trail and was talked into riding a horse. He later wished he hadn't. He kept warmer walking, and ended up leading the nag the last 14 miles. Tony returned safely and Mrs. Smith paid him the 25 dollars he had been promised. Tony then returned to Pandachuk's place, north of the Wapiti River. His journey to Grande Cache and back, alone and in the dead of winter, had taken 13 days.

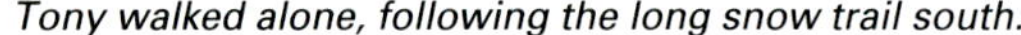

Tony walked alone, following the long snow trail south.

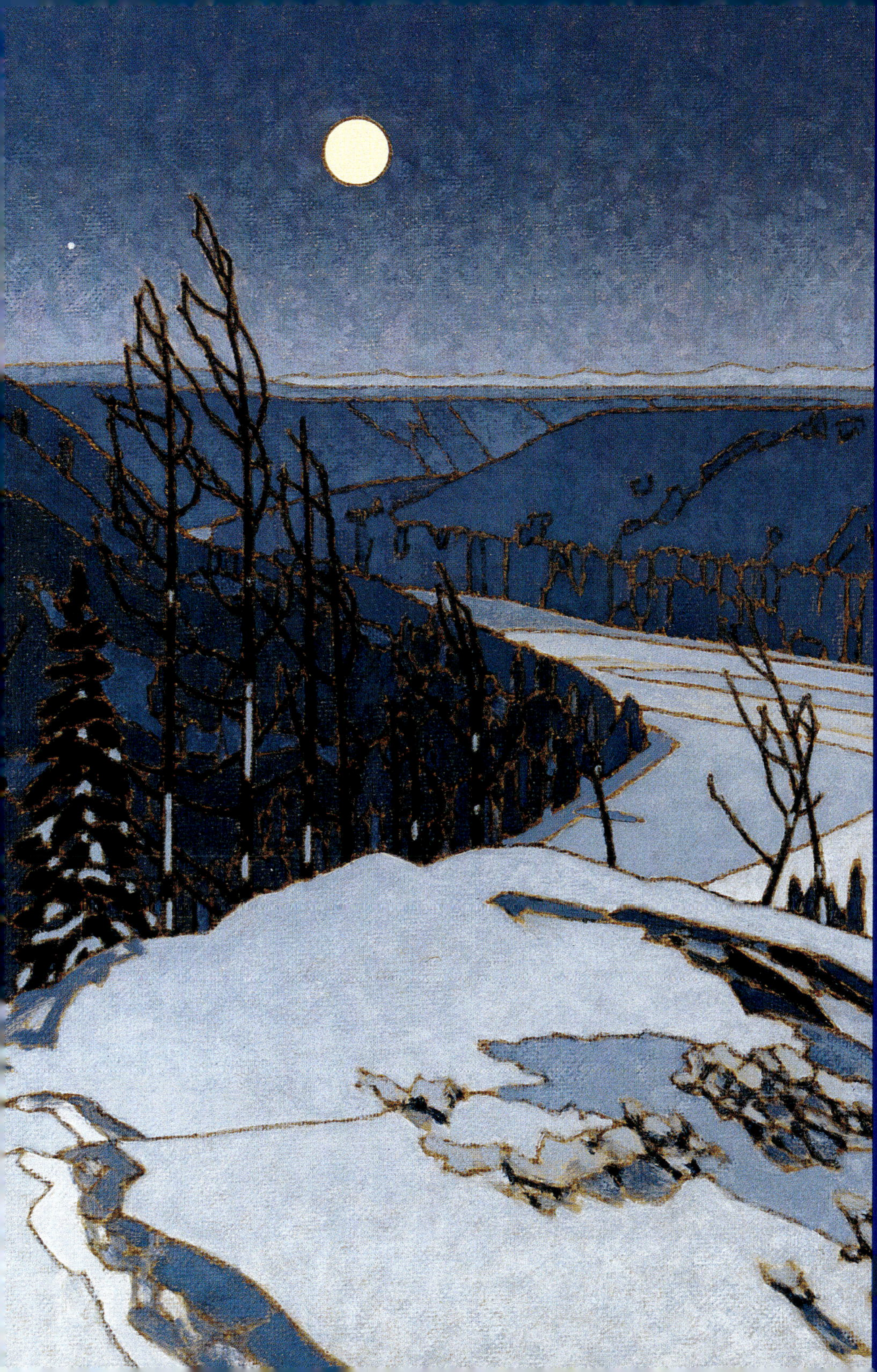

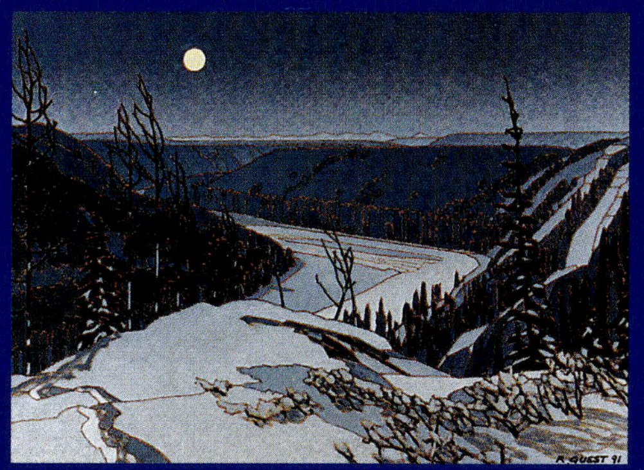

Jasper Crossing on the Wapiti, Full Moon

"THE WESTERNER *is imminently practical, and any unnecessary expenditure of energy he looks upon as silly. Nor it is considered heroic to walk when one could save time and fatigue by riding, or to live in a tent in the winter when a little pains would erect a log shanty"*

J. B. Bickersteth, 1914

Trail, North Bank of the Wapiti

The Trail heading up the north bank of the Wapiti is still in its original condition. Like most of the old trails in the area, this one started as a hunting path and was finally discontinued in the 1950s when other trails and roads opened up vast areas of the back country to mechanized travel. Compared to a trail through the bush, a hillside trail is wider, and the sides tend to flatten as if horses or cattle had scrambled for footing. In spots, this part of the Trail is about eight feet wide, and near the top of the hill there is a braided part where independent animals made their own detours. Marks can be found on some boulders, as if horseshoes had struck them and left metallic streaks. The painting shows a fall setting, complete with two grouse.

FISH FOSSILS FORCE A FRACAS

In the mid-1950s, rare fish fossils were found at Fish Fossil Lake, a short distance from Wapiti Lake. Not only was this information valuable to the petroleum people, but it also created a stir with two museums: the American Museum of Natural History, and the National Museum at Ottawa. By August 1961, crews had already removed some of these fossils, with 14 packhorses carrying out as much as 1500 pounds of rock in one trip. It was a long haul back to civilization. The fossil find stimulated research in other parts of the country, and specimens were found further south, around Willmore Wilderness Park. Even though modern forms of transportation were becoming more available, traditional packtrails were still needed to gain access to the research area.

Fish fossils near Wapiti Lake

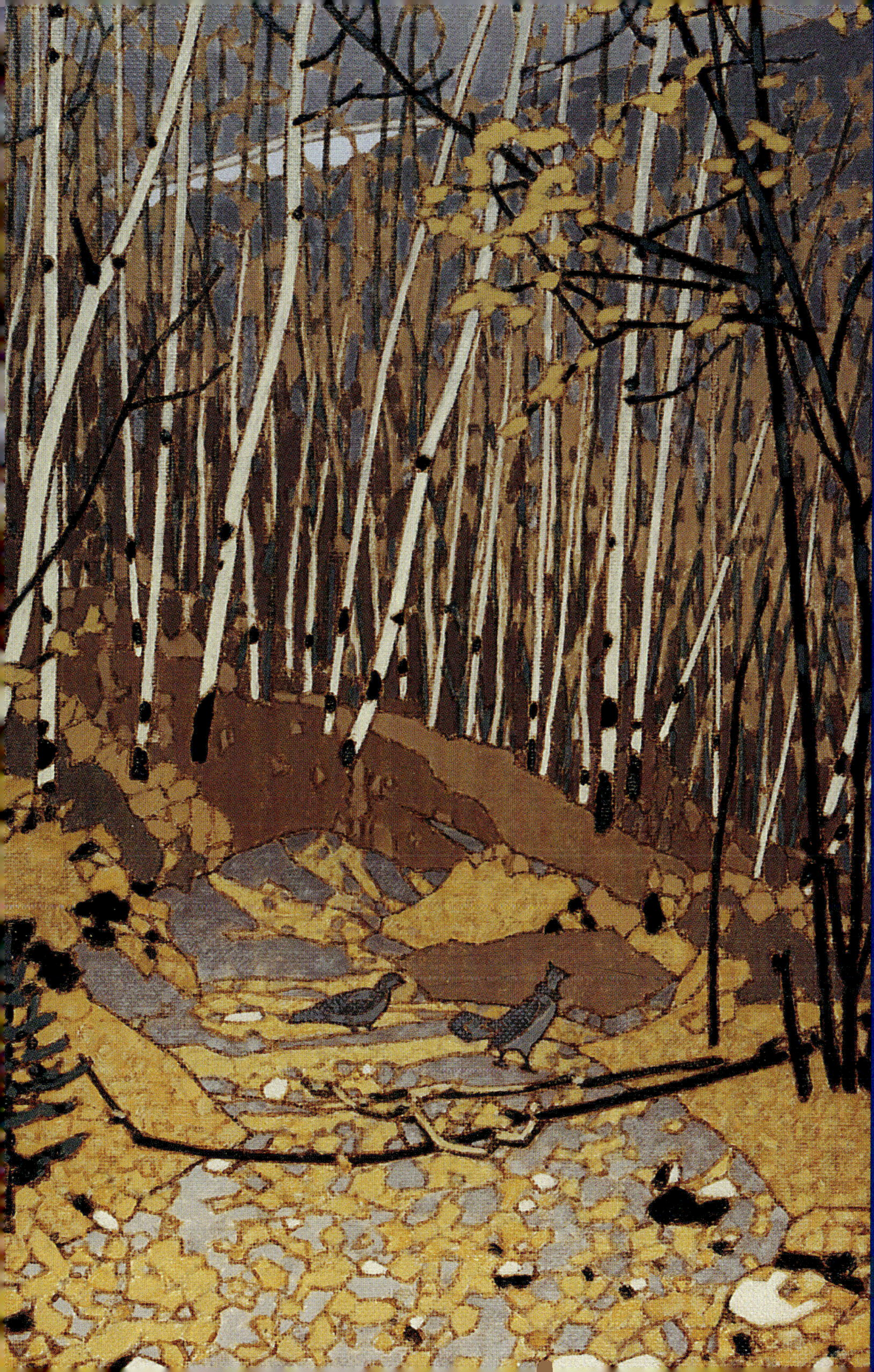

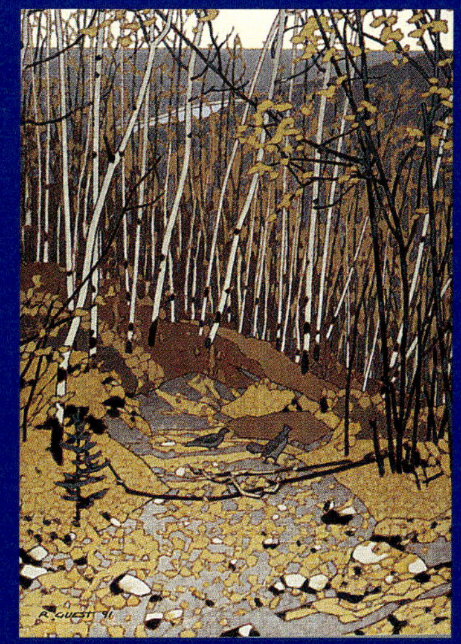

Trail, North Bank of the Wapiti

"THERE CAN BE *no doubt at all that the glory of the West is the 'fall' of the year when the days are absolutely clear and the sun shines brilliantly in an unclouded sky. The leaves of the millions upon millions of poplar trees turn a bright gold; the wet swampy growth of the muskeg reddens."*

J. B. Bickersteth, 1911

Cold Night Trail, Smith's Farm

Packtrails started in two ways: as game trails or as Indian pitching trails. They were followed and, in time, became regular routes. The packtrail on the north side of the Wapiti River most likely started as a pitching trail, and it was a portion of a much longer route. It was a recognizable track through the bush, crossing what in later years would be known as Bill Smith's farm. In the early years travellers would go for miles without seeing any sign of human life, not even the occasional trapper's cabin. In winter it was a challenge to survive and care for pack animals, but the moon provided light and made winter camping and travel easier. The painting shows a section of the Trail at Smith's that has been widened over the years so that carts and wagons could use it during summer. The moose tracks have become an added feature each winter.

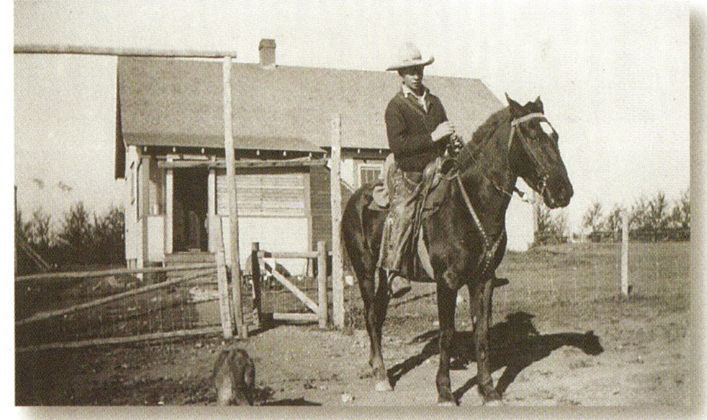

Bill Smith at 18, on his saddlehorse, Max, c.1938.

BILL AND BERT

Bill Smith had his first taste of the Hinton Trail (also known as the Jasper Trail) in 1940, while still in his teens. He made the trip with his older brother Bert, who had gone down the Trail several times. Together, over the years that followed, they made the trip to Grande Cache on at least three different occasions, with an average of 14 packhorses each time. They used army packsaddles, which were better for horses climbing steep hills, and panniers made of wood and stretched cowhide.

Bill and Bert hauled supplies where needed, carrying the occasional load of furs out to market for Fletcher Smith, hiring each horse out for a dollar a day. Their operation continued all winter, if necessary, but usually they preferred to freight in the summer or late fall. During the early years of the Second World War, some of the trading posts began to close down. Their journeys ceased as the old packtrail became a thing of the past.

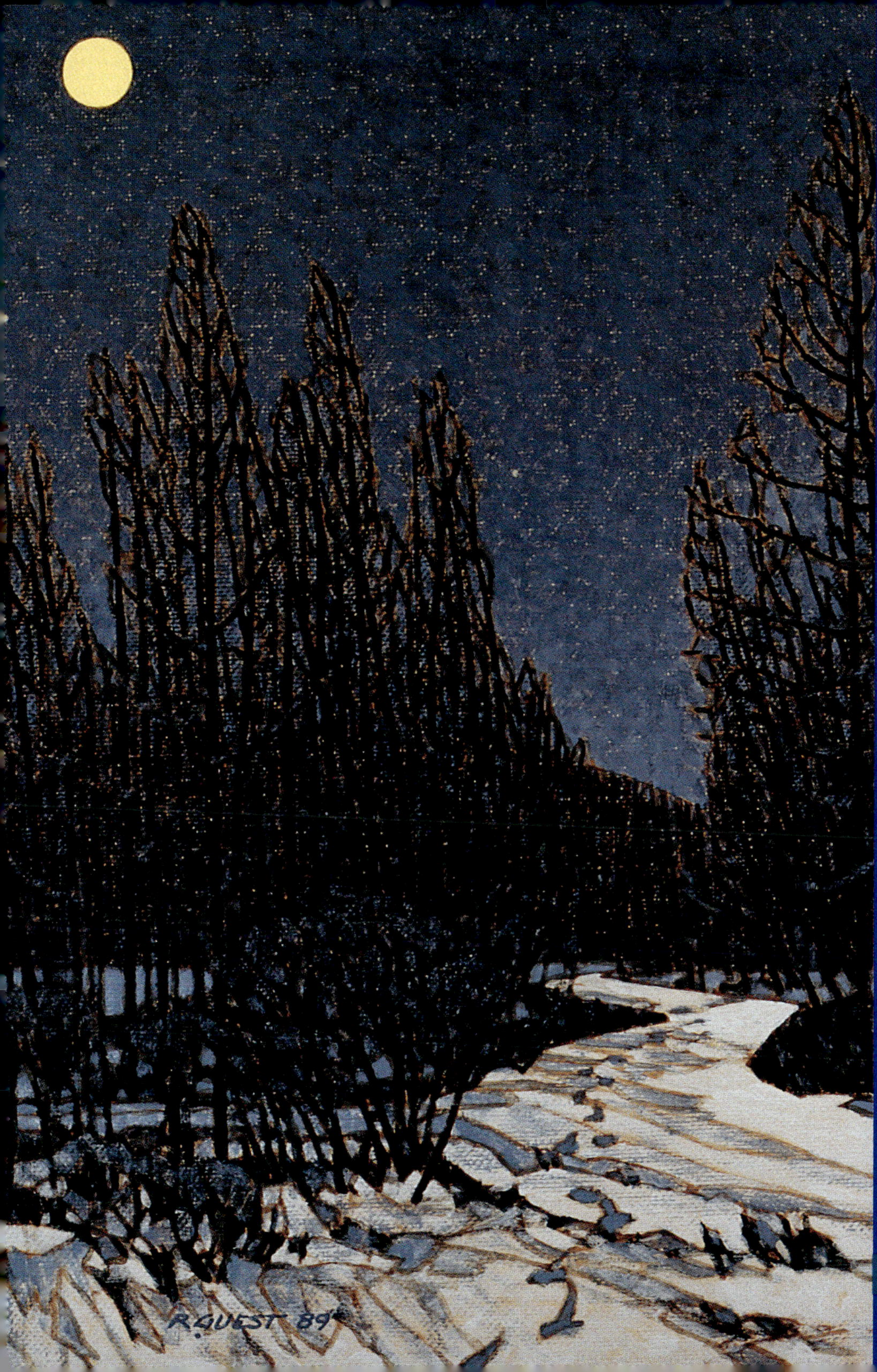

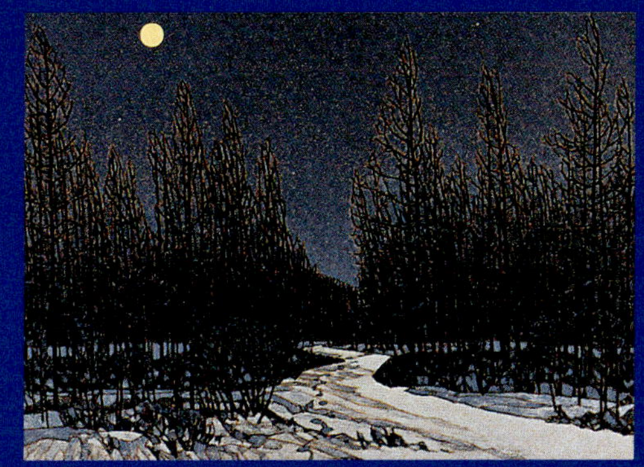

Cold Night Trail, Smith's Farm

"And then we too said goodnight and groped out to find our own tents, far more afraid of stubbing our toes in the darkness than in fear of the spirits which the Indians think wander around after dark."

Mary T. S. Schaffer, 1911

Tree by the Trail, Scorgie's Farm

The packtrail went through the community called Hinton Trail. The district post office was incorporated in 1923. Perhaps the most notable spot along the Trail in this area is where it crossed the creek near the Scorgie houseyard, heading in a northerly direction. There, a gnarled old poplar grows close to the road allowance. It is believed to have been there when the Trail was being used. The Trail eventually wound its way through the bush to a ford on the Redwillow River. There was mention of an old beaver dam, where a wall of logs and sticks caused the creek to back up almost to where Scorgie's garden is today. There are few signs of the original packtrail now. The painting shows the tree in early July, with tiger lillies and gathering clouds.

FLETCHER SMITH

In the 1930s, probably more than any other individual, it was Fletcher Smith who influenced the amount of traffic on the old Hinton Trail, particularly from the Peace River country down to Grande Cache. He had various business interests, and also owned two trading posts, one on Victor Lake and the other at Sheep Creek. He employed Sam and Betty Unruh to manage these posts. His centre of supply, or general store, was situated in the community of Hinton Trail, almost a half-mile west of Scorgie's. From here, sometimes for months at a time, Fletcher would leave home to oversee the operation of his distant stores. In spite of his dedication to his work, he was still quite a family man. One year, Fletcher received severe frostbite when he walked out over the Trail a far distance to be with his wife and four children for Christmas.

Beaver's house along the Wapiti

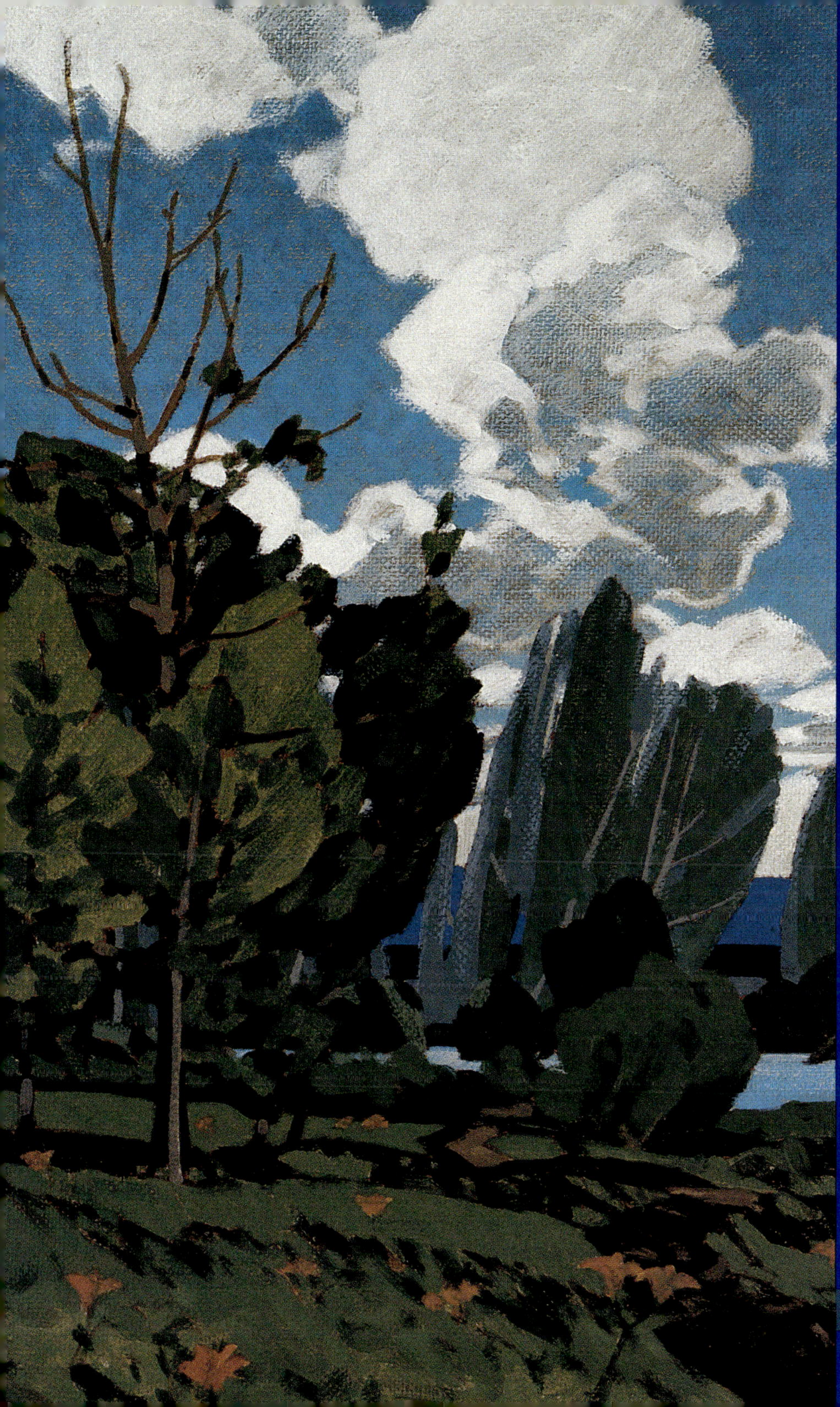

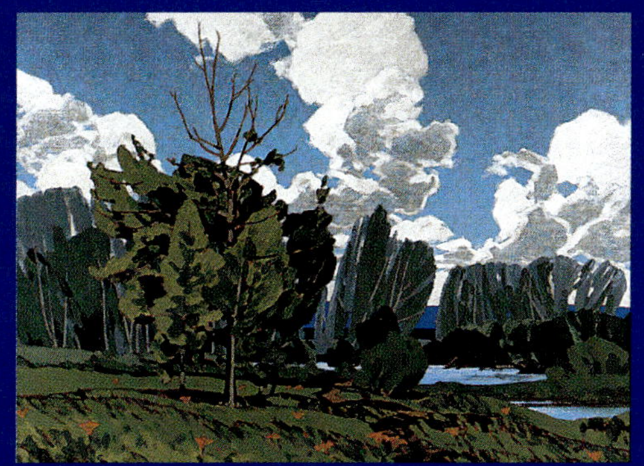

Tree by the Trail, Scorgie's Farm

*"T*HE REDWILLOW, *for instance, was in spring flood and barely fordable. We crossed the river on to a large flat on the west side of the river. This flat was known as Indian Flat as Indians had camped here for years in the fall. It was the old Hinton Trail crossing too. We got to the cabin on Scorgie's about May 10th, 1917."*

Ian McEachern, 1976

"...my mind went back to the first carpenters who had cut logs in these waters, the busy little beavers whose work was still visible, but whose pelts have been the cause of their extermination."

Mary T. S. Schaffer, 1911

Crossing on the Redwillow

Usually the Redwillow was easy to ford. There were two crossings to the old Trail, one for people on horseback, and another more suitable for wagons. But, like other rivers and creeks in the area, there were times when the water would rise without much warning. There were lush meadows on either side of the river valley—ideal pasture for such wildlife as deer and moose, and for domestic stock. Sometimes, camping on the flats for weeks at a time, groups of natives would stop on their way through. Quite often their destination was the trading post at Lake Saskatoon, and they would have come all the way from the Kakwa River area. Only a few could speak any English at all. I made sketches for a painting to depict a rainy day in early summer.

◆

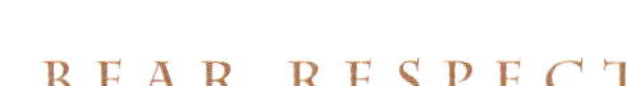

BEAR RESPECT

At one time, most trappers' cabins had sod roofs. During the summer, when the trapper was away, a bear could enter the cabin by climbing on the roof and digging in. It would invariably exit through a window.

No evening campfire would be complete without at least one bear story, preferably one about a grizzly. Grizzlies are to be taken more seriously than black bears, as they appear to have no natural enemies. These animals, capable of turning over large boulders in search of ground squirrels, with the strength to rip logs apart for insects, can make quick work of a mere human. They have generated respect, even fear, because of their size and unpredictability, and tales about them have contributed to a frontier tradition. Grizzlies are magnificent to observe—preferably through binoculars.

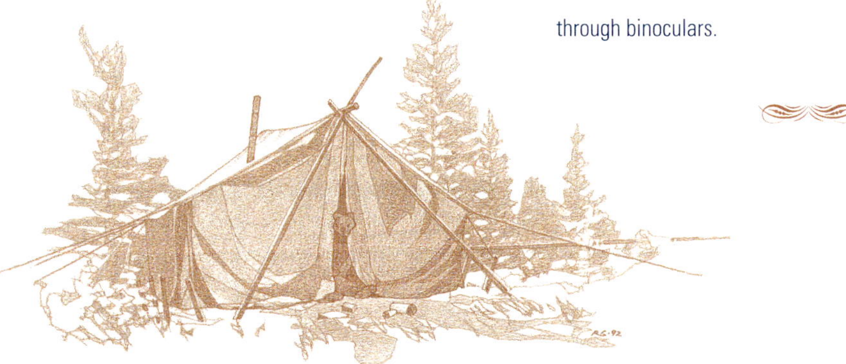

Bear in the tent, alone!

TOP: Tracks of a grizzly bear

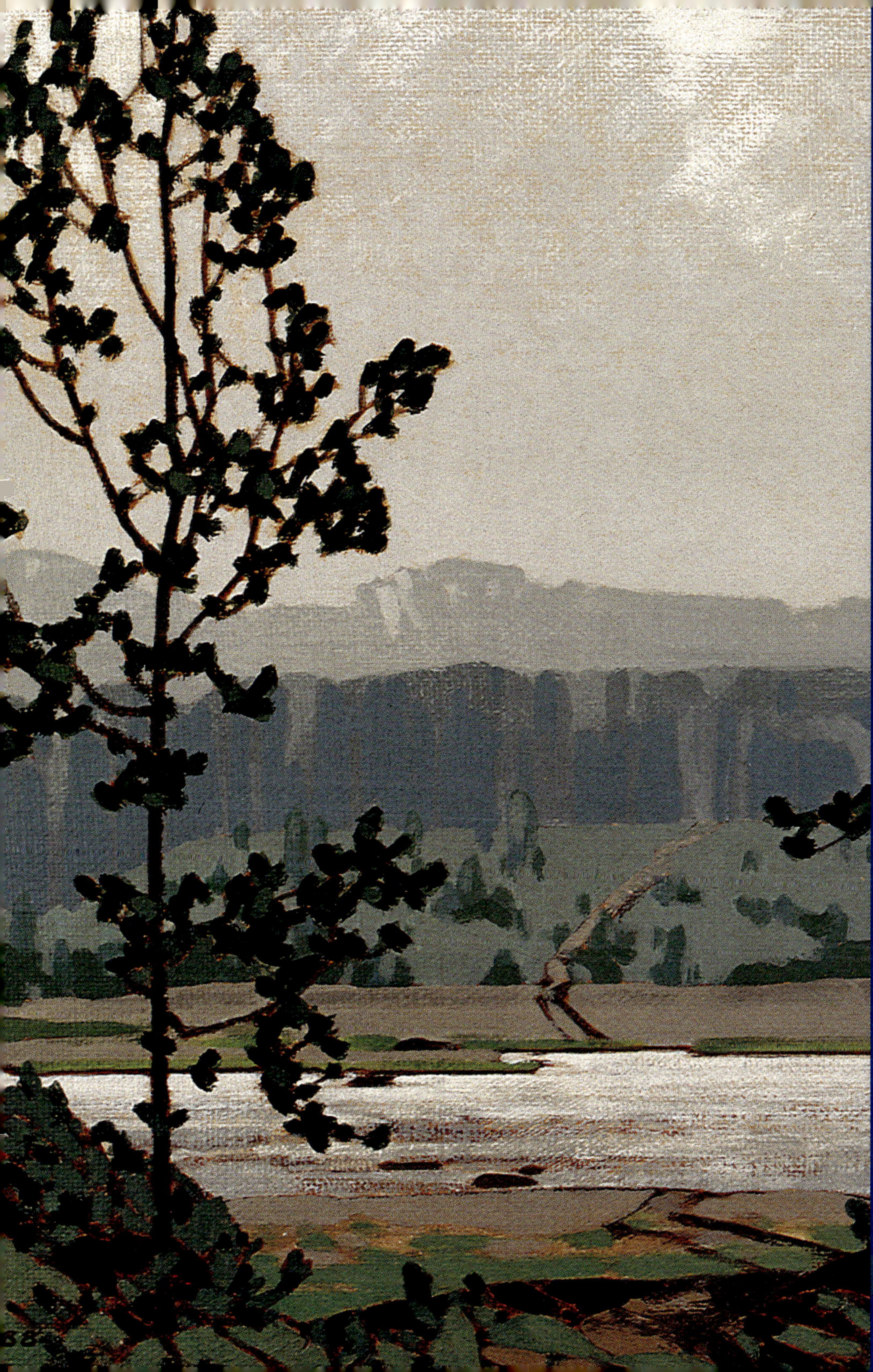

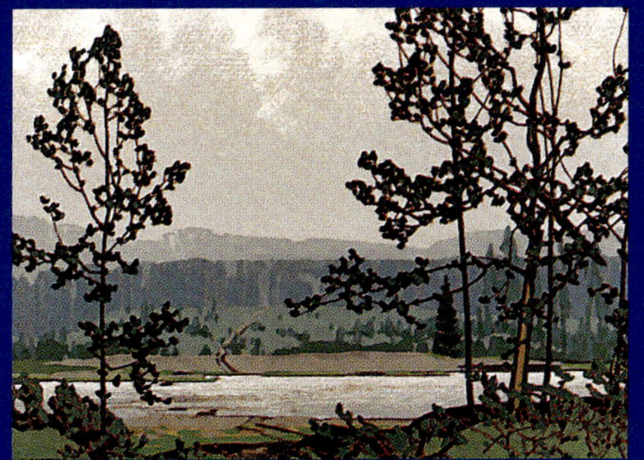

Crossing on the Redwillow

"HUNTERS have told me that a grizzly courts a stand-up fight and fears no one; also that he fails in one accomplishment—he cannot climb a tree. Neither can I."

Mary T. S. Schaffer, 1911

"The best damned watchdog we ever had. No one would come near the place!"

Pete McCullough

First Spence Farm on the Redwillow

The William Spence house was built around 1915, and was likely the first substantial log building south of the Redwillow River. He had walked into the country all the way from Lake Saskatoon, and was among the earliest settlers. He had checked on land suitable for mixed farming, and after he filed for homestead, he returned with a wagon, a team of horses, and his family. The fine log house still stands on the flats along the river, a short distance from the original Trail. Through the years, the Spence family became well acquainted with the Indians who passed back and forth, preferring the upper crossing. Eventually the Trail was improved and widened in places to allow for some of the first carts and wagons heading further south. I sketched the old house and farmyard just as the new leaves were breaking out on a bright day in May, and used the sketches for the final painting.

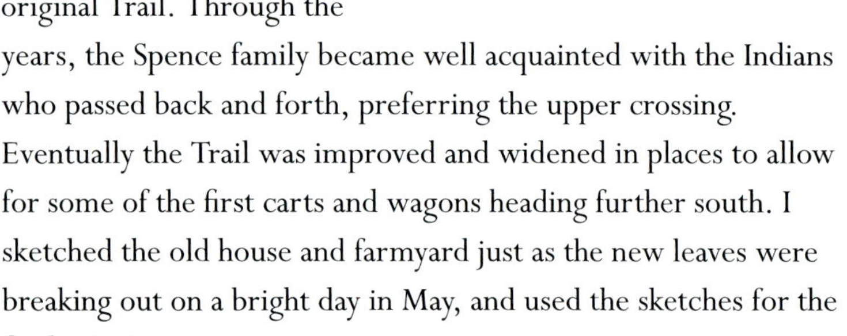

With horses and wagons, Indians make their seasonal journey to the Little Smoky, c.1936.

SPLITTING UP

The old Trail became braided as it passed through the Redwillow valley near Spence's farm. This was characteristic of the packhorse area where groups of Indians occasionally travelled along parallel paths. It was noticed along the river that the Indians had a twin-trail system that separated the hunters (men) from the women and children. This was partly for safety and partly to help them obtain fresh meat. The men would ride ahead along the hilltop, on the lookout for possible trouble or game. Meanwhile, lower down and at a slower pace, the women and children would follow along a different path, mostly out of sight and more sheltered. Eventually, once the main trail left the valley, it would again become a single path.

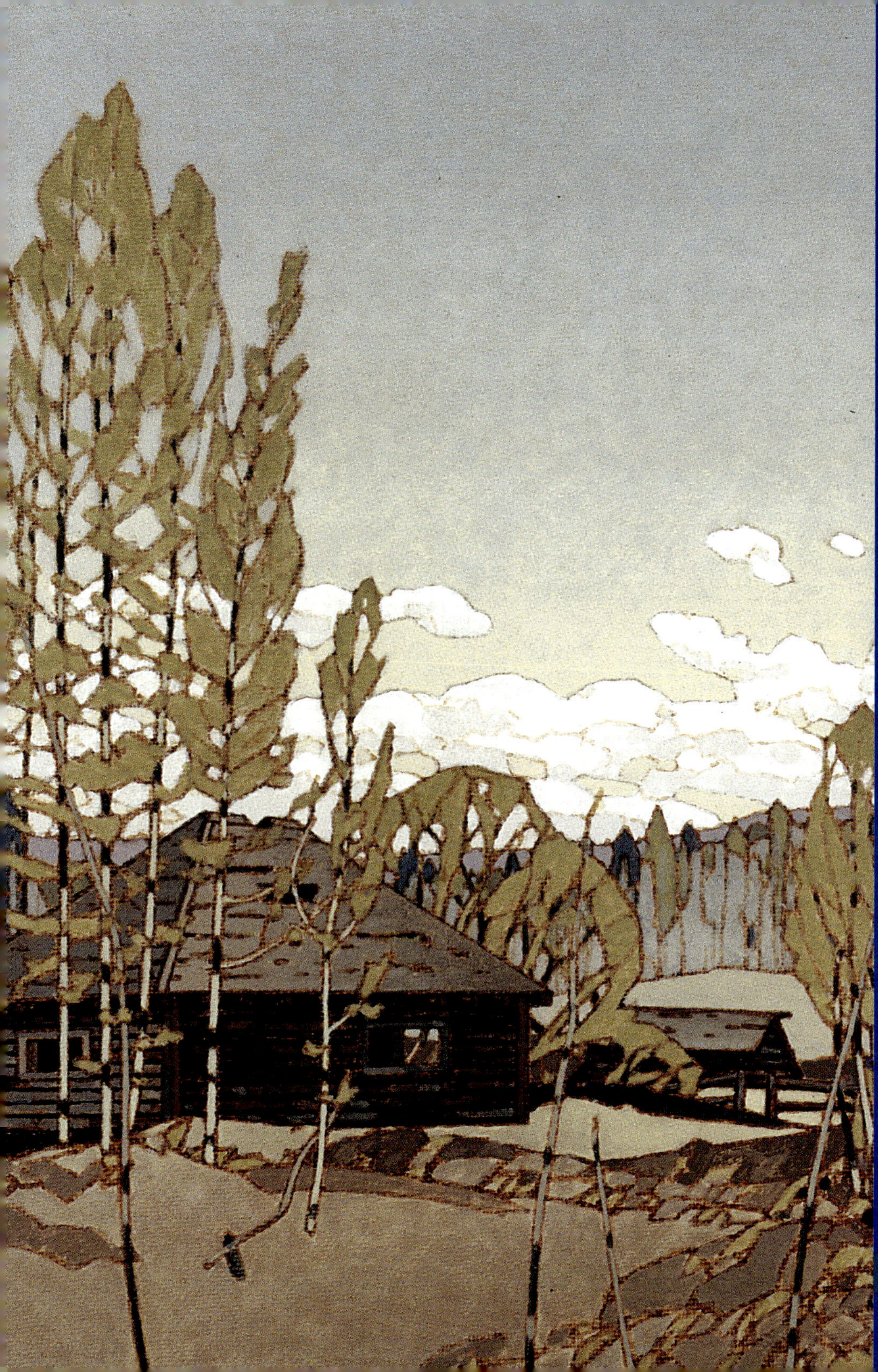

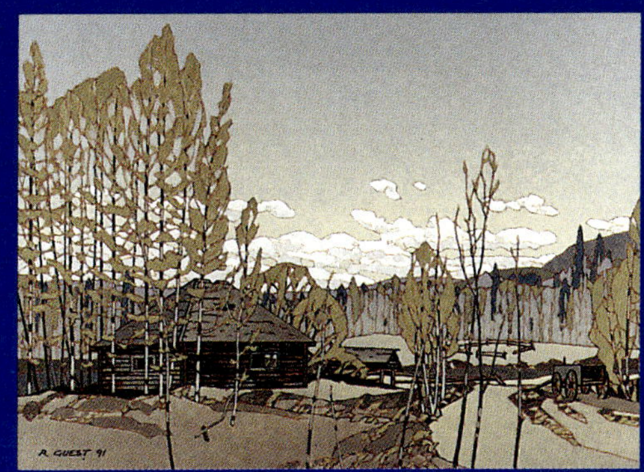

First Spence Farm on the Redwillow

"When the cabin was finished they took the precaution of having Finnegan plow a fire-guard. That was all that saved the cabin from a fire that swept the country that fall."

Jim McEachern, 1916

Nose Mountain Seen from Halcourt Hill

One of the best views of Nose Mountain is from the settlement in the north. Having left the miles of bush and low country behind, it must have been exhilarating for travellers to be out in the open again. Glancing back they could enjoy a beautiful panorama, from the edge of today's farmland, where the gradual elevation gives a fine view of the surrounding country. One of the most striking features was, and still is, the long blue outline of Nose Mountain with an endless range of silvery snow peaks to the west of it. This stands out in all seasons, a magnificent backdrop to the southern edge of the Peace River country. The old pack-trail went over Halcourt Hill, a little east of the present road allowance. Except for the foreground pattern of grain fields and gardens, the view hasn't changed very much. I made the painting based on sketches and a small pre-study. It was in the late spring.

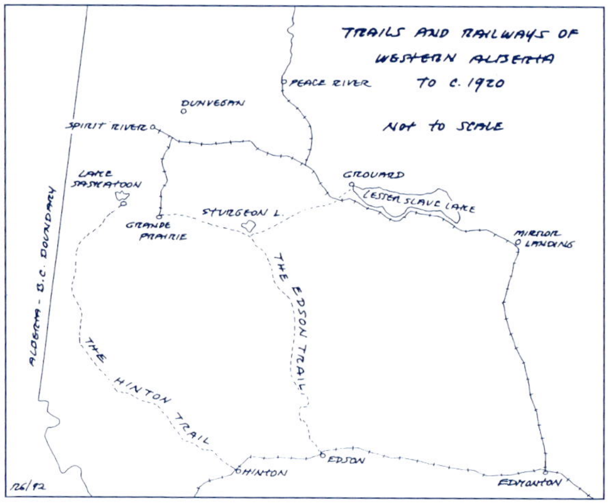

◆

Trails and Railways of Western Alberta

SETTLING OF THE PEACE RIVER COUNTRY

Two things affected the number of settlers coming to the Peace River country: the opening of the Edson Trail in 1911, and the arrival of the first train in Grande Prairie in 1916. Until the Edson Trail was complete, people coming into the country by wagon were confronted with a long and frustrating ride over the Grouard Trail. Groups like the "Bull Outfit" used oxen, 36 of them, because they were believed to be better adapted to rough travelling than horses. Like most wagon trails it was an exhausting, difficult, and dangerous journey.

The first trains were a contact with the outside world. It worked both ways—settlers came into the country and residents went out to visit the large centres, and to do business. In fact, the railroad lines of the Yellowhead Pass became the main drawing card to have the Edson Trail put through. By an odd stroke of irony it was also a train, the Edmonton–Dunvegan & British Columbia, that led to the demise of the same trail after only six years of use.

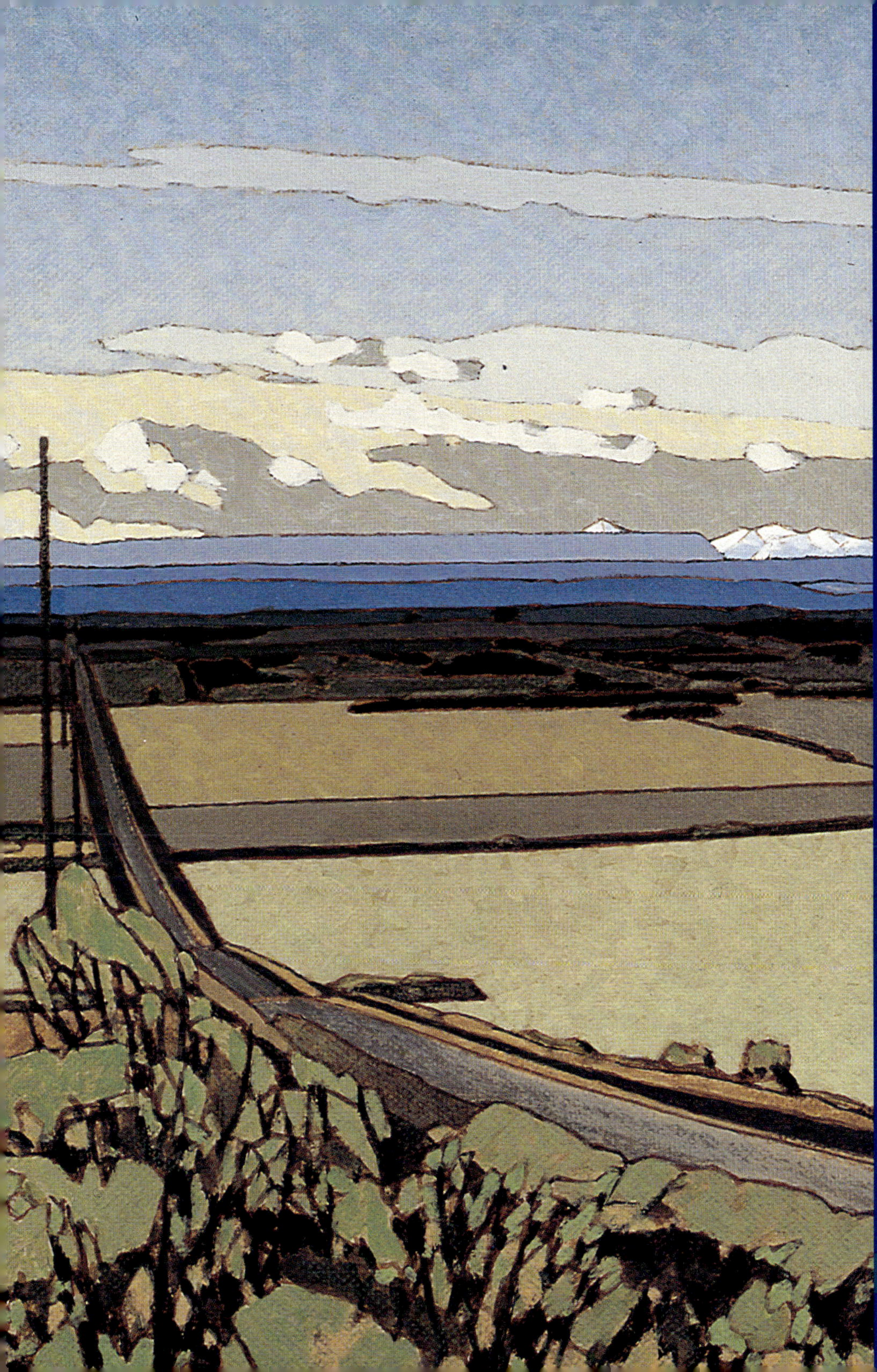

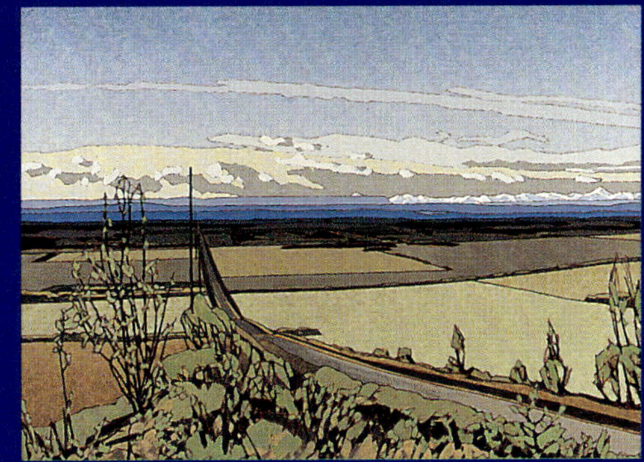

Nose Mountain Seen from Halcourt Hill

AN OLD *Indian told him that around the turn of the century, north of the Wapiti River, there was little besides grass, especially from the Redwillow River all the way to Lake Saskatoon. People travelling through this country on the old Trail had to carry firewood with them if they wanted to make a campfire as none could be found along the way. But, on the other hand, in the dry season, Indians themselves were scared to light fires of any kind in case they got away in the grass.*

From Dave Schenk

Upper Crossing on the Beaverlodge

Where the Hinton Trail meets the Beaverlodge River there were two well-known crossings. As on other streams, the decision of where to cross would depend on such conditions as flooding or ice breakup. Even washouts on the hills, if serious enough, could change plans. The upper crossing seems to have been close to the present-day Cassidy farm, where the packtrail angled across country toward the "Indian Quarter" on Sherk's place. It appears that this was as close as the Trail ever got to Beaverlodge. Although there isn't much forest left, there is evidence that there must have been some heavy bush along the river at one time. The painting was based on an evening in late fall, when the moon was rising.

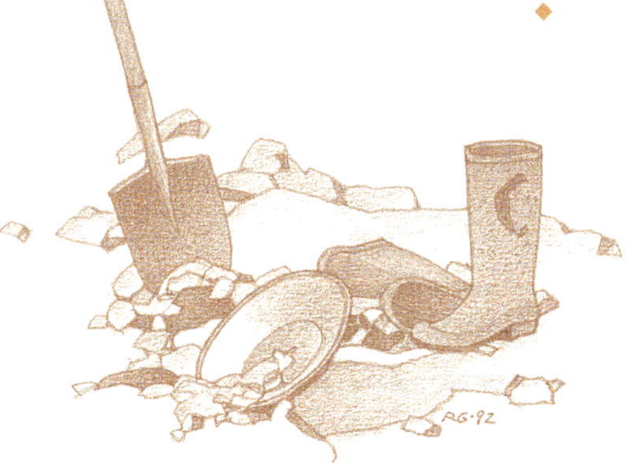

Prospector's tools and bear-bitten boot

MISGUIDED GOLD SEEKER

A pioneer of the area, J. J.(Jim) Brooks first arrived in the Peace River country as part of an expedition headed for the Yukon Gold Rush of 1898. It seems logical that the western branch of the "Backdoor to the Klondike" overlapped with some of the northern trails. It must have passed very close to the present-day hamlet of Rio Grande and to Kelly Lake on the British Columbia side of the border. Evidently his group did not get beyond Fort St. John where they turned back in the fall of 1900 and stopped in the valley of the Beaverlodge River. At the time, the men were exhausted and sick after a rough journey, and they followed a group of Beaver Indians to their wintering grounds close to the lower ford on the river. They built a fair-sized log house, complete with a fireplace and large stone chimney, and there they passed the winter months.

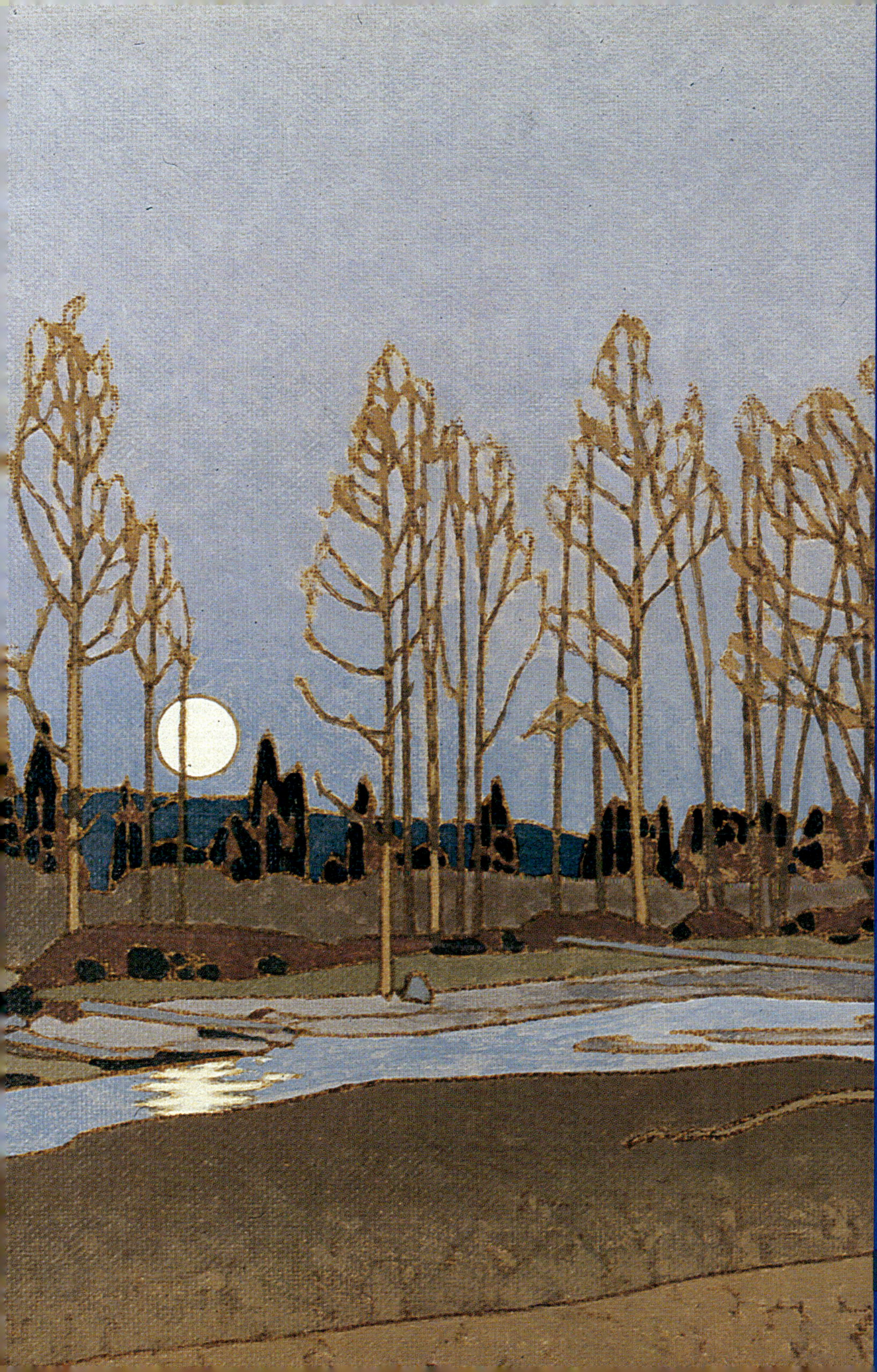

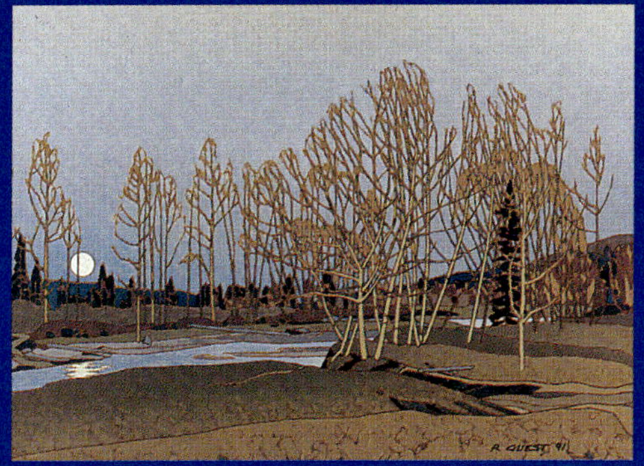

Upper Crossing on the Beaverlodge

"IN THE spring the party built a boat and started to follow the river down to Peace River Crossing, but misfortune dogged them all the way. At a point on the Wapiti River near the present ferry crossing at Pipestone Creek, their boat was damaged by rocks and they had to make camp on a sand bar. One of the party had been hurt and after the chill and exposure of the icy water he became delerious and committed suicide. He was buried on the sand bar."

Hugh W. Allen, c.1915

Indian Quarter in Early Winter

Early settlers in the south Peace talked about an old Indian trail heading southwest. This was before the turn of the century, and was a reference to the well-travelled horse path that angled toward the mountains and Grande Cache. According to old maps, this trail crossed the Beaverlodge valley in the vicinity of an Indian campground on the northeast side of the Beaverlodge River. The natives and the odd trader in the area preferred this spot, and, from time to time they set up camp there on their way across country to the trading post at Lake Saskatoon. Today the land is farmed by the Don Sherk family, and the camping spot is referred to as the Indian Quarter. The painting is mostly a reconstruction. The location was observed during a day in early winter when it was snowing, and a cold wind came out of the northwest.

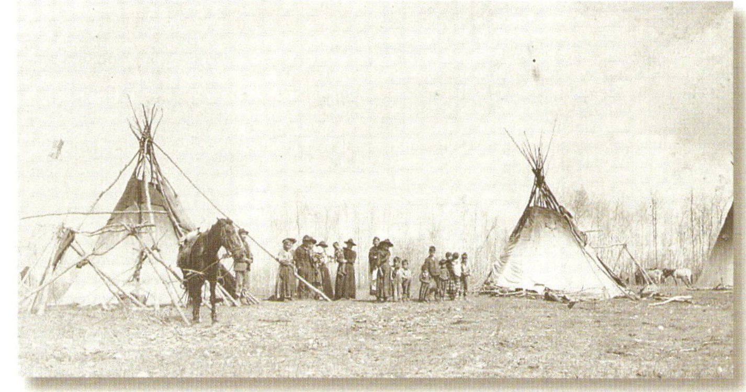

Tipis on the Indian Quarter on the Beaverlodge, 1911

DOUBLE-TRAILING THE PRAIRIES

Wherever a travois was used, the trail had to be wider. These portable lodges could be moved for many miles, especially in the open grasslands. In the bush this process was slow, and for years after in some places, wide, wagon-like ruts remained in the sod from the dragging ends of travois pulled by horses "double-trailing the prairies." Lawrence Locke pointed this out on his own property at the junction of the Redwillow and Beaverlodge rivers. There, in the early 1920s, Indians came through, bringing their travois with them. Even today a faint swath, up to eight feet wide in places, can be seen where travois were pulled. In his book *The Great North Trail,* Dan Cushman points out that it took, on average, three horses to move a standard tipi or lodge with 18 poles and a cover made from 11 buffalo hides.

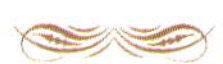

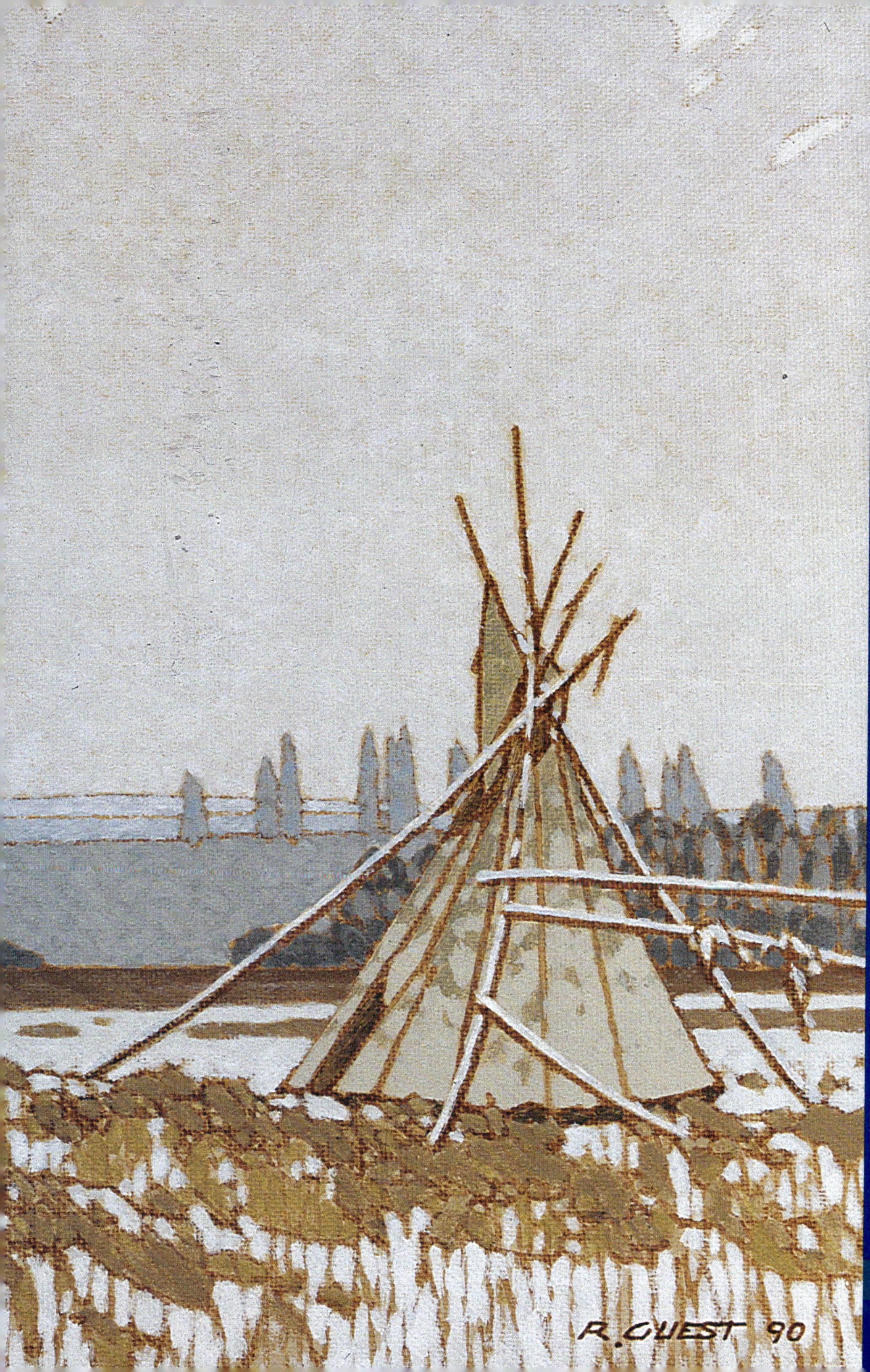

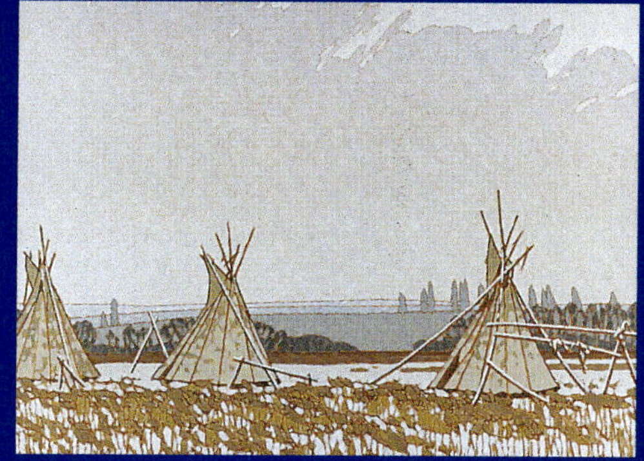

Indian Quarter in Early Winter

“THE LUCKY ones had to chew pine and gather frozen cranberries, thus tending to escape the scurvy which was a worse killer than starvation.

“The Indians hunted siffleurs, skinned them, dried them near fires, and stacked them like mummified bats against the hungry time of winter.”

Dan Cushman, 1966

Wapiti Crossing at Pipestone Creek

In the 1930s it must have been a sight to watch a string of packhorses climb the "hog's back" on the south bank of the Wapiti River. When the ice was safe, the crossing was likely almost as well-travelled in the winter as in the summer. In those years, freetraders, like Alan Watts, would haul supplies out to trading posts while the ground was frozen, and there were no spongy, unpredictable muskegs to worry about. At that time of year, trappers would be most active as well. Until fairly recently, the bush was kept down and thinned out by forest fires. Visibility was better and one could see for a long way. Eventually there was a ferry at the crossing, often referred to as Osborne's Crossing. The painting is based on sketches done in the fall, while there were still a few leaves and ice was already forming on the river.

Mima (on rocks) and Mrs. St. Arnault, shown here in 1935, were neighbours along the Wapiti River.

THE SPECIAL TOUCHES OF A TRAIL WEDDING

Mima (Jemima) Osborne was noted for her hospitality. On one special occasion in 1945, her neat house down by the river was the scene of a wedding party. To make room for the three-day celebration and dancing that followed, Mima cleared all the furniture out of her cabin and stacked it outside, praying it wouldn't rain. The wedding was a colourful affair, with sardines as one of the special items on the menu. Almost everyone was wearing new, beaded buckskin jackets and other accessories. The weather was very warm, and in the air there was the aroma of newly smoked moose hide. Mima said with a smile when she told me the story later, "Every time I smell moose hide, I can smell sardines."

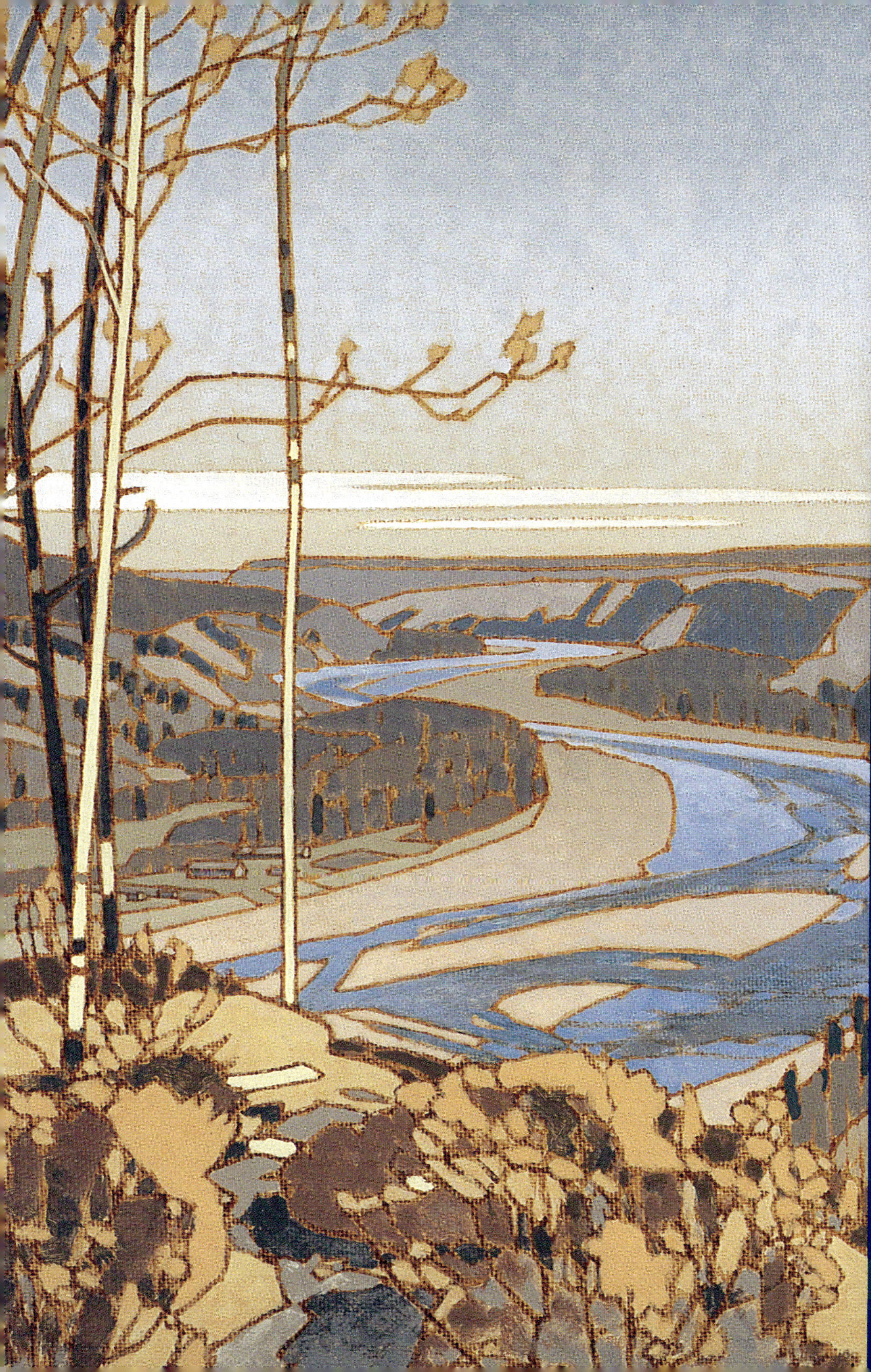

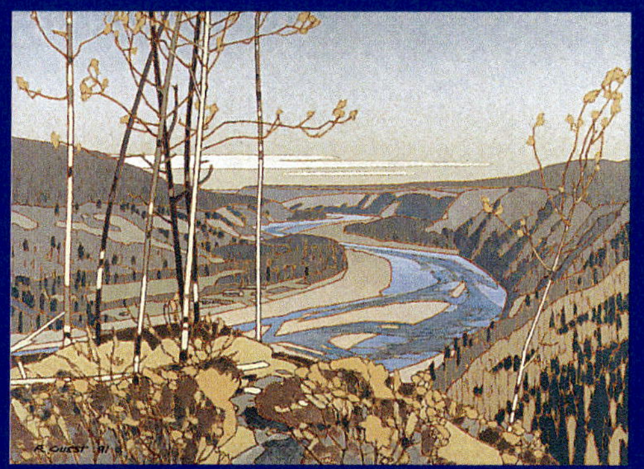

Wapiti Crossing at Pipestone Creek

"Just a few years after we moved to the river, the first settlers began settling on the south side of the river, moving their belongings over in a rowboat or rafting when the river was high. When the water was low they could ford. Some stock had to swim..."

Mima Osborne

Night Tipis on Flyingshot Lake

Flyingshot Lake, marshy with bush around its shores, was a fine habitat for waterfowl. The name "Flyingshot" refers to the narrows where ducks and geese could be shot "on the wing." The Metis settlement of Flyingshot Lake was probably the first of its kind to be established in the south Peace country. Some residents were in the vicinity before the turn of the century. The Metis families came from Lac Ste. Anne, bringing their tradition of trapping and hunting, and the skills that enabled them to survive in the harsh climate of the northwest. Cabins were the preferred homes, but during the warm months of late spring through September, tipis were often used, and provided a wonderful silhouette along the shores of the lake. To get to the main Trail, it was necessary to travel a few miles over open prairie to the trading post at Lake Saskatoon. The painting, in part, is a reconstruction, combining the actual location, seen on a moonlit night, with historical imagery. The time of year is late May.

Tipi in Alpine Meadows

TOP: Canada Geese in V Formation

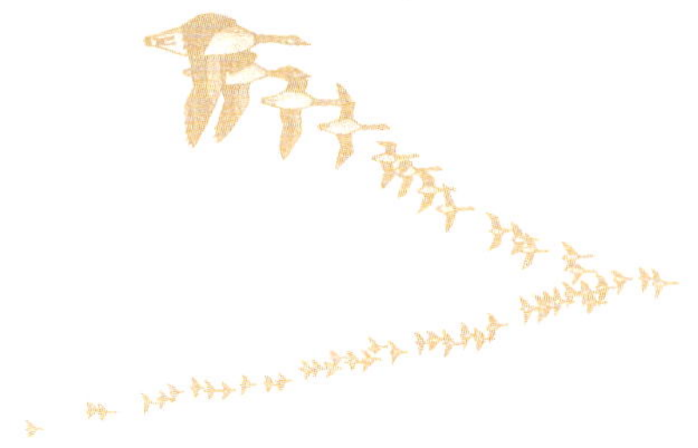

ON THE WING AT FLYINGSHOT LAKE

Many of the Flyingshot Metis got to know the network of trails, and some of them made the long trip to Grande Cache or Hinton, at the turn of the century before some of these places had names. Among the early Metis to settle there were Adam Calliou and his brothers Esau and William, who came from Lac Ste. Anne in 1894. A 1907 survey of the Flyingshot Lake settlement was one of the first conducted in the south Peace country, and a school was built where the children learned to speak English. For many their stay was short-lived after the first land surveyors came into the Grande Prairie area in 1909 followed by displacing settlers. In 1916 another flood of settlers arrived with the railroad. In an attempt to leave civilization behind them, many Metis set out for the semi-isolated spot of Kelly Lake where they could again establish their own community.

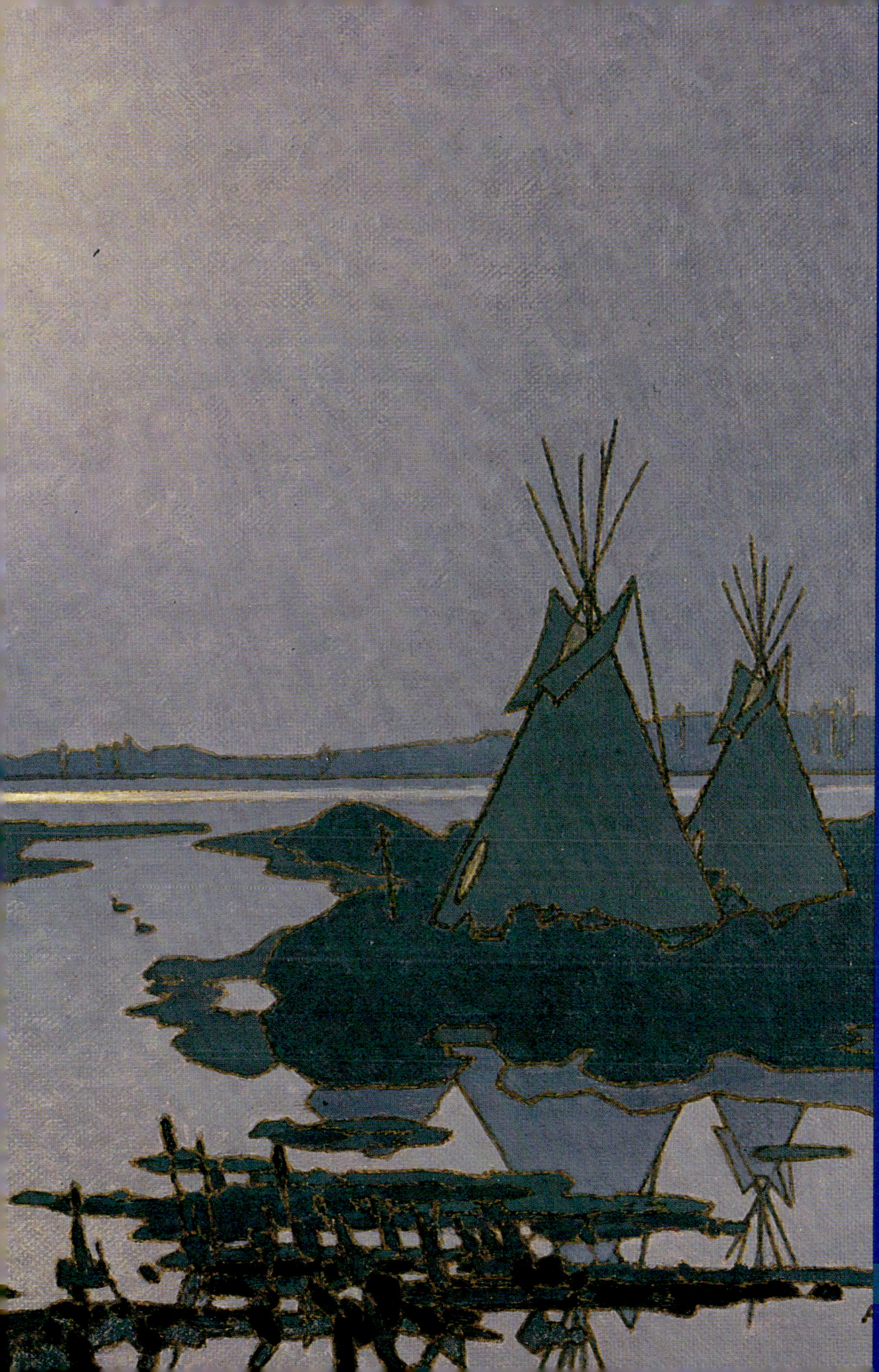

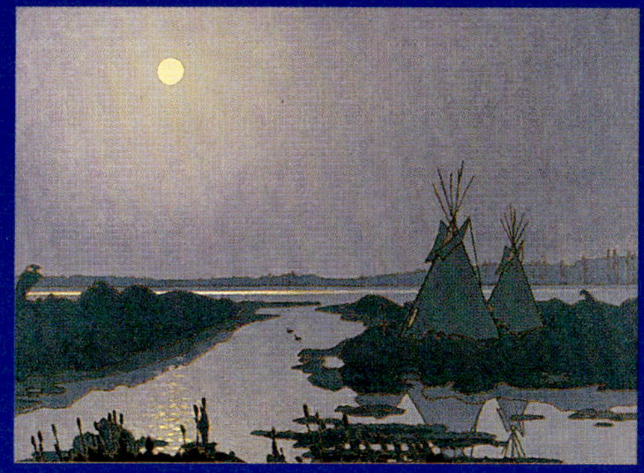

Night Tipis on Flyingshot Lake

"THERE IS *no voice, however famed, that can attune itself to the lonely corners of the heart, as the sigh of the wind through the pines when tired eyes are closing after a day on the trail."*

Mary T. S. Schaffer, 1911

Sentinel Poplar, East Branch Of The Trail

Today, there is almost no trace of the east trail because of farming. But along the route a single, large poplar tree stands close to where the old trail passed. Having inspected the tree close up, it appears to be about 100 years old, and is in good condition in spite of its lonely, windswept location. Among the various stories told about the 'Lone Tree on the Hill,' two in particular stand out. One mentions it marking the grave of the first white woman to die in the Grande Prairie area. Another story has the tree marking a special cache belonging to a group travelling through the country before there were roads. There must be some reason why a single tree was left in the middle of a grain field. The poplar, in a symbolic way, is a sentinel, and many questions are raised about its reasons for being there.

◆

WORKING TOGETHER—AGAINST THE TRAIL

Today, a map of west-central Alberta and the territory north of it shows that farmland has claimed most of the original Trail. This large zone extends south as far as the edge of the county of Grande Prairie and the 18th base line—the Hinton Trail was literally ploughed under.

Aside from the encroachment of civilization, with its pressure for new land, nature itself is partly to blame. Once the horse traffic stopped, the bush began to close in. Other facets of nature—forest fires and renewal, flooding that can alter complete river flats, erosion and landslides—helped eradicate it. For a modern hiker without a map of the Trail, it would be pure chance to attempt to follow it through on its original course.

Joachim's hay cradle

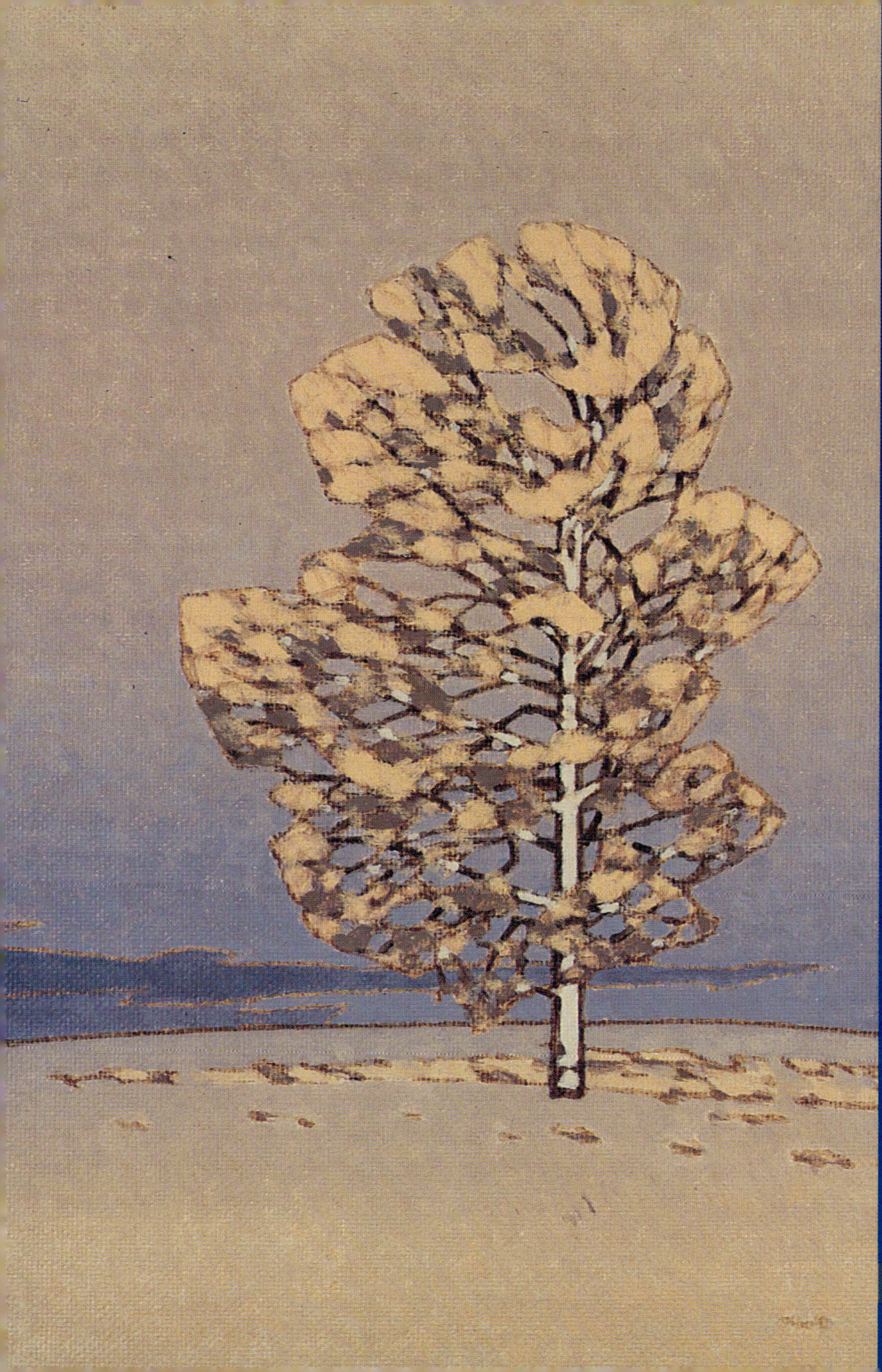

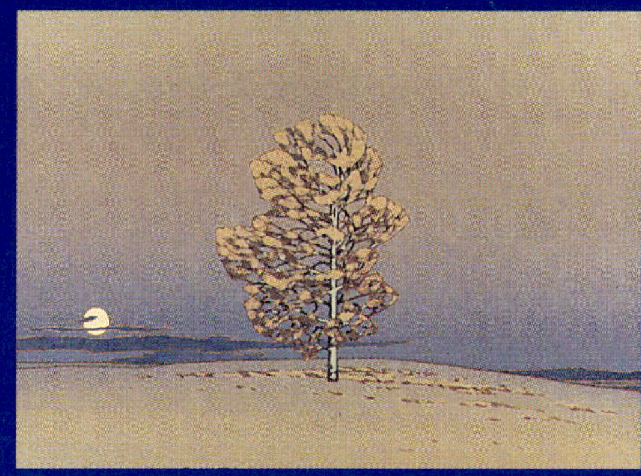

Sentinel Poplar, East Branch Of The Trail

"WE STRUCK *the ghost of a trail, and just hoped it would go on and lead us to our destination. It was a very forlorn specimen on which to base our hopes, it never got worse, and it certainly never got any better."*

Mary T. S. Schaffer, 1911

Monkman Stopping Place on Cutbank Lake

For practical purposes, the end of the Hinton Trail in the north was at Lake Saskatoon. When the railroad came through the south Peace country to Wembley it bypassed Lake Saskatoon, and eventually most of the residents and business people left. But a few miles further north, the Monkman family operated a stopping place on the west end of Cutbank Lake. Many travellers destined for the Hinton Trail would stop there first. The stopping place was in farm country, and there was good food and lodging for weary travellers, as well as a large barn for their horses. The Monkman family was widely known and liked. Today some of the original buildings are still there, and, even though the large barn and house are beginning to show the effects of time, they serve as a reminder of the trail era in this part of the country. Sketches were made for a painting in the late fall of 1989, when Bill Monkman was still living there.

BARN RAISINGS AND SEED SOWINGS

As far back as 1900, while he was in charge of a trading post at Lake Saskatoon, Alex Monkman had a garden as well as plots of grain. Among the first to take land in the Beaverlodge valley was Oliver Johnson, in 1908. Mr. Johnson became known as Rutabaga Johnson, for his success at growing Swede turnips, the first perennial vegetable in the district.

As well as successfully growing grain, some of the early settlers decided it might be profitable to raise livestock. As early as 1906, partners by the name of Grant and Mead established their "cow camp" on the north side of the Bear Lake, where they tried to raise 125 head of cattle in the harsh winter of 1906–07. They were preceded by Jim McCreat who, in 1906, brought cattle into the Beaverlodge area. Harry Adair, who filed north of Lake Saskatoon, was part of a group who attempted to bring in a large herd of horses over the Grouard Trail from Stettler in southern Alberta.

Moose in cabbage patch, Wapiti River

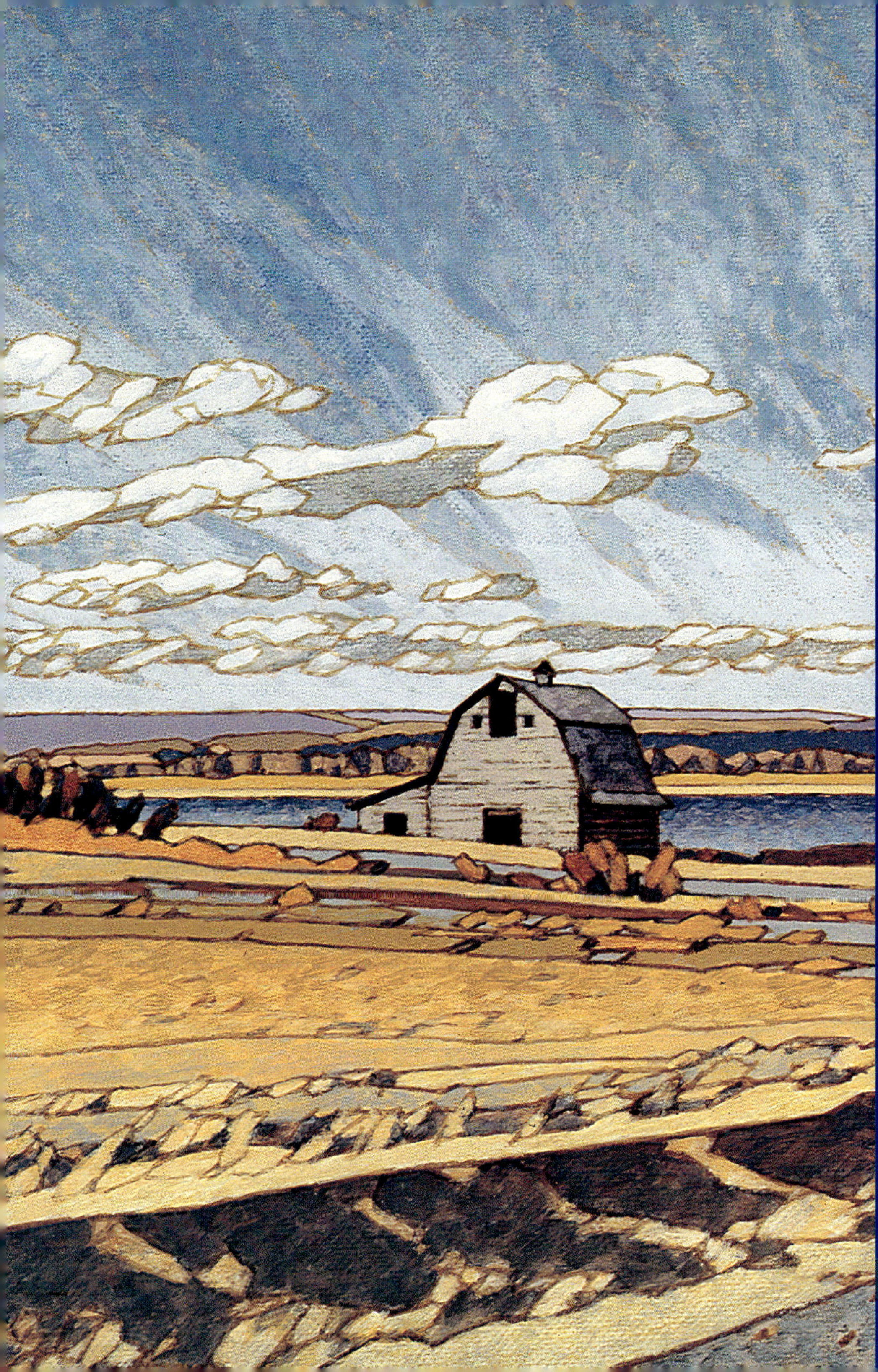

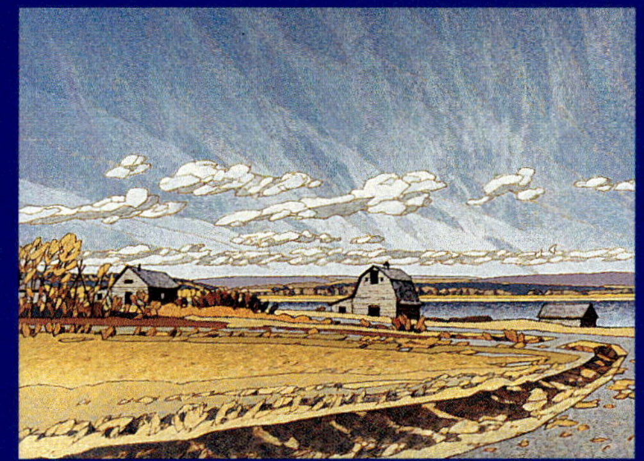

Monkman Stopping Place on Cutbank Lake

ANOTHER aspect of encroaching civilization was the land survey system. In the Peace River country, particularly north of the Wapiti River, this led to the introduction of fences and road allowances. Those things marked the end of a long packtrail tradition.

From Harold Spence

Original Townsite on Lake Saskatoon

The Hudson's Bay trading post was one of the first buildings at the west end of Lake Saskatoon. For some years, the post represented the official fur trade in the area, based on their long tradition in western Canada. But there were others in the business as well. Some were successful freetraders who were responsible for the setting-up of independent posts, eventually establishing stores as far away as Grande Cache and Pierre Greys Lakes. At Lake Saskatoon, other commercial interests developed and, within a few years, there were such things as a church, at least one school, a North-West Mounted Police barracks, and a host of other community-minded organizations. Annually, for many years, treaty Indians came to Lake Saskatoon to collect treaty money, and while in the area they took part in celebrations that lasted several days. Lake Saskatoon was the terminus of the Hinton Trail. The painting shows the western corner of the lake in early summer.

THE EARLY DAYS OF LAKE SASKATOON

The hamlet of Lake Saskatoon started in the late 1890s when, at the west end of the lake, a trading post was established and operated by freetraders who evidently opposed the Hudson's Bay Company. A permanent trading post was built at the west end of Lake Saskatoon, and operated by Alex Monkman, a local resident. The post was part of an arrangement with two other businessmen, Jim Cornwall and Fletcher Bredin, who had other financial interests in the Peace country at the time. In 1901, the Hudson's Bay Company also built at the west end, and the posts together started the first settlement of Lake Saskatoon. The hamlet was well situated, with trails converging from all four directions of the compass. By 1911 early settlers had filed on land in the Lake Saskatoon area, as well as around Grande Prairie, Sexsmith, and Spirit River. Grande Prairie was known as Prairie City in those days.

Last original Hudson's Bay building still standing at old townsite

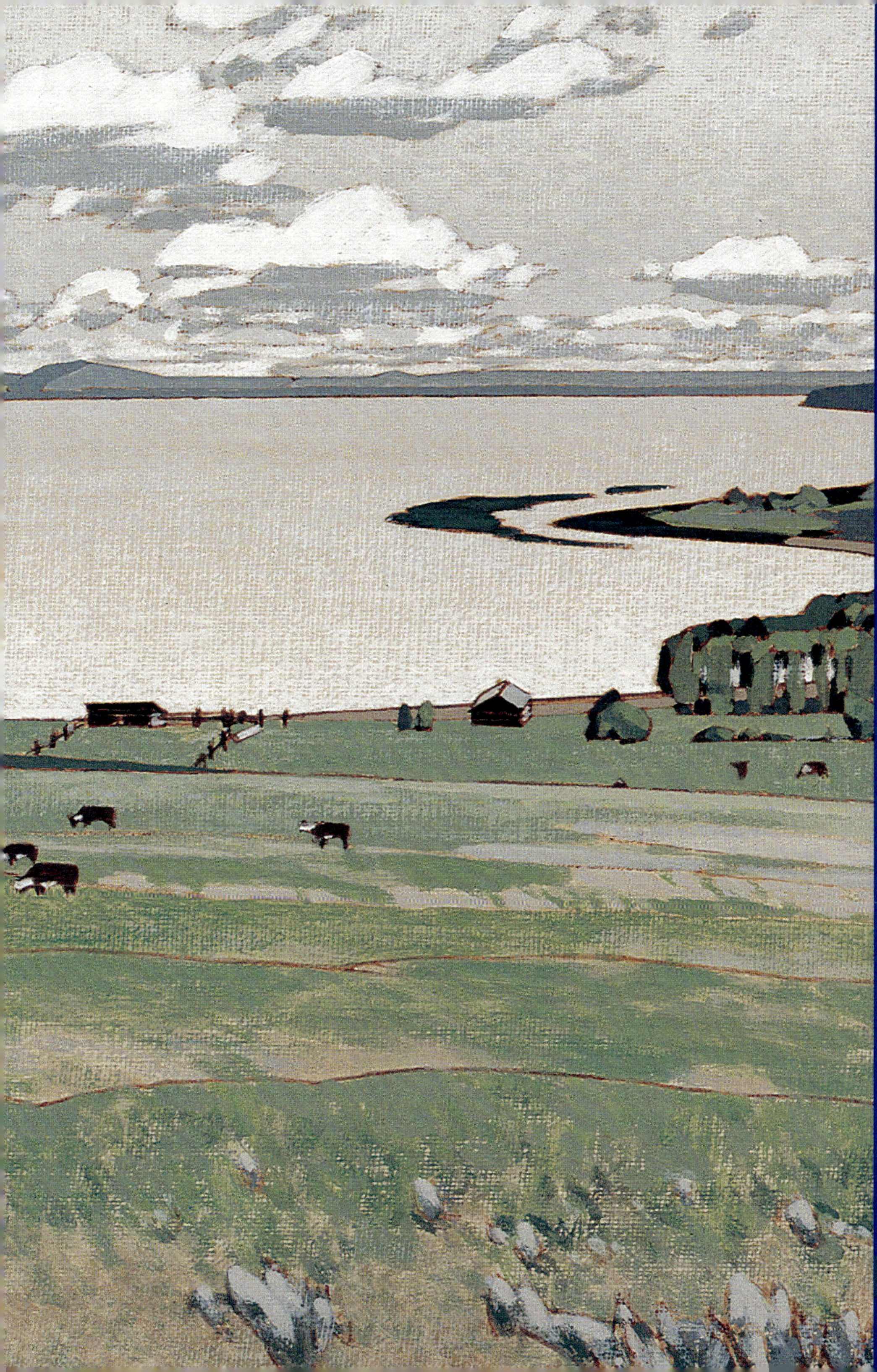

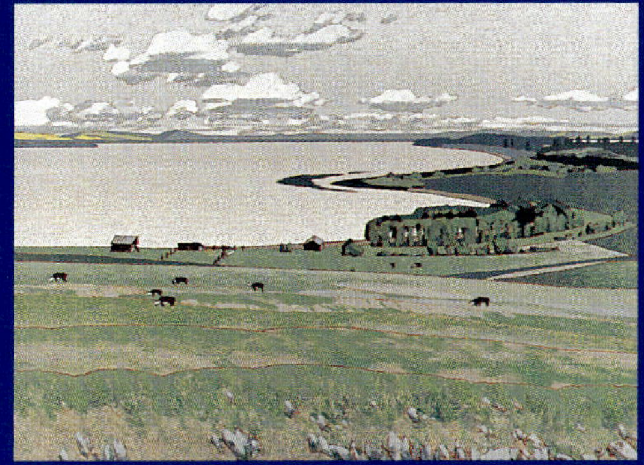

Original Townsite on Lake Saskatoon

"WHEN I *realized that our recently brushed-up garments were frayed and worn and our buckskin coats had a savage cast, that my three companions looked like Indians, and that the lady gazing at us belonged to another world. It was then that I wanted my wild life back again, yet step by step I was leaving it behind."*

Mary T. S. Schaffer, 1911

Acknowledgments

From the planning stage of my Hinton Trail project through to the completion of this book and fine art collection, a few very special individuals stand out. Without their vision and faith in my work, this project would never have been possible and I offer my sincere thanks. In particular I would like to mention Mr. Grant Kennedy, President of Lone Pine Publishing Ltd., Mr. Robert Doull of Westmount Press Ltd., Mr. Richard McCallum of Quality Color Press Ltd., Mr. Jean Poulin of Pièce de Résistance Graphics Ltée., and Mr. Glenn Rollans, Editor-in-Chief, Lone Pine Publishing Ltd. I would also like to thank Graham Sheard of Lone Pine for his long hours and good judgement and Kim Johansen of Résistance for her harmonious design.

I am indebted to my wife, Myrtle, for her support of the Hinton Trail project from the start. Her help with driving, editing and typing did much to pull the whole thing together.

In trying to piece together the Hinton Trail project, I was fortunate to have the interest and active support of many people, many of whom knew the Hinton Trail from first-hand experience. Although approximately 150 men and women gave their time and knowledge, space will not allow me to mention them all by name. But I wish to thank everyone and sincerely hope the finished product is a credit to their participation. Without their support this historical publication and collection of over 272 works of art would not have been possible. I thank the following people for their help, their stories, and their photographs:

Alberta Forest Service (Grande Prairie), Alberta Historical Resources Foundation, Art Allen, Gerry Andrews (photos p. 116), Mary Andrews, Gordon Blackmore, Tom Brown (photo p. 108), Isabel Campbell (photos pp. 102, 112), Denis Chailler, Fred Comeau, Gavin Craig, Dorcas Dalgleish (photo p. 98), Jean and the late Bert Dalgleish (photos pp. 8, 66, 92), Gordon Delorme, the late Louis Delorme, Walter Delorme, Martha Dunbar, Joe Dupuis, Harry Edgecomb, Dr. R.C. Elliot, Sue Feddema, Ray Ferguson, Deome and Rose Findlay, Sam Fomuk (photo p. 94), Forest Technology School (Hinton, photos pp.12, 26, 68), Charlie and Jean Fox, Betty Gaudin, Dewdney Gladu, Glenbow Archives (Calgary, photo p. 138), Grande Prairie Daily Herald-Tribune, D. Grant, Ivor Guest, Hazel Hart (photo p. 22), Stella Holtz, Dr. E.J.W. Irish (photo p. 32), Day Isley, Alice Joachim, Kelly Joachim, Ernie Karakonti, Basil Leonard, Dr. David Leonard, Frank Letendre, Ed Lightfoot, Frank Liszczak, Lawrence Lock, Carl Luger (photos pp. 60, 76), Paul Marshall, Ian and Alice MacDonald, Dr. Grant MacEwan, the late Henry McCullough, Pete McCullough, Alex McEachern, Euphemia McNaught, the late Edward Moberly, Henry Monkman, Edna Moyer, Dr. W. Nassichuk, Clarence Norris, the late Mima Osborne (photos pp. 58, 78, 100, 110), Lena Ouellette, the late George Pandachuk, Jack and Vi Patterson (photos pp. 72, 82, 106), John Patton, Isobel Perry, Paul Pivert of Panda Camera (Grande Prairie), the late Felix Plante (photo p. 38), Proctor and Gamble Cellulose Limited (Grande Prairie), Provincial Archives of Alberta, Evelyn Rose, Tony Roteliuk (photo p. 122), Steve Sawchuck, Dave Schenk, George Schultz, Laverne Scorgie, E. Sheehan (photo p. 90), Don Sherk, Bernie Simpson, Bill and Elsie Smith (photos pp. 54, 126), Jack Smith, N.W. Smith, Terry Smith, Harold Spence, John St. Arnault, Vic Stapleton, Frank Stoll, Mort Timanson, the late Al Traux, R. Tubb (photo p. 10), Roman von Tiesenhausen, Betty and the late Sam Unruh (photo p. 56), Tom Wanyandi, Lynn Watson of Paquin Photographs (Grande Prairie), Sela Watts (photos pp. 132, 140), Pat Wearmouth, Whyte Museum of the Canadian Rockies (Banff), Milt Wright.

Robert Guest, December 1994

I would like to thank the following authors and agencies for their generous permission to quote from their works. Every reasonable effort has been made to make these acknowledgements complete. The publishers welcome any information enabling them to correct any omissions or errors in future printings.

Anderson, Frank W. *The Rum Runners*. Surrey: Heritage House Publishing Co. Ltd., 1968.

Andrews, G.S. *Metis Outpost*. Victoria: G. Smedley Andrews, 1985.

Bickersteth, J. Burgon. *The Land of Open Doors: being letters from Western Canada,* 1911—1913. Toronto: S. Rancourt, University of Toronto Press, 1976.

Bronson, Anne et al. *Willmore Wilderness Park*. Calgary: Alberta Wilderness Association, 1973.

Calverley, D. *Monkman Pass and Trail; A Brief History*. Calgary: Petro-Canada Coal Division, 1982.

Campbell, I.M., ed. *Pioneers of the Peace*. Grande Prairie: Grande Prairie District Old Timers Association, 1975.

Cushman, D. *The Great North Trail*. New York: McGraw-Hill Book Company, 1966.

Fomuk, S. personal communication.

Glenn, John, Sr. *Mountain Trails*. Saskatoon: The Western Producer, 1969.

Hart, H. *History of Hinton*. Hinton: Hazel Hart, 1980.

Helgason, G. *The First Albertans: An Archeological Search.* Edmonton: Lone Pine Publishing, 1987.

Irish, Dr. E.J.W. *Geology of the Rocky Mountain Foothills, Alberta.* Calgary: Geological Survey of Canada, Department of Energy, Mines and Resources. Reproduced with the permission of the Minister of Supply and Services Canada, 1992

MacGregor, J.G. *Packsaddles to Tete Jaune Cache.* Toronto: McClelland and Stewart Limited, 1962.

McEachern, I. *How the Hinton Trail was Born: The Early Years.* Original Manuscript, 1967.

Miracle, Leonard. *Complete Book of Camping.* New York: Outdoor Life. Harper and Brothers, 1961.

Moberly, Henry John. *When Fur was King*. London: J.M. Dent and Sons Limited, 1929.

Moyles, R.G., ed. *Challenge of the Homestead: Peace River Letters of Clyde and Merle Campbell*, 1914-1924. Calgary: Historical Society of Alberta, 1988.

Schaffer, M.T.S. *Old Indian Trails of the Canadian Rockies*: New York: G.P. Putnam and Sons, 1911.

Schoonover, C. *The Edge of Wilderness: A Portrait of the Canadian North.* Agincourt: Methuen Publications, 1974.

Selwyn, A.R.C. *Reported Trail from Peace River to Jasper House*. Ottawa: The Queen's Printer, 1977.

Seton, E.T. *The Book of Woodcraft.* Garden City, N.Y.: Garden City Publishing Co. Inc., 1912.

Smith, N.W. *Thanks - For the Memories.* Vancouver: Veterans' Advocate, 1981.

Stacey, E.C. *Beaverlodge to the Rockies and Supplement* (2 vols). Altona: D.W. Friesen and Sons Ltd., 1976.

Taylor, W.C. *Tracks Across My Trail: Donald (Curly) Phillips, Guide and Outfitter.* Jasper: Jasper-Yellowhead Historical Society, 1984.

Timanson, M. Letter to author, 24 April 1992.

Weir, Joan, *Backdoor to the Klondike*. Erin: Boston Mills Press, 1988.

White, M. *Lake Saskatoon Reflections.* Sexsmith: Lake Saskatoon History Book Committee, 1980.

Yates, J.G., Lowe, A.J., eds. *Along the Wapiti.* Grande Prairie: Wapiti River Historical Society, 1981

"Fossil Hunters Enthusiastic over Discoveries." Grande Prairie: Herald-Tribune, 1961.

"Hazelmere Man's Packhorses Spot Search for Oil." Grande Prairie: Herald-Tribune, 1954

"May Have Met Foul Play." Grande Prairie: Grande Prairie Herald, 1913.

"No News of the Police Yet." Grande Prairie: Grande Prairie Herald, 1913.

"Sargt. Harper and Party Safe. Followed and Arrested Asa Hunting Near Grande Cache, B.C." Grande Prairie: Grande Prairie Herald. 1914.

"Sargt. Harper and Party Return after Hard Trip with Hunting as Prisoner and 15 Year Old Shaw Girl." Grande Prairie: Grande Prairie Herald. 1914.

"Summer Road from Prairie Creek Into Grande Prairie." Edmonton: Edmonton Bulletin. 1911.

"Trail Too Close to the Rockies." Edmonton: Edmonton Bulletin. 1910.

Robert Guest, B.Ed., A.C.A. Dip.

Robert was born in Beaverlodge, Alberta in 1938. After working for the Alberta Forest Service, and then as a college instructor for ten years, he returned to his studio in the wilderness on the banks of the Wapiti River in 1984. There he worked on the Hinton Trail project concurrently with a 66-piece collection of paintings entitled "Winter on the Wapiti."

Robert has been involved in several environmental and conservation concerns. In 1968, he founded the Canadian Wolf Defenders, a conservation society that achieved success internationally in improving the image and protection of wolves. In 1970, he founded Wild Kakwa, an environmental society dedicated to establishing a wilderness park.

Robert has contributed greatly over the years to the strengthening of Alberta's artistic community. He is a member of the Alberta Society of Artists, and was one of nine founding members of the Alberta Art Foundation in 1972. He was also a founding member of Grande Prairie's Prairie Art Gallery in 1975 and the founder of the Peace Watercolour Society in the Peace River country in 1976.

For many years Robert has hiked through the mountains and foothills of the eastern slopes of the Rockies, where he gets his inspiration. Robert's drawings and paintings have been represented in many exhibitions, including the collection of Her Majesty The Queen. He is best known for his research and artwork related to the Hinton Trail.

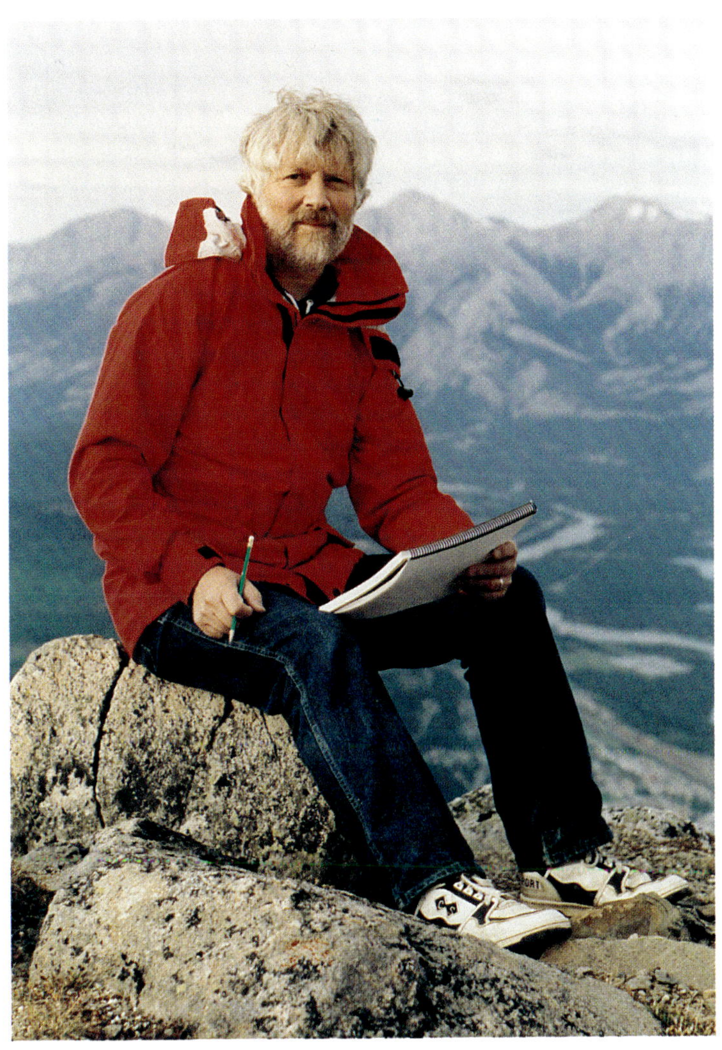

More Great Books For Those Who Love Adventure In The Outdoors!

The Canadian Mountaineering Anthology

edited by Bruce Fairley

Journey through the history of Canadian mountaineering, from the pioneer to present day. The guides on your journey will be such mountaineers as Conrad Kain, Reverend William Spotswood Green, W.D. Wilcox, Arthur Wheeler and Sharon Wood. They, along with a long list of others, recount their attempts to conquer Canada's most majestic and perilous peaks in this book of triumph and tragedy. A great book for history buffs and adventurers alike.

5.5" x 8.5" • 414 pages • 25 B&W photographs
Softcover • ***$16.95*** *(Canadian)* • ***$14.95*** *(U.S.)*
ISBN 1-55105-041-2

Compact Guide to Birds of the Rockies

by Geoffrey Holroyd and Howard Coneybeare

This habitat-based guide includes unusual and useful notes for more than 100 birds. It lists typical locations for sighting each bird, and a never-before-published species checklist for five Rocky Mountain parks. Its convenient size and full-page colour illustrations make this guide a must for your knapsack.

4.25" x 5.75" • 144 pages
120 colour illustrations
Softcover • ***$9.95*** • *ISBN 0-919433-52-9*
A Selection of the Canadian Parks and Wilderness Society

Compact Guide to Wildflowers of the Rockies

by C. Dana Bush

This habitat guidebook describes 100 species of wildflowers commonly found in the Rockies, classified according to elevation and topography to assist in identification. It includes information on propagation, ecology and growing seasons. Easy to flip through and small enough to carry with you, this guide makes wildflower discovery a breeze.

4.25" x 5.75" • 144 pages
120 colour illustrations
Softcover • ***$9.95*** • *ISBN 0-919433-57-X*
A Selection of the Canadian Parks and Wilderness Society

Hoofed Mammals of Alberta

edited by J. Brad Stelfox

This comprehensive, in-depth look at Alberta's ungulates examines white-tailed deer, mule deer, caribou, wapiti, moose, pronghorn, mountain sheep, bighorn sheep and bison. An invaluable resource written for recreationalists, sport hunters, research scientists and conservationists, this book is full of useful information.

8.5" x 11" • 256 pages • 10 colour maps
9 colour illustrations • 18 colour photographs
over 175 B&W charts and illustrations
Softcover • ***$19.95*** • *ISBN 1-55105-037-4*
Hardcover • ***$39.95*** • *ISBN 1-55105-035-8*

"[The] best reference book ever published on the subject."

-Andy Russell, noted author and outdoorsman

Gift Cards—Birds of North America

illustrated by Gary Ross

This series of illustrated gift cards highlights 16 birds common to North America. Each card features a colour illustration of a single bird on the cover and information on the characteristics of that bird on the back of the card. Sets include: Birds of Alberta, Birds of British Columbia, Birds of Canada and Birds of the West.

5" x 7" • 8 sets of cards with envelopes - 2 sets per region • 6 different cards per set • colour illustration on each card • blank stationery
$9.95 *(Canadian)* • ***$8.95*** *(U.S.)*

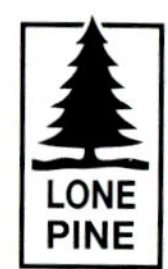

Edmonton
#206, 10426 - 81 Avenue
Edmonton, AB T6E 1X5
Phone (403) 433-9333
Fax (403) 433-9646

Vancouver
#202A, 1110 Seymour Street
Vancouver, BC V6B 3N3
Phone (604) 687-5555
Fax (604) 687-5575

Washington State
16149 Redmond Way, #180
Redmond, WA 98052
Phone (206) 343-8397

Or Call Toll-Free 1-800-661-9017